Augsburg C---
George Sverdr---
Minneapolis, Minn---
WITHDRA---

D0648069

The Curriculum Field:
Its Formative Years

The Curriculum Field:
Its Formative Years

Mary Louise Seguel

Associate Professor of Education
Northern Illinois University

Teachers College Press
Teachers College, Columbia University, New York

© 1966 by Teachers College, Columbia University
Library of Congress Catalog Card Number: 66–20115
Manufactured in the United States of America

Cover design by Felix Cooper

TITLE IN BCL 2nd ED.

LB
1570
S36

To Alice Miel

8 49 08

Preface

Educators, whether teachers or members of that large supporting cast that supports the teacher's classroom work behind the scenes, are as a rule so absorbed in current action as to give only intermittent thought to the past. There is something very "daily" about the act of educating, and reflective thought can easily be shelved, though not permanently. There are frequent reminders that present action may best be understood as an outgrowth of the past.

A group of curriculum makers, for example, who are completely absorbed in developing a curriculum for a particular time and place feel a stimulating shock when the lay person, with the terrifying innocence of the child in the fairy tale, asks: "Why are you always developing the curriculum? Why don't you ever get it 'developed' so that you can settle down and teach it?" A similar challenge may come to a professor of curriculum making from a neophyte teacher who balks at a college course designed to teach her how to make the curriculum. "I'm willing to let you experts make those decisions," she wails. "All I want to know is how to teach children." Sometimes the professional curriculum maker himself is sharply brought out of his absorption in his current professional task by an educational proposal that sets his teeth on edge. The very outrage that he feels is a warning to him to check again the origins of those ideas with which he is most comfortable.

The questions, "Should we do what we are doing?" "Is it a good thing to do?" "Should we be doing it at all?" lead easily to historical questions —"How did we begin to do this, anyway?" "What got us started, and why did we think it necessary and important?" "Are the conditions the same now as then?" Of course, the historical answer is not the complete one; questions of value must be referred to the present as well, but a look at the past can reveal whether curriculum makers are still doing what they set out to do. It can show whether new proposals are really new or only trips down a road already traveled. And, at the very least, knowledge of the past drains off that sense of frantic immediacy that so often plagues new professions. If good men and true have struggled with these questions before, they will probably have to do so again. History seems to show that the most worthy problems are perennial.

•

The writer wishes particularly to acknowledge the contribution of Alice Miel. Her grasp of the potential of the American educational enterprise, both broadly and in detail, has informed the whole of this work from its inception. Arno Bellack's searching theoretical analysis of the curriculum was directly influential, both on the writer's undertaking of this study and on any analysis that has been made. The writer is also indebted to Lawrence Cremin, whose high standards of historical scholarship proved a constant inspiration.

Gratitude is also due all those who read the manuscript. James McClellan, in particular, pointed out the importance to the curriculum field of the struggle for power among the newly emerging specialists in education. Walter Wernick suggested helpfully that creative and aesthetic forces constantly challenged the technological approach to the curriculum.

Among the host of devoted fellow educators who gave substantial help to the project, grateful mention must be made of Dorothy McGeoch and Mabel Brantley. Constance Carr McCutcheon, Miriam Selchen Dorn, and Murray Deutsch—student members of the writer's project committee —were also most helpful. Personal gratitude goes to Mireya and Leo Seguel, whose understanding support was at all times indispensable.

Mary Louise Seguel
DeKalb, Illinois

Contents

1   Introduction   1

2   The McMurrys   7
    THE MC MURRYS AS REPRESENTATIVE HERBARTIANS   7
    UNEASE ABOUT THE CURRICULUM   9
    GERMAN EXPERIENCE   16
    STRATEGY ON THEIR RETURN   23
    AN ASSESSMENT   38

3   John Dewey   47
    DEWEY'S INTRODUCTION TO EDUCATION   47
    CRITIQUE OF THE HERBARTIANS   50
    THE CURRICULUM OF THE LABORATORY SCHOOL   56
    REORGANIZATION OF THE HERBART SOCIETY   58
    DEWEY'S TEACHING CAREER   58
    CHALLENGES TO THE PROFESSION   60
    AN ASSESSMENT   62

4   Bobbitt and Charters   67
    BOBBITT   67

THE EFFICIENCY MOVEMENT IN EDUCATION		67
BOBBITT'S BACKGROUND		76
METHOD OF CURRICULUM MAKING		80
CHARTERS		90
CHARTER'S BACKGROUND		90
JOB ANALYSIS		93
AN ASSESSMENT		99
MEETING DEWEY'S CHALLENGES		99
JOINT CONTRIBUTION		101

5 Harold Rugg — 105

THE EDUCATIONAL SITUATION	105
RUGG'S BACKGROUND	112
EFFORTS AT SYNTHESIS	117
AN ASSESSMENT	134

6 Hollis L. Caswell — 137

CASWELL'S BACKGROUND	137
STATE CURRICULUM REVISION PROGRAMS	141
THE CURRICULUM SOCIETY	156
LANDMARK WORKS	161
APPOINTMENT TO TEACHERS COLLEGE	170
AN ASSESSMENT	171

7 Summary — 177

THE PROBLEM	177
CONCLUSION	179

Bibliography — 185

Index — 197

1 Introduction

Today's curriculum maker, whether theorist or practitioner, should probably be forgiven for assuming without question that curriculum making is something worth doing and that it must be studied in order to be carried out properly. He picks up these assumptions forcefully from several sources. When he studies to be a teacher, he usually takes courses in curriculum making, and he finds a curriculum specialist functioning in most school systems. If he does graduate work, he may choose curriculum making as a field and become a curriculum specialist himself. As a specialist, he may then teach his specialization to others or may coordinate curriculum making in a school system. The educational libraries he uses contain much literature on curriculum making, both theoretical and practical, creative and critical. He may become recognized as an authority on curriculum making by writing some of this literature. With other curriculum makers he may join a professional organization which supports and fosters improved curriculum making. In all this experience, there is much that suggests, first, that curriculum making is a valuable task and, second, that it must be studied in order to be well done. There is little or nothing in this experience that hints at the sources of these assumptions about curriculum making or the reasons that justify them. Everyone connected with curriculum making seems less deliberate in his neglect of these assumptions than inattentive to them.

If the curriculum maker is moved by that curiosity that takes shape as a sense of history, he will discover that curriculum making was not always consciously conceived of and studied by interested school people. For example, in 1890 neither professional preparation, literature, organization, nor expert opinion on curriculum making existed in the United States. Yet by at least 1940, curriculum making was a recognized field of specialization, and it has continued to be so until now. Clearly something took place during the past seventy-five years to make curriculum making today identifiable and considered valuable.

It seems important to understand the development of such thinking, especially if the sources and the reasons for the development can be discovered in the tracing of it. An attempt to re-create the past in order to discover who engineered this development, what its course was, and what influenced it, should help today's curriculum maker. As he becomes more aware of the sources of his current assumptions and the process by which they reached him, he is better able to understand them and to judge their value. He is also helped to speculate usefully about the future. For example, might hindsight not show how thinkers in this period of time missed opportunities, struggled with ambiguities or depended upon their historical context? Could this knowledge help to free current thought on curriculum making from tendencies to be uncritical and dogmatic? Might other thinkers have backed different ideas, basing them on different reasons? Do some of these alternatives suggest new directions for today's educators?

It seems valuable, then, to try to describe the course of thought that ended by bringing to professional awareness the nature and value of curriculum making. This course of thought began by being little distinguishable from thought about the growing educational enterprise and continued to be closely tied to educational thought as a whole. There is little doubt that the concerns and proposals of all who interested themselves in education during this period—and they represented a wide variety of purposes—influenced in a unified and profound way the development of several specialized concerns, only one of which became curriculum making. For a complete and comprehensive understanding of the birth and growth of the field of curriculum making or of any other specialized field, one would need to examine the whole story of the transformation of the generalized educative tasks of the culture into responsibilities delegated primarily to a body of professional educators. The very term, professional educator, as used today, is misleading when applied to many in our educational past whose devotion to education was matched by a nonspecialized attitude which is now unusual.

In the same fashion, all those who interested themselves in the curriculum, and they numbered many whose educative concerns were general ones, were influential to some degree on the eventual appearance of the field of curriculum making. The history of this influence is, however, more a history of the whole developing educational enterprise than the chronicle of the development of this one specialized aspect of it. An illustration may show how difficult it is to disentangle the roots of this growing specialization. Throughout the period, college teachers who wrote public school textbooks in subject matter fields and whose students taught those fields in high schools undoubtedly had a method of making the curriculum, although if asked they might not have been able to formulate it or been interested in doing so. Those teachers made decisions on what and how to teach, based on criteria whose worth seemed to them and to many unarguable. Since such an assumed point of view precluded any study of the criteria or the way these criteria were used in selecting content, college teachers of academic subjects were only indirectly involved in helping shape the specialization of curriculum making. The attention of the developing curriculum maker, on the other hand, was directed toward the act of decision itself, whether based on traditional criteria or on newer competing ones. He was not primarily a curriculum maker, as was the man who wrote the textbook. He was a student of the act of curriculum making, striving to become aware of its nature and to improve its performance. For this reason, he was directly involved in shaping the new field. Although a comprehensive treatment should attempt to place this budding student of the process of making the curriculum within the larger setting in which he developed, it seems important to concentrate first upon him and to discover the nature of his particular concern, as a step toward understanding how his ideas differed not only from what had gone before but from what was going on around him.

A helpful strategy here is to look at the writings of some of those individuals whom the profession itself later came to identify as having been interested from the outset in curriculum making, and to see what clues can be gained from their earlier concerns and proposals. What were such thinkers saying and writing that was not at the time consciously recognized as curriculum making but that has since shown itself to be related? At what moment did they catch the profession's attention in a particularly effective way, and when did this attention shift from them toward a new emphasis? Did these influential positions function somewhat as sequential steps in a chain of cause and effect? Or rather were these emphases, originally captivating and stimulating, superseded but never quite discarded? Did they often remain as forms in the background of reflection, casting long shadows of influence on the course of thought they had originally affected? In short, a look

3

at influential positions taken in the past by some leaders in curriculum making should cast light on the general course of thought that led to the eventual awareness by the whole profession of the nature and value of curriculum making.

Six leaders were chosen as the most promising few with which to begin. Dewey, whose position was important but different, was added later. The six chosen were all well known, were representative usually of a much larger group of equally significant figures, and enjoyed periods of influence fairly evenly distributed over a rough time span of fifty years (1890–1940). Each one's particular writings chosen as influential were analyzed to discover: 1) how each perceived the educational situation and why he became interested and involved in the study of the curriculum; 2) what proposals he made about the curriculum; and 3) how relevant to the educational situation his proposals proved to be.

In 1895, Charles and Frank McMurry joined with other leading Herbartians to form the National Herbart Society for the Scientific Study of Teaching. The Herbartians were a group of American educators who advocated elements of Herbartianism for American schools. They did so after studying the educational theory and practice of Johann Herbart in German universities and schools in the late eighties and early nineties, or after reading and discussing Herbartian literature in the United States. Charles and Frank McMurry were chosen to represent the Herbartian influence on curriculum making.

The study of these changing emphases soon showed the need to consider the influence of John Dewey. He did not directly concern himself with the thinking about curriculum making, but his interest and competence in educational matters throughout this period were comprehensive in range and depth and were lasting in effect. Unlike the other six, who enjoyed successive short periods of greatest effectiveness, Dewey early achieved a position which was not lost sight of but which continued to be challenging to educators with special concerns in curriculum. Thus Dewey cast a long shadow of influence which touched the work of all the rest.

In 1913, Franklin Bobbitt published an essay drawing an analogy between curriculum making and industrial processes,[1] which proved to be seminal for the later development of a movement in curriculum

---

[1] Franklin Bobbitt, "The Supervision of City Schools," *Twelfth Yearbook of the National Society for the Study of Education,* Part I (Chicago: University of Chicago Press, 1913).

study known as activity analysis. Bobbitt and Werrett Wallace Charters were chosen as representatives of this emphasis on the tabulation of social behavior.

In 1926, the National Society for the Study of Education, the former National Herbart Society, made a landmark attempt to draw together all the ideas on curriculum making which had been elaborated upon and tested up to that point. Harold Rugg, editor of the yearbook which resulted,[2] was chosen as representative of this effort at order and synthesis.

An example of the eventual recognition of curriculum making as an important professional responsibility was the establishment in 1938 at Teachers College, Columbia University, of a Department of Curriculum and Teaching. This administrative change unified educational concerns which had previously been scattered throughout professional preparation in all areas and at all levels of education within the college. The organizing head of the new department, Hollis L. Caswell, was selected as representative of the new specialist in curriculum making.

By now the reader, sensing how easily curriculum makers are confounded with students of curriculum making, must realize that these six were chosen chiefly because they were interested in the study of curriculum making itself. For this reason, they can give us the clearest picture of the essential nature of the field they helped to shape. There were a number of others like them whose contribution was quite as valuable. There were even others who thought an interest in curriculum making was unnecessary and undesirable. A study of their position would be interesting and helpful as well. The history of this period appears to be an exciting and fruitful one, which the present study of a few of its leaders has only begun to explore.

[2] National Society for the Study of Education, "The Foundations and Technique of Curriculum-Construction," *Twenty-sixth Yearbook* (Bloomington, Ill.: Public School Publishing Co., 1926).

2   The McMurrys

THE McMURRYS AS REPRESENTATIVE HERBARTIANS

The group from which to select a significant and influential "American" Herbartian in the nineties is large and contains a number of interesting and important men.[1] The colorful and prophetic artist-teacher, Francis Wayland Parker; William Torrey Harris, leader in American education and one of the Herbartians' most friendly and able critics; Charles DeGarmo, witty polemicist, President of Swarthmore; Elmer E. Brown, scholar and later United States Commissioner of Education; C. C. Van Liew, student of both the child-study and Herbartian movements, and President of the State Normal School, Chico, California; James Earl Russell, Dean of Teachers College, Columbia University; Edmund James, President of the University of Illinois; Herman Lukens of Clark University; the list rolls on, composed of persons whose influence on American education at the turn of the century was unique. They appear to be a company of men of such nearly equal stature that the choice of one outstanding figure is difficult. Even the contribution each made to the new Herbart Society does not

[1] A contemporary account which is a good source on the Herbartian movement and outstanding members of it is Charles DeGarmo, *Herbart and the Herbartians* (New York: Charles Scribner's Sons, 1895). Two histories of Illinois State Normal University give a good background on leading Herbartians; David Felmley, *Semi-Centennial History of the Illinois State Normal University, 1857–1907* (Normal, Ill.: David Felmley, 1907), and Helen E. Marshall, *Grandest of Enterprises, 1857–1957* (Normal, Ill.: Illinois State Normal School, 1956). A fuller account of Herbartian figures is found in Henry Hugh Edmunds, "History of the Herbartian Movement in the United States and its Relation to Present Trends in Education" (Milner Library, Illinois State Normal University, 1929, Typewritten), and in Charles A. Harper, *Development of the Teachers College in the United States with Special Reference to Illinois State Normal University* (Bloomington: McKnight and McKnight, 1935).

give us a useful clue. Most of them not only endorsed the organization but worked devotedly to give the meetings vigor and critical intellectual leverage.

Although Charles and Frank McMurry shared with other Herbartians a concern for the fate of the elementary school curriculum they were unusually successful in calling the attention of the profession to the curriculum in action in the classroom. The following quotation typifies their focus on instruction. "The teacher," Charles commented once, "is working at the very smelting process, the point of difficulty where new, uncomprehended knowledge meets this tumult of the child's mind."[2] Their colleagues and students remembered both men especially for their constant insistence that theory be tested in terms of whether it would work with children.[3] Since this concern for the improvement of instruction later became widely shared by leaders in curriculum, the McMurrys appear to be especially good Herbartians with whom to begin our study of the developing curriculum field.

UNEASE ABOUT THE CURRICULUM

It is no exaggeration to say that at the time the Herbart Society was formed in 1895, American educators felt that the curriculum, or the program of studies and their content, was in great need of attention. In the period of consolidation that had ensued after Horace Mann revitalized the school in 1837, school organization had been given the lion's share of attention by schoolmen. During these stabilizing years, the basic functional machinery of the school had been worked out.[4] This achievement had been cause for real satisfaction, but in the process less attention had been paid to the curriculum and there was a growing feeling by 1880 that something should be done. A general

[2] Charles A. McMurry, *Conflicting Principles in Teaching and How to Adjust to Them* (Boston: Houghton Mifflin Co., 1914) p. 258.

[3] Samuel A. Kruse, "Late Charles A. McMurry Met the Acid Test of the Master Teacher," *School and Society*, LVIII (Sept. 4, 1943), pp. 171–72. See also Ullin Leavell, "Peabody's Modern Founders," *Peabody Journal of Education*, XXII (March, 1945), pp. 262–63. George D. Strayer, a colleague of the McMurrys, corroborates this when he says Frank always insisted "that the principles which he advocated must be carried out in the classroom and that their validity was in considerable measure to be determined by the degree to which skillful teachers were able to embody these ideas in their everyday work." George D. Strayer, "Tribute to Frank McMurry," *School Executive*, LVI (Sept., 1936), p. 4.

[4] Vivian T. Thayer, *The Passing of the Recitation* (Boston: D. C. Heath and Co., 1928), Chap. I; Harold Rugg, *Foundations for American Education* (Yonkers-on-Hudson, New York: World Book Co., 1947), pp. 522–23.

sense of unease at this time led educators to take stock, especially of the content of the school program and the methods then in use.[5]

Pressure of content

One of the problems connected with the curriculum had been that its content had greatly expanded, but not in an orderly and systematic way. There had been a persistent pressure for change in this content since the Civil War. It was based in part on the very real presence in the culture of a number of new, systematically developing, scholarly disciplines. One gets a hint of the extent of this explosion and classification of knowledge, scholarly and technical (quite as impressive as anything in our own era) by glancing at the dates of the establishment of the major learned societies in the United States. Within a forty-year period before 1890, national societies had been founded in geography, history, mathematics, and eight scientific fields, almost always coincidentally with the appearance of the corresponding university chairs and departments.[6]

The pressure to include these subjects in the curriculum was also caused by a developing cultural attitude toward the usefulness of knowledge in individual and social improvement. The rise of the academies in the middle of the nineteenth century in America testifies to the growing conviction that knowledge was useful in preparing youth for the "work of life." The academies offered whatever courses anyone wanted taught for any practical reason. Their lists of subjects came to include a wide variety of technical and scholarly studies designed to fit young people for the changing social, commercial, industrial, and political conditions.[7] No fewer than 149 new titles had found

[5] D. L. Kiehle, "The New Education," *Education*, IV (July, 1884), pp. 612–18; C. H. Levermore, "The 'New Education' Run Mad," *Education*, VI (Jan., 1886), pp. 290–98; C. D. Adsit, "The New Education in California," *Education*, X (Oct., 1889), pp. 118–26.

[6] In the period between 1852 and 1899 the following learned societies were established in the United States: American Geographical Society (1852); Mechanical Engineers (1857); Entomologists (1859); Chemical Engineers (1876); American Historical Association (1884); Electrical Engineers (1887); Geologists (1888); Zoologists (1890); American Mathematical Society (1894); American Physical Society (1899). *Encyclopedia Britannica* (14th ed.), XVIII, 309–19.

[7] Edward Elliott, "The Education and Training of Secondary Teachers," *Fourth Yearbook of the National Society for the Study of Education*, Part I (Chicago: University of Chicago Press, 1905), p. 19. See also Elmer E. Brown, *The Making of Our Middle Schools* (New York: Longmans, Green and Co., 1902) Chap. VIII; Paul Monroe, *A Text-Book in the History of Education* (New York: The Macmillan Co., 1920).

their way into printed programs of study in the academies between 1787 and 1870.[8] The same pressure to add socially useful content was felt by the elementary schools from which the students in the academies came.

Emphasis on memorizing

Usually this new content was introduced into the curriculum of the elementary schools by way of a text. The growing efficiency of the publishing industry in this period made texts gradually cheaper and more available. More technical change took place in the production of books in the fifty years after 1839 when Daguerre first published his manual on photography than had occurred in the previous three centuries. Between 1830 when Scribners was founded and 1869 when Duttons began business, twenty-one major publishing houses were established in the United States. Book publishing rose in value in the thirty years before 1900 from eight million to forty-three million dollars.[9]

The new knowledge arrived in the classroom in textbook form cheaply and easily, but it was abstract in formulation and specialized in content.[10] The books, authored mostly by university scholars, had been written first for the college, then watered down for the high school, and finally simplified for the elementary school to such an extent as to reduce them to a virtual outline of knowledge, robbed of the very rich and illustrative detail that would have given such an outline meaning. Examples of such textbooks multiplied since the scholar found it easy and tempting to write books on three levels of difficulty from substantially the same content.

Teachers tended to rely on these texts for both content and method. Entrance to teaching was not yet well stabilized, and a number of young people began to teach immediately on leaving the high school or academy if they succeeded in passing the certification examinations.

[8] Harold Rugg, "The School Curriculum, 1825–1890," *The Foundations and Technique of Curriculum-Construction, Twenty-sixth Yearbook of the National Society for the Study of Education,* Part I (Bloomington, Ill.: Public School Publishing Co., 1926), p. 20.

[9] *Encyclopedia Britannica* (14th ed.), Vol. XX. *Encyclopedia Americana,* Vol. XXII, 1962.

[10] Later, Harold Rugg was to label this kind of knowledge morphological, since it consisted principally of the names of the parts of a scheme of classification and the description of forms. Harold Rugg, "The School Curriculum, 1825–1890," "The Foundations and Technique of Curriculum-Construction," *Twenty-sixth Yearbook of the National Society for the Study of Education,* Part I (Bloomington, Ill.: Public School Publishing Co., 1926), pp. 20–22.

Many of them knew little more about the subjects they were teaching than they had learned earlier from the same texts they were now using with their pupils or from a simplified version of them. As Francis Parker fumed at the time:

> Thousands of girls without culture, with very deficient education, manage, after repeated trials, to pass cram examinations met by quantity drills . . . these same girls, the daughters, friends and relatives of ward politicians with a pull, are put in charge of fifty or more immortal souls to repeat as best they may the wretched process of quantity teaching.[11]

These teachers were accustomed, because of their preparation, to considering memory as a substitute for knowledge, and they found nothing in the abstractly worded textbooks to disabuse them of their conviction. The textbook did not usually offer illustrative details, suggestions for applying the content, or interrelationships with other subjects. Rather, most texts furnished questions and answers to be employed in the recitation and tended to encourage the teacher to emphasize memorization. Drill in these questions and answers frequently impeded a real understanding of the material on the part of the child. A report of a supervisor in 1885 gives us some insight into this matter:

> [The teacher] repeated the questions in Geography in the exact order found in the book, and as the children could answer but few of them, he would look at the map, or the text, and read the answer from the book; when a pupil or pupils could give the expected answer, he or they answered abruptly, or in concert.[12]

As a result, learning for the children came to be a process largely of memorizing words and parroting them back, rather than acquiring new meanings.

In addition, the general enthusiasm for subject matter that would exercise the mental faculties led schoolmen to hail these compendiums of content as especially useful for developing the memory and reasoning powers. As Frank McMurry was to remark many years later:

> There was no uneasiness about the curriculum in those days. Anything that was a fact might well be included, because it at least "trained the mind."[13]

[11] Francis W. Parker, *Talks on Pedagogics* (New York: E. L. Kellogg and Co., 1894), pp. 442–43.

[12] John Trainer, *How To Grade and Teach a Country School* (Decatur, Ill.: Burgess, Trainer and Co., 1885), p. 17.

[13] Frank M. McMurry, "Some Recollections of the Past Forty Years of Education," *Peabody Journal of Education,* IV (May, 1927), p. 325.

Growth of the curriculum

As each new variety of text was added to the school offering, the curriculum or course of study began gradually to be enlarged in many school systems. The textbook furnished the content of each new subject in these curricula as well as a method of teaching it. The subjects themselves constituted the course of study, and their orderly arrangement determined the daily program. The curriculum which grew in this unsystematic way became an assembly of parts, each one of which was included in responses to the demand that new content be taught and that such content develop the child's mental powers.

Haphazard adoption of methods

Changes were made in this period in the methods of teaching the older, better established subjects in the curriculum, the skills in literacy and mathematics. In the absence of scholarly study and teaching in pedagogy on the university level in the United States, these innovations in method had been "borrowed" mostly from Europe. In general, these new methods tended to isolate the mathematical and literary skills from the content areas, rather than to relate them functionally. A common element of these methods had been the belief that the learner should begin with the simplest elements of the subject and proceed step by step to acquire more complex notions. Pestalozzi, who started the movement by a search for an alphabet of every subject, described his work as follows:

> . . . I sought by every means to simplify the elements of reading and arithmetic, and by grouping them psychologically, enable the child to pass easily and surely from the first step to the second, from the second to the third, and so on. The pupils no longer drew letters on their slates, but lines, curves, angles, and squares.[14]

When an observer commented, "I see, you want to mechanize instruction," Pestalozzi enthusiastically agreed, adding, "He had hit the nail on the head and supplied me with the very word I wanted to express my aim and the means I employed."[15]

Several examples will show that American enthusiasm for these methods was widespread. The staff of the Oswego Normal School after 1860 urged that the child be taught to read by having him learn the

[14] Samuel Chester Parker, *A Textbook in the History of Modern Elementary Education* (Boston: Ginn and Co., 1912), p. 365.

[15] Samuel Chester Parker, *A Textbook in the History of Modern Elementary Education* (Boston: Ginn and Co., 1912), pp. 365–66.

phonic values of the letters first, and then combine the letters on cards to make words.[16] The teaching of writing was affected in the same way by an influential book written by N. A. Calkins in 1860, called *Primary Object Lessons*. He recommended that the child practice the common elements of basic geometric forms such as straight and curved lines and acute and obtuse angles as a preliminary step in learning to draw and write.[17] Judging by a comment made by Frank McMurry many years later, we may conclude that this method must have been widely used:

> Penmanship was taught by learning the "principles" of the letters, the right curve, the left curve, the straight down-stroke, etc. . . . and after long practice on these principles, one was allowed to combine them into words of one syllable, such as *if, in, for,* etc.[18]

Grube, a German, had proposed that the teaching of arithmetic be improved by insisting on the complete mastery of all possible operations with one number before taking up the next. Louis Soldan first popularized this method in 1870 by reading an essay on it before the St. Louis Teachers Association. Reprints of this essay were widely read and influential in spreading Grube's idea.[19]

Lack of pedagogy

We may suppose that scholarship in pedagogy on the university level would have been influential in ordering and directing any changes made in curriculum and method during this period. But pedagogy was not yet a university discipline in the United States in 1890, although attempts had been made for fifty years to make it so. For example, the University of Iowa had established a Normal Department as early as 1855. Although several other universities had followed suit, all of these were eventually discontinued.[20] There had also been agitation for university chairs in pedagogy since the work of Horace Mann. New York University had had a chair in the Philosophy of Education for teachers of the common schools as early as 1832, but it was not

[16] Samuel Chester Parker, *A Textbook in the History of Modern Elementary Education* (Boston: Ginn and Co., 1912), pp. 367–68.

[17] Samuel Chester Parker, *A Textbook in the History of Modern Elementary Education* (Boston: Ginn and Co., 1912), p. 368.

[18] Frank M. McMurry, "Some Recollections of the Past Forty Years of Education," *Peabody Journal of Education,* IV (May, 1927), p. 326.

[19] Samuel Chester Parker, *A Textbook in the History of Modern Elementary Education* (Boston: Ginn and Co., 1912), p. 370.

[20] Newton Edwards and Herman Richey, *The School in the American Social Order* (Boston: Houghton Mifflin Co., 1947), p. 787.

permanent.[21] When in 1879, at the end of at least two decades of agitation, President Angell finally succeeded in establishing the first permanent university chair in education at the University of Michigan, a change of attitude ensued.[22] By 1890, there was something like a chair in pedagogy in over one hundred institutions. But a chair, representing the ideas of a single individual, lacked the power and resources for influencing practice that a university department of education would have had. Without a model school in which to test theory, the chairs of education in the nineties were still not much more than attempts in the right direction. At best, their holders did not take pedagogy for the elementary schools seriously. When Frank McMurry was appointed Professor of Education at the University of Illinois in 1893, he sensed this. As he commented, years later:

> I was advised by good authority not to let it be known that my chief interest was in the primary school, for fear I might lose my position. It was then beneath the dignity of any university to identify itself with training for the instruction of young children.[23]

Sensitive to the need for a model school in which to test pedagogical theory, he rigged up at the University of Illinois in 1893 what was probably the first practice teaching experiment in any American university (two teachers in the basement of Old Main).[24] It was a noteworthy pioneering effort, but model schools, established in connection with a university department of education, were not to be generally accepted for a decade at least.

The normal schools were still too absorbed in building their reputation for quality in teacher training to give much attention to the critical evaluation of new teaching methods. Their leaders, men of exacting standards, had placed at the center of the curriculum of the normal school the subjects usually studied in the almost-forgotten years of childhood. Reading, writing, spelling, arithmetic, and grammar had become objects of a most thorough and persistent struggle for mastery on the part of the normal school students. As a result, the graduate of the normal school was often the most relentless at securing mastery

---

[21] Newton Edwards and Herman Richey, *The School in the American Social Order* (Boston: Houghton Mifflin Co., 1947), p. 786.

[22] Newton Edwards and Herman Richey, *The School in the American Social Order* (Boston: Houghton Mifflin Co., 1947), p. 790.

[23] Frank M. McMurry, "Some Recollections of the Past Forty Years of Education," *Peabody Journal of Education,* IV (May, 1927), p. 332.

[24] The project was killed the following year, as a result of a change of administration. *Bulletin No. 7* (University of Illinois, School of Education, 1912), p. 3.

14

of the fundamentals on the part of the pupils.[25] A recollection by Frank McMurry is pertinent:

> In the fall of 1889, in asking for the privilege of visiting the best primary school in Chicago, I was directed to the Doolittle School. There I spent one entire day in the first grade, where the pupils were having Reading, Writing, Spelling, and Numbers, each four times a day and nothing more.[26]

Some scholarly guidance was available from works on education both native and European, but it was scattered in character. In 1872, an observer reported that everything of value published in America on education filled comfortably three long bookshelves.[27] These works were a varied assortment, including translations of philosophical books on education by noted Europeans and handbooks of suggestions for practice by gifted American teachers. The handbooks on practice had been popular during the first decades of school consolidation. David Page's *Theory and Practice of Teaching* had gone through twenty-five printings by 1860. He was imaginative and resourceful in his approach, and his book had the virtue of speaking directly to the problems of the improvement of instruction. But his was not a theoretical approach, and educators had begun by 1880 to turn to more systematic works on pedagogy. A good example of a book of the latter kind is one which was widely used in the normal schools in this period, a treatise on *Pedagogics as a System* by Rosenkranz, a German theorist. William T. Harris, an influential figure in American education after the Civil War, had selected it for translation because it expressed a philosophy which he strove to incorporate into school practices while serving as Superintendent of the St. Louis Public Schools.

President Edwards of Illinois State Normal University, which the McMurrys attended, had introduced Rosenkranz as an antidote to the other books on systems and methods, which were "epigrammatic and racy, but of little solid pedagogical worth." He admitted that the German book was "full of strange terminology and was written in a peculiar style . . . but it was not shallow."[28] Frank McMurry recol-

[25] Charles A. Harper, *Development of the Teachers College in the United States with Special Reference to Illinois State Normal University* (Bloomington: McKnight and McKnight, 1935), p. 89.

[26] Frank M. McMurry, "Some Recollections of the Past Forty Years of Education," *Peabody Journal of Education*, IV (May, 1927), p. 326.

[27] Charles A. Harper, *Development of the Teachers College in the United States with Special Reference to Illinois State Normal University* (Bloomington: McKnight and McKnight, 1935), pp. 133–34.

[28] Charles A. Harper, *Development of the Teachers College in the United*

lected later that when he had read Rosenkranz in normal school it had violently repelled him.[29] Possibly if he had studied it within the context of an American scholarly tradition in pedagogy, he might have found it more illuminating. As it was, the literature in education available to students then consisted either of theoretical books like that of Rosenkranz, or practical books like that of Page. University scholarship in pedagogy in the United States was as yet insufficient to guide the teacher in bridging this gap between theory and practice and in applying theory to the problems facing the American public schools.

Summary

We can see then that the changes in content and method that had occurred were largely unsystematic and made in response to various outside pressures. Efforts to improve the curriculum had been vigorous but had lacked guidance and direction. The application of American ingenuity to educational problems was typical and praiseworthy, but there was a growing feeling that some attempt at a critical evaluation was long overdue.

GERMAN EXPERIENCE

Purpose

We can safely assume that Frank and Charles McMurry were familiar with the curriculum of the late eighties—disjointed, abstract, wordy, and crowded. Both brothers, after attending Illinois State University in the early eighties, had taught for several years in the elementary school. We can not be sure whether they felt it incumbent on them to improve the state of the schools, however. It is true that they decided to go abroad to study in Germany, a country noted for the excellence of its educational system. But in the nineteenth century, Germany appeared to the American scholar in search of top-notch higher education much as the United States appears today to students from the underdeveloped countries.[30] Although Frank had enjoyed

---

States with Special Reference to Illinois State Normal University (Bloomington: McKnight and McKnight, 1935), p. 131.

[29] Frank M. McMurry, "Some Recollections of the Past Forty Years of Education," *Peabody Journal of Education*, IV (May, 1927), p. 327.

[30] Ten thousand American students are estimated to have matriculated in German universities in the nineteenth century. They studied philosophy, medicine,

the contacts with boys and girls, he testified that he had felt no particular call to teach, and Charles had originally planned to study theology abroad.[31] When they joined the throng going to Germany in the late eighties, they may still have been somewhat uncommitted. They knew Germany to be a Mecca in education. They had even heard from a friend in Jena that "there is a new and distinct school of Pedagogics at that place. It is the most noted school of its kind in Germany."[32] If they were to attempt to improve American education, Germany would certainly be the place to study. Yet they may have been skeptical of the scholarly potential to be found in pedagogy. As Frank remarked many years later:

> Not one of my old teachers encouraged me to go abroad to study. . . . They did not see enough theory back of the educational process to make extensive study necessary.[33]

Herbartian theory

During the initial year of learning the language and getting accustomed to German life, their biggest surprise seems to have been that no one took attendance in a German university. After the first shock, Frank recalls that he began to "bolt" his courses and read, sketchily in some books, over and over in others, marking and re-marking passages. Two of them, Karl Lange's *Apperception* and Christian Ufer's *Formale Stufen,* were to have a profound influence on his thinking and eventually on that of his Herbartian colleagues in the United States. Each book developed in detail one of the principal points in the pedagogical theory of Johann Herbart, German philosopher, psychologist, and pedagogue. Herbart's ideas, which had been current for thirty years in Germany, had recently been revived by Tuiskon Ziller, a disciple. In 1865, Ziller published *Basis of the Doctrine of Instruction as a Moral Force,* in which he expounded and elaborated Herbart's

---

theology and law. In 1880 there were more than two thousand abroad. Bulletins of the United States Bureau of Education 1880–1900.

[31] Frank M. McMurry, "Some Recollections of the Past Forty Years of Education," *Peabody Journal of Education*, IV (May, 1927), p. 327.

[32] The friend was Edmund James, later President of the University of Illinois. Quoted from a letter from DeGarmo to Edmunds, April, 1929. Henry Hugh Edmunds, "History of the Herbartian Movement in the United States and its Relation to Present Trends in Education" (Milner Library, Illinois State Normal University, 1929, Typewritten), p. 6.

[33] Frank M. McMurry, "Some Recollections of the Past Forty Years of Education," *Peabody Journal of Education*, IV (May, 1927), p. 327.

ideas. From this time on, they became increasingly influential in Germany, particularly in teacher training.

As a pedagogical theory, Herbartianism was noteworthy because it was carefully rationalized by a set of philosophical ideas and a system of psychology. In order to follow the McMurrys' experiences in Germany more intelligently, a general background statement of several essential notions of this theory may be helpful.

To begin, Herbart described the mind not as a bundle of faculties to be exercised, as popularly conceived, but as a unity creating knowledge out of the raw materials of ideas and presentations. This unity was active not passive. According to the theory, without ideas there would be no mind. This "creating" process, called apperception, was rhythmic (a process of mental breathing). Former ideas, constituting an apperceptive mass, went out to meet new ideas and interact with them. As William Kilpatrick pointed out once:

> Any suitably organized aggregate of ideas (called by Herbart the apperceptive mass) assumed therein a certain autonomy in the child's experience, favoring thereafter any ideas that fitted suitably with the apperceptive mass and opposing those that did not.[34]

The key in teaching was to develop the apperceptive mass properly so that it would help, not hinder, the child to assimilate the new ideas in the best way. To do this the teacher must give the desirable experiences to the child and not assume that he has had them. He must constantly check and revise the child's perception (that is, the way he "sees" the idea at the time) so that the child will "see" the new idea correctly. This process was thought of in a series of steps. As originally elaborated by Herbart, they were:

1. Clearness (in presentation).
2. Association (by comparison).
3. System (by organization).
4. Method (by application).

These were the steps involved in the total mastery of the subject. The steps were reformulated by Ziller to fit the stages in the recitation, and were commonly known in America in the following form:

1. Preparation: stating the aim of the lesson, recalling related facts,

[34] William H. Kilpatrick, Dewey's Influence on Education," *The Philosophy of John Dewey*, edited by Paul A. Schilpp (Evanston: Northwestern University, 1939), pp. 454–55.

and taking other precautions to put the children in the right frame of mind for the new material.

2. Presentation: securing new data or experiences from reading, lecturing, conversing, experimenting, questioning, etc.

3. Association, comparison, and abstraction: discussing and interpreting the new material, relating it to previous experiences, comparing, classifying, arranging, noting common characteristics, perhaps reaching a vague feeling of the general principles involved.

4. Generalization: formulating a statement of the general principles which have been worked up to in step three.

5. Application: interpreting other situations or experiences (new or old) in terms of the generalization reached, working particular problems, judging special cases of all sorts.[35]

The ease or pleasure felt by the apperceptive process developed into interest as it became attached to the ideas which gave the pleasure.[36] There were six of these interests or motives of mental action, and each one categorized the ideas which evoked it. They were:

Interests related to experiences with things.

1. Empirical interest: observation of things.
2. Speculative interest: reflection about natural laws.
3. Aesthetic interest: contemplation of and feeling for the beautiful.

Interests related to experiences with people.

4. Sympathetic interest: kindly disposition toward people.
5. Social interest: participation in public affairs.
6. Religious interest: contemplation of human destiny.[37]

Interests of this kind characterized the life activities appropriate

---

[35] Samuel Chester Parker, *A Textbook in the History of Modern Elementary Education* (Boston: Ginn and Co., 1912), pp. 425–26.

[36] Frank McMurry commented years later on the difficulty teachers had with this concept of interest. "Heretofore we had tried to get the child interested so that he would learn," he would explain. Then he would go on to recommend to them that, "what we should do, however, is to get the child to learn so that he will become interested . . . The confused expression on the faces of many persons at such times was proof that they did not quite get the point," he added. Frank M. McMurry, "Some Recollections of the Past Forty Years of Education," *Peabody Journal of Education.* IV (May, 1927), p. 330.

[37] Samuel Chester Parker, *A Textbook in the History of Modern Elementary Education* (Boston: Ginn and Co., 1912), p. 392.

to the cultivated man. For example, a sympathetic interest was shown by a kindly disposition toward people. It might be fostered by studying historical materials which illustrated "good" behavior (for example, kindly acts). The child would, as a result, develop a kindly attitude or interest in relations between people which would tend to get stronger as it was more often experienced, through the study of appropriate historical materials.

As a result, knowledge was considered crucial to the action of the will. The contents of the mind controlled the "interests" and ultimately the child's behavior. A favorite summarizing statement was, "The mind leads the will captive." The central aim of education was the moral aim of good action or behavior. Guided by the correct ideas and motivated by interest, the educated person would be prepared to discharge his duties in life properly.

One should notice that the aim of this education was to prepare man for life in an idealized culture conceived of as a prototype of the essential truth of the universe. That Herbart absorbed this view from the Humanistic revival of his times is suggested by the following comment:

> Neo-Humanism rested on the conviction that the true civilization and education sought after by Rousseau was to be found in full perfection in the Hellenic world. It regarded Greek culture as the consummation and idealization of Nature and the Hellenic type of man as the full and unrestricted realization of the idea of human kind as conceived by the creative spirit of Nature.[38]

Such a position is essentially conservative since it assumes some preexisting standard for human life, whether embodied in Greek life or in that of another culture, and judges human actions in terms of the standard of this idealized culture. Within this assumed framework, moral action is the highest goal. Changes in the cultural framework are irrelevant and ignored by the theory.

Herbart had been primarily interested in secondary education, but his disciple Ziller had applied these same ideas to the curriculum of the elementary school. In so doing, Ziller had added two new ramifications to Herbart's theory which deserve some attention since they were to be the subject of much discussion in American educational circles.

One was the doctrine of concentration (in its modified form known as correlation). Inspired by a revived wave of national enthusiasm at

[38] F. Paulsen, *German Education* (New York: Charles Scribner's Sons, 1908), p. 161.

the time of the rise of Bismarck (1870), Ziller used history and literature as the core of the work in the elementary school. He had adapted a suggestion made by Herbart that they were superior subjects for the development of moral ideas and sentiments. By a concentration on this central core of history and literature, Ziller hoped to develop an integrated ethical character, based on a proper apperceptive mass. He intended in this way to produce the greatest effect on moral development.

In order to achieve concentration, Ziller devised the scheme of arranging this sequence of topics in literature and history according to the stages in the evolution of cultures. This plan was based on the current theory of culture epochs, which stated that the child in his development recapitulated the cultural evolution of the race.[39]

Later the plan of concentrating all school work around one core subject was to be dropped in favor of correlating relevant material from various subjects around the study of selected topics in any one subject.

Teacher training

As we have seen, the McMurrys' first introduction to Herbartian theory was through Lange's book, the theme of which was apperception, and through Ufer's, which discussed the steps of the recitation. Both books had opened their eyes to the possibility that pedagogy might have a philosophical and psychological rationale of real breadth and depth. Frank's comment years later was:

I know I experienced an educational conversion, and that the time of it was in the winter of 1887–8. It was those two books that did it.[40]

In connection with the work in pedagogy at the University of Jena, the McMurrys attended training classes in the practice school as well. For forty years there had been at this university a program of teacher training intimately connected with the activities of the practice school. There was little novelty in this program in Germany. A practice school run in connection with a pedagogical school under the wings of a

[39] There was far from unanimity among Herbart's disciples on the nature of his basic doctrines. Karl Stoy, another of Herbart's disciples, with whom DeGarmo had studied, rejected Ziller's formulations and called the theories of concentration and culture epochs, "Ziller's novelties . . . wrecks from the great structure of Herbart." Charles DeGarmo, *Herbart and the Herbartians* (New York: Charles Scribner's Sons, 1895), p. 185.

[40] Frank M. McMurry, "Some Recollections of the Past Forty Years of Education," *Peabody Journal of Education*, IV (May, 1927), p. 329.

21

great university had been part of the German tradition in education ever since Herbart had first established the pattern at Koenigsberg in 1809. The particular vitality of the program at the University of Jena was due to the vigorous work of its director, Wilhelm Rein, a disciple of Ziller. Two years before the McMurrys attended the school, he had begun a program of teacher training that surpassed all previous ones in the thoroughness with which the Herbartian doctrine was applied. The doctrines of concentration and the culture epochs received special emphasis. The teachers in training observed and analyzed the teaching done in the practice school, using Herbartian ideas as their criteria. They saw the mammoth course of study which Rein had worked out for the whole elementary school program, used as a guide to the teaching of the desired content.[41]

The McMurrys were familiar enough with practice schools. But the scope, depth, and pace of this one astounded them, as did the fact that the methods of selecting content and organizing the curriculum were so consistently Herbartian. The class in pedagogy consisted of three sessions. The first one, called the Practikum, was held usually on Wednesday and consisted of a model recitation conducted by a student teacher about which the class members were to make full notes. One member was appointed each time to bring in a written critique. Frank later made this comment:

> The first recitation observed was a very simple one in second or third-grade Reading, with a class of not more than twenty children. It was the simplest thing in the world, and I could have said all that needed to be said about it in five minutes.[42]

The second session, called the Theoretikum, was usually held from seven to eight Friday evening. Here the critiques were read.[43] A member recollected that the Professor had been kind but had called his effort valueless because it was "merely an *observation about* a psychological analysis of the observation of natural objects, not an *analysis* at all."[44]

---

[41] For the first grade alone the course of study filled 198 pages, and the whole work constituted two large volumes. See Samuel Chester Parker, *A Textbook in the History of Modern Elementary Education* (Boston: Ginn and Co., 1912), p. 403.

[42] Frank M. McMurry, "Some Recollections of the Past Forty Years of Education," *Peabody Journal of Education,* IV (May, 1927), pp. 328–29.

[43] There were in all some thirty students from possibly a dozen different countries, Charles and Frank being the first American members. Everyone's turn came for the critique, a great labor in German!

[44] Charles DeGarmo, *Herbart and the Herbartians* (New York: Charles Scribner's Sons, 1895), p. 182.

For the third session, called the Conference, the members adjourned to a nearby hotel. The tables having been arranged in the form of a "T" with the Professor on a sofa at the head, the discussion was thrown wide open. Dr. Rein summarized the whole and expressed "much regret that lack of time prevented any consideration of some half dozen additional vital questions which he briefly but pointedly enumerated." The impression made on the students was a deep and lasting one. Frank reported years later:

> That evening was a revelation to me. Even though I suspected that it was only by accident that so much theory related itself to that particular thirty-minute recitation . . . it carried me a long way toward the conviction that I would get in Germany what I had gone there for.[45]

This work with Rein convinced Frank that pedagogy had a rationale of a very respectable breadth and depth. He also recognized in the Herbartian theory something which American schools so far had lacked. At the core of the Herbartian pedagogy was a systematic method of selecting, arranging, and organizing the curriculum, that put the child and knowledge in a pedagogical relationship. Closely related to the pedagogy were a systematic philosophy and psychology. Frank and Charles had seen the pedagogy at work in a highly successful program of teacher training based on a well worked out course of study. Curriculum matters seemed to be in the hands of men who possessed a University tradition of educational scholarship and who took a thoroughly professional attitude toward their specialization. Herbartianism appeared to the McMurrys to be a made-to-order solution for the heterogeneity and confusion of the American common school curriculum.

STRATEGY ON THEIR RETURN

Charles's writings

The chief strategy of the McMurrys on returning from Germany was to try to get the beneficial effects of the Herbartian viewpoint on the curriculum into actual practice in the schools as rapidly as possible. One of Charles's first moves on his return from Jena was to set down in book form some of his thoughts on the application of Herbartian doctrines to the American curriculum problem. Rather than work his

---

[45] Frank M. McMurry, "Some Recollections of the Past Forty Years of Education," *Peabody Journal of Education*, IV (May, 1927), p. 329.

ideas out at length, one by one, he arranged for the private printing of three small volumes and began to collect data for another. The four would represent in miniature four kinds of books he felt would be useful and needed. The first was called a book on method,[46] but, unlike the usual books on methods of teaching, it gave a short outline of the method of selecting and organizing content which he had observed in use in Jena. Based on the Herbartian doctrines of apperception and correlation, the book showed how to control the child's active assimilation of knowledge by developing the recitation in the proper order. He described how the teacher must select and arrange the ideas in the lesson, tailoring them to fit the active mind process observed in the child.

In the second work, he applied this general method to the subject of geography.[47] He suggested that the teacher might foster apperception by beginning with geographical objects and activities within the children's direct experience, such as the food products of their own gardens, or a visit to a sawmill, etc. As an illustration of the doctrine of correlation, he recommended that related geographical facts be presented when the children studied topics on the history of Illinois.

His third work was for children, a collection of narrative and biographical materials on the pioneer history of the Middle West, selected from first-hand sources and suitably arranged.[48] Here was the "meat" of history instruction, the wealth of detail which would bring children close to the actual historical experience. This was the kind of content in history which was ideal for developing the apperceptive mass.

Fourth, he began to work out by experimentation in the practice schools of both the normal schools in which he was a professor[49] an American version of the celebrated course of study of Rein.[50] When the volume appeared in 1895 it was sent especially to superintendents

[46] Charles McMurry, *How to Conduct the Recitation and the Principles Underlying Methods of Teaching in Classes* (Chicago: A. Flanagan Co., 1890).

[47] Charles McMurry, *A Geography Plan for the Grades of the Common School* (Winona, Minn.: Jones and Kroeger, 1891).

[48] Charles McMurry, *Pioneer History Stories for Third and Fourth Grades.* (First Series; Winona, Minn.: Jones and Kroeger, 1891). He wrote two more volumes on the history of the East Coast and the Far West. The series was to prove unexpectedly successful, and to become a prototype for later factual materials for children.

[49] Winona State Normal, Winona, Minnesota, 1889–92; Illinois State Normal University, Normal, Illinois, 1892–99.

[50] Charles McMurry, *A Course of Study for the Eight Grades of the Common Schools, Including a Handbook of Practical Suggestions to Teachers* (Bloomington, Ill.: Public-school Publishing Co., 1895).

of schools, accompanied by the request that they use it, comment on it, and send him theirs for comparison. He implied that a course of study was not static but needed to be actively worked out in close connection with the process of actual instruction.

Remembering the impact on their own thinking made by the books of Ufer and Lange, both Charles and Frank encouraged a small group of enthusiasts in Illinois to translate or arrange for the translation of a number of fundamental books on Herbartian doctrine.[51]

Help to committees

The McMurrys tried also to give what help they could to current efforts being made by the National Education Association to improve the curriculum.[52] This body had traditionally conducted what is now called educational research by means of committees of special investigation, and by 1890 there had already been several such committees appointed to study problems connected with the school curriculum. Beginning in 1875 with a Committee on a Unified Course of Study from Primary to University, the Association had appointed a new committee in each succeeding decade to struggle with the question of the best means of accommodating the new subjects in the curriculum.

[51] Members of this group were the most active of all the returning scholars. As the historian Samuel Parker commented, in assessing the waning Herbartian movement in 1912, "The geographical center of this interest in Herbartian principles was northern Illinois, especially in the normal schools." Samuel C. Parker, *History of Modern Elementary Education* (Boston: Ginn and Co., 1912), p. 404. Among the translations of works on Herbartianism which were sponsored by this group were: Gustav Lindner, *Empirical Psychology*, trans. C. DeGarmo (Boston: D. C. Heath and Co., 1889; Johann Herbart, *Psychology*, trans. M. K. Smith (New York: D. Appleton and Co., 1891); Johann Herbart, *The Science of Education: Its General Principles*, trans. Henry and Emmie Felkin (1892); Wilhelm Rein, *Outlines of Pedagogics*, trans. C. C. and Ida J. Van Liew (New York: E. L. Kellogg and Co., 1893); Karl Lange, *Apperception*, trans. C. De-Garmo (Boston: D. C. Heath, 1893); Christian Ufer, *Introduction to the Pedagogy of Herbart*, trans. J. C. Zinser (Boston: D. C. Heath, 1894). DeGarmo edited the latter two works which were translated and sponsored by the original Herbart Club whose members were as follows: Levi Seeley, Elmer E. Brown, Eudora Hailmann, Florence Hall, George James, Margaret K. Smith, Theo. Noss, L. R. Klemm, Ossian Lang, Herman Lukens, Charles McMurry and Frank McMurry. Further sources on Herbartianism include: Samuel C. Parker, *A Textbook in the History of Modern Elementary Education* (Boston: Ginn and Co., 1912), Chap. XVII; Dorothy McMurry, *Herbartian Contributions to History Instruction in American Elementary Schools* (New York: Teachers College, Columbia University, Bureau of Publications, 1946); Charles DeGarmo, *Herbart and the Herbartians* (New York: Charles Scribner's Sons, 1895).

[52] From the beginning the McMurrys worked principally in the Department of Superintendence, a very powerful arm of the National Education Association,

As we have already noted, these committees were faced with the problem of an increasingly heterogeneous school population, demanding a curriculum that was practical as well as cultural. Although there was no truly effective pressure for two educational ladders, as in Europe, the two groups of subjects, the cultural and the practical, did represent a conflict within the curriculum of a school which professed to give equal opportunities to all. The problem was to prevent the study of subjects in one group from interfering with the study of subjects in the other, in preparation for the day when the student would finally decide whether to leave school for work or go on to the university. The first committee[53] explored the idea of a unified program which would somehow include all the subjects. A second study of the problem[54] resulted in the proposal to rate all the subjects on a value scale so that a core of the most worthwhile ones could be selected. This idea was lost when it was then suggested that perhaps all subjects would be equally useful if all were so well organized and taught that they provided the necessary mental discipline. This recommendation was elaborated upon by the most famous committee of them all, the Committee of Ten, appointed in 1893.[55] They concluded, among other things, that all the subjects could be considered to be of equal educational value, if well taught. To be well taught, they contended, the newer studies should enjoy the same "advantages the older subjects

---

rather than in the Department of Elementary Education, which owed its creation to the efforts of the Department of Superintendence. The Department of Elementary Education had been associated primarily with methods, since Edward Sheldon, of Oswego fame, was its first president. An examination of some eighty-five speeches given to the Association from 1871 to 1906 on topics which seem related to the curriculum reveals that only five were given under the sponsorship of the Department of Elementary Education. Apparently from the very beginning, the study of the curriculum had a wider scope than that furnished by any special level of education.

[53] The Committee on a Course of Study from Primary School to University. An account of its work is given in: National Educational Association, "Report of a Committee on a Course of Study from Primary School to University," *Addresses and Journal of Proceedings* (1876), pp. 58–68.

[54] National Educational Association, "Report of the Committee of Educational Value of Common School Studies," *Journal of Proceedings and Addresses* (1886), pp. 403–20.

[55] National Educational Association, Committee of Ten on Secondary School Studies, *Report.* U.S. Bureau of Education (Washington, D.C.: Government Printing Office, 1893). Chaired by Charles W. Eliot, President of Harvard, it included the United States Commissioner of Education, William T. Harris, five university presidents, one college professor, two headmasters, and one principal of a public high school. Eventually some ninety college and normal school professors of the established branches participated in its deliberations.

have always possessed," that of their early introduction into the elementary school curriculum by means of "perspective views or broad surveys."[56] If the young child meets the subject early, they stated, he will acquire the necessary facts and mental habits so difficult and painful to acquire later. To guarantee that all subjects would enjoy equal value, it was proposed that all subjects should qualify the student equally well for entrance to college.

This recommendation relieved the conflict in the secondary curriculum but sharpened the problem of a crowded curriculum in the elementary school. The Committee, largely composed of experts in subject matter, had arrived at a solution which guaranteed the continued presence of each subject in the curriculum but put the burden of selection on the learner. Such selection was not recommended for the elementary curriculum, however. As a result, the committee action almost demanded that someone adjudicate between the various claims of each subject in the name of the learner in the elementary school. That the committee members had a twinge of conscience is shown by the promise in their report not to increase the demands of the established subjects and by their formal recommendations that "every subject should help every other."[57]

The work of the Committee of Ten had been closely watched by the Herbartians. While they disapproved on principle of the disregard the Committee showed for content by permitting the learner to select at the secondary level, this criticism did not apply to the recommendations for the elementary school, since no selection was to be allowed. The Herbartians saw that the learner in the elementary school, faced with a crowded curriculum now officially sanctioned by this influential committee, needed help. Francis Parker thought the report very important and urged that it be at the heart of discussions in teachers meetings. An advocate of the correlation of studies as a way of relieving crowding in the curriculum,[58] he suggested that a special committee on correlation be appointed in the Department of Superintendence to make recommendations. The result was that a Committee of Fifteen was

[56] National Educational Association, Committee of Ten on Secondary School Studies, *Report.* U.S. Bureau of Education (Washington, D.C.: Government Printing Office, 1893), p. 16.

[57] National Educational Association, Committee of Ten on Secondary School Studies, *Report.* U.S. Bureau of Education (Washington, D.C.: Government Printing Office, 1893), p. 15.

[58] Francis Parker had just published *Talks on Pedagogics: an Outline of the Theory of Concentration* (New York: E. L. Kellogg and Co., 1894).

formed to explore, among other matters, the question of correlation.[59] The subcommittee charged with the study of crowding was chaired by William T. Harris. The members of this subcommittee tried to answer carefully the questions which had been posed them by the Herbartians and others. Typical questions and answers are the following:

Q. What is the pedagogical value of each subject?

A. All are of equal value if they help the child gain insight into the civilization of the age.

Q. Which subjects should be taught, when, and how long?

A. Music should be taught throughout, writing only through the sixth year.

Q. What should be the sequence of studies?

A. Studies should be arranged to provide the best exercise of the faculties and the unfolding in the natural order.

Q. Should the subjects be treated differently if the child leaves school at twelve?

A. Neither omissions nor optional studies are recommended.

There were other questions which the Committee answered vaguely if at all and these were probably of special interest to the Herbartians. Examples of these questions were: Should the sequence of studies be determined by the child's apperception? Is the purpose of correlation to develop apperception or to build ethical purpose? What are the best methods of correlation?[60]

The disappointment the Herbartians felt with the work of the Committee was clearly expressed by Frank McMurry in his comments during the discussion which followed the report. The Committee, he said, had been too preoccupied with the studies, or divisions of learning, to deal properly with the correlation of ideas or thoughts within the studies.[61] DeGarmo's remarks on this occasion were even more pointed:

Those who expected other things of the report may be excused for not

[59] National Educational Association, *Journal of Proceedings and Addresses* (1895). A complete account of the formation of this Committee is found on pp. 232–37; the text of the report on Correlation of Studies, pp. 287–332; discussion of the report, pp. 343–50. In contrast to the Committee of Ten, this Committee consisted of thirteen superintendents of schools, and only one university president as well as the United States Commissioner of Education, W. T. Harris.

[60] National Educational Association, *Journal of Proceedings and Addresses* (1895), p. 233.

[61] National Educational Association, *Journal of Proceedings and Addresses* (1895), pp. 343–44.

having classified the evaluation of educational values under the head of correlation of studies at all. The whole consideration is static and *a priori* . . . this Hegelian exposition of the reasons for teaching the common branches does not touch the real problem involved in their correlation. . . . Just as, until in his maturity [the child] studies Dr. Harris's "Introduction to Philosophy," he will be totally unconscious of the fact that he uses the second figure of the syllogism every time he recognizes his father in the distance, so he must wait until he reads Dr. Harris's report on the correlation of studies to know the philosophical reason why he studied grammar and arithmetic.[62]

DeGarmo went on to say that the sequence of topics within a study and their mutual relations with each other had not been discussed at all. No clear method of giving unity to the content had been presented. He approved of the Committee's proposal to select content that would help the child meet the demands of civilization, but he warned against the too hasty conclusion that such a selection would guarantee that the child was "correlated" with his environment:

Correlation . . . extends to the daily work of the schoolroom as it appeals to the child's mind, to his capacity to grasp and assimilate knowledge; it includes the formation of his mental habit whereby conduct becomes the resultant of correlated knowledge, not the effect of isolated impulse.[63]

Nicholas Murray Butler summarized the objections by saying that the child sees the environment as correlated; the adults have analyzed it into subjects; and the advocates of correlation are simply trying to put the course of study back where they found it, from the child's point of view. After commenting that "for one hundred years . . . we have been trying to extract the curriculum from a philosophical discussion of this sort," he concluded by insisting that the ideas of the correlationists needed to be heard.[64]

Francis Parker, the originator of the idea for a committee, was almost incoherent in his disappointment:

When in Boston, two years ago, I moved that a committee be appointed to report on correlation, I had in mind a full and complete treatment of

[62] Charles DeGarmo, "The Principles upon Which the Co-ordination of Studies Should Proceed," *Journal of Proceedings and Addresses of the National Educational Association* (1895), pp. 88–89. DeGarmo had studied in Germany at the same time as the McMurrys and was as influential a figure as they. His interest was principally in secondary education.

[63] Charles DeGarmo, "The Principles upon Which the Co-ordination of Studies Should Proceed," *Journal of Proceedings and Addresses of the National Educational Association* (1895), p. 90.

[64] National Educational Association, *Journal of Proceedings and Addresses* (1895), p. 348.

the subject. I had confidence in the ability of the committee. I supposed they would make a careful study of every phase of the subject; that they would make themselves familiar with Herbart, Ziller, Stoy, and Rein. They have ignored the very subject which they were intended to treat. The report is a grand restatement of facts long known to all of us. But it is like the play of "Hamlet" with Hamlet left out; or, as I might better say, with Hamlet kicked out. Too many teachers at the present time think that Herbartian doctrine seems to furnish a grand working hypothesis. . . . The report leaves no margin for the research of the teacher. Can abstract philosophy direct her? Shall we not be directed by our experience? Just think of six years of regular books. Is there no relief? I shall accept this report respectfully; I shall take it home and study it prayerfully; but I move that a committee of fifteen be appointed to revise it.[65]

Formation of Herbart Society

This was the moment when a good clear exposition of Herbartian doctrine would be interesting and profitable, and something of this kind was in the offing. Three years before, in 1892, at the Saratoga meeting of the Department of Superintendence, a small group of interested men and women had formed what they called simply a Herbart Club. They had done so principally for their own professional improvement.[66] We can guess that the disappointment caused by the report of the Committee of Fifteen fanned the modest spark of interest in Herbartian doctrines shown when the club was organized. At any rate, in the same year as the appearance of the report, the group acquired an official name, The National Herbart Society for the Scientific Study of Teaching, a distinguished executive council, a membership,[67] and funds for a yearbook.

Although Herbartian doctrine was of special interest, the organization planned a wide, scholarly approach to current educational issues by soliciting papers and reports for the meetings from members seriously and patiently at work upon the study of some problem arising

[65] National Educational Association, *Journal of Proceedings and Addresses* (1895), p. 344.

[66] There was a precedent in Germany for this kind of group. As one means of bringing about a revival of interest in Herbartian doctrines in 1868, Ziller had started a movement for the foundation of Herbart Clubs. Rein as Ziller's student continued the practice at the University of Jena.

[67] The Council: Charles DeGarmo, Nicholas Murray Butler, John Dewey, Wilbur Jackman, Elmer Brown, Frank and Charles McMurry, Levi Seeley, and C. C. Van Liew. Charles McMurry was the first secretary. Membership by 1899 had grown to seven thousand and included teachers, students of education, and parents.

out of their immediate labors.[68] In this way, they tried to combine questions which were current and controversial with topics which represented particular areas of inquiry being pursued by individuals.[69] All papers were put in the hands of the members before the meetings, as well as printed afterwards in the Yearbook, together with reports of the discussions. It was hoped that by this means the discussions could be more "vigorous and thoughtful."

Discussion of correlation

As we might expect, one of the principal topics to which the meetings of the Herbart Society were devoted in its first few years was that of correlation. Discussion of this subject began with DeGarmo's keynote speech in 1895, in which he briefly outlined the setting of what he considered to be the school's chief problem. He referred to the impetus to extend universal schooling in America, which we have already reviewed, and to the success in establishing the basic machinery of the school at the expense of systematic attention to the curriculum. There had been a multiplication of both knowledge and learners, he said, and the unsuitability of some of the subjects for the newly received "sons of toil" had centered the educator's attention on the question of what to teach.[70]

"Many and various are the schemes for solving the problem," he said, proceeding to demolish them with his usual wit and penetration. He showed scorn of "surgical pedagogy"—omitting old studies so that new might be added. "To reduce weight it amputates limbs." Plans to "let the child choose what he fancies," he continued, reflected the outmoded doctrine of formal discipline which asserted that "study of any kind has a disciplinary value for the mind, without much regard

---

[68] *First Yearbook of the National Herbart Society for the Scientific Study of Teaching* (Bloomington, Ill.: Pantagraph Printing and Stationery Co., 1895), p. 204.

[69] They stipulated that Herbartian doctrines were to be discussed but that they were by no means limiting themselves to Herbartian topics.

[70] Charles DeGarmo, "Most Pressing Problems Concerning the Elementary Course of Study," *First Yearbook of the National Herbart Society for the Scientific Study of Teaching* (Bloomington, Ill.: Pantagraph Printing and Stationery Co., 1895), p. 4. DeGarmo's educational philosophy had a strong socioeconomic cast. "The future . . . belongs neither to the humanist nor to the scientist as such, but to both combined in the economist," he wrote in 1896. He warned that if current economic problems were not solved, "hunger and economic servitude will cause the masses to change evolution into revolution." Charles DeGarmo, *Herbart and the Herbartians* (New York: Charles Scribner's Sons, 1895), pp. 237, 239.

to its content." Obviously, taking all good things into the course of study was self-defeating unless some provisions were made for their accommodation. No mind, much less the untrained mind of the child, could organize the enormous number of unrelated topics.[71]

After indicating his agreement with DeGarmo, Frank McMurry suggested that the way to solve the problem was to provide for a proper correlation of subjects. In so doing he touched off a controversy on the true nature and meaning of the term that was to last several years. Frank first described the doctrine of apperception in such a way as to connect it closely with the stages of child growth. He contended:

> that what one can know and feel and will depends on what he has already known and felt and willed, or that past experiences are the sole basis for intellectual, emotional, and ethical growth. . . . The first requisite . . . is that the subject-matter of instruction be intimately related both to the kind of thinking, and to the topics of thought which most naturally occupy the child's mind. Suitable matter will vary according to age and stage of development. If we could only discover and take advantage of this most opportune moment for offering every bit of knowledge, what a wonderful economy of effort would result![72]

While there was a good deal more to the doctrine of apperception than this, Frank insisted that its relevance to the crowded curriculum lay in its suggestion that content would be most economically taught if it were selected to fit the stages of child growth. The theory of the culture epochs, i.e. that the child passes through the same general stages of development through which the race passes, suggested that what specially interested the race at a certain age would appeal with most force to the child at the corresponding age. By this arrangement the content of each study could be fitted more closely to the child's past experiences and become more fully a part of him.

These culture epochs, he went on, were best represented in the early years of schooling by some classical work in literature and history —such as the stories of Ulysses and Robinson Crusoe, or the fairy tales—and in later grades, by more diversified historical materials. The work of the school could be "concentrated" in these classics, and all

---

[71] Charles DeGarmo, "Most Pressing Problems Concerning the Elementary Course of Study," *First Yearbook of the National Herbart Society for the Scientific Study of Teaching* (Bloomington, Ill.: Pantagraph Printing and Stationery Co., 1895), p. 5.

[72] Frank McMurry, "Concentration," *First Yearbook of the National Herbart Society for the Scientific Study of Teaching* (Bloomington, Ill.: Pantagraph Printing and Stationery Co., 1895), p. 28.

the studies organized around them. Thus, a well-integrated curriculum tailored to the child's stage of growth would solve the problem of an overcrowded program of studies as described by DeGarmo.[73]

The theory of the culture epochs was to have an interesting career,[74] but it is not to be confused with the doctrine of correlation itself. By 1896, a number of papers had been prepared to defend or attack the culture epoch theory. More important, efforts had been made to discuss correlation without using the culture epoch theory, which "mixed" the studies in a way alarming to many.

Among those who had viewed correlation with suspicion was William T. Harris, who defended the inviolability of the basic divisions of the structure of knowledge. He had categorized knowledge into five co-ordinate groups: (1) mathematics and physics; (2) biology; (3) literature and art, chiefly the study of literary works of art; (4) grammar, leading to logic and psychology; and (5) history, as the study of sociological, political and social institutions. He had contended that "no one of these groups could be spared from a symmetrical whole without destroying the pupil's view of the world."[75] He was probably as influential as any other person in making the idea of concentration unpopular. Nevertheless, the Herbartians stuck to their guns on the doctrine of correlation.

In addition, a considerable group agreeing with Harris had contended that correlation was a function of the child's mind itself and was not hindered but furthered by clear, logical instruction in each branch of study, according to the natural sequence within the study. Such instruction would make the content of each subject properly available to the child's mind as it naturally unified itself. They feared that a forced unification, attempted too early, would disturb and perhaps destroy this natural unifying process.[76]

The advocates of correlation tried to pin down the nature of this

[73] Frank McMurry, "Concentration," *First Yearbook of the National Herbart Society for the Scientific Study of Teaching* (Bloomington, Ill.: Pantagraph Printing and Stationery Co., 1895), pp. 28–69.

[74] Its proponents recommended, among other things, the following: the use of literature and history in the grades; the study of primitive life, such as Indian units; and the organization of content around a given culture during a certain period of its development, such as Greek culture, life during the Middle Ages, etc.

[75] Charles McMurry in a discussion of correlation quoted Harris approvingly as saying the above at Jacksonville. Charles McMurry, "A Reply to Dr. White's Paper," *Second Yearbook of the National Herbart Society for the Scientific Study of Teaching* (Bloomington, Ill.: Pantagraph Printing, 1896), p. 28.

[76] Emerson E. White, "Isolation and Unification as Bases of Courses of Study," *Second Yearbook of the National Herbart Society for the Scientific Study of Teaching* (Bloomington, Ill.: Pantagraph Printing, 1896), p. 16.

33

unity. According to Charles McMurry, it consisted of "the relation of knowledge to the practical world of men and things," and he could quote Harris in support of this statement.[77] Charles insisted that the natural movement of the child's mind is toward a unity which is accidental, irrelevant, and often opposing, since it is the result of an unmediated jumbling of total experience in the immature being. The problem for the educator, as Charles saw it, was to devise ways by which this totality which is naturally disorganized would develop toward a totality which is properly organized.

Charles agreed with DeGarmo that "every subject of instruction has some essential function in fitting the child for life"[78] and that the ideas of history were related to the ideas of geography in dealing with the problems of nature and man. But, for the child, these historical and geographical ideas were mixed up in a welter called, for example, the Mississippi Valley. The Mississippi Valley might be cut up for him into a series of historical and geographical ideas. He contended that teachers should help children "organize" their thoughts by grouping the studies around topics, at the same time distinguishing carefully for the child the characteristic contribution of each study to the topic.

That teachers did not do this at present, he continued, was regrettable but must be faced. For example, teachers customarily presented in one morning the history of the Mississippi Valley, the geography of South America, the science of the parts of a flower, and the literature of Greece. Charles quoted Herbart himself to show the confusion that necessarily ensued from such practice:

> In consideration of the unmediated jumbling together of thought masses as a condition common to anomalous mental states, I cannot refrain from wondering what sort of a process is being worked out in the heads of schoolboys, who in a single forenoon are driven through a series of heterogeneous lessons, each one of which, on the following day, at the regular tap of the bell, is repeated and continued.[79]

[77] Charles McMurry, "A Reply to Dr. White's Paper," *Second Yearbook of the National Herbart Society for the Scientific Study of Teaching* (Bloomington, Ill.: Pantagraph Printing, 1896), p. 22. Charles referred to remarks Harris had made in a speech entitled "The Essential Differences of Elementary and Higher Instruction," *Addresses and Journal of Proceedings of the National Educational Association* (1890).

[78] Charles DeGarmo, "The Principles upon Which the Co-ordination of Studies Should Proceed," *Journal of Proceedings and Addresses of the National Educational Association* (1895), p. 92.

[79] Charles McMurry, "A Reply to Dr. White's Paper," *Second Yearbook of the National Herbart Society for the Scientific Study of Teaching* (Bloomington, Ill.: Pantagraph Printing, 1896), p. 46.

As an advocate of correlation, Charles agreed with Emerson White that "children are not philosophic spiders that gather knowledge by excursions over a web of philosophic causation."[80] He contended that the child was, rather, trying to analyze and then synthesize his totality of knowledge and that the teacher could help him. The architectural plan for this synthesis of content which the children were building consisted of a set of topics arranged in such a way that they gradually developed some central unifying ideas, and of a set of relationships between these ideas, worked out for the child as he went along.

For example, an historical topic like the discovery of the Mississippi might be developed together with the relevant geographical and scientific understandings. Or a strictly geographical topic such as the Falls of Minneapolis might be used as a focus for a variety of aspects drawn from the different subjects. In a "type study" of this kind, the following aspects might be studied:

> the rock strata and the cañon below the falls (geology); the mills and turbine wheels (physics); sawmills and pineries (pine trees); and early history (Indians and Hennepin); besides the strict geographical relations of commerce, railroads, Minneapolis, etc.[81]

There was danger that the doctrine of correlation would be misunderstood. As DeGarmo commented wryly, "We could, of course, associate butter with butter-flies and cows with cowslips."[82] Later, Louis Soldan was to caricature this same kind of misunderstanding of the theory. He was to describe a lesson in the early grades in which the teacher had the children read about, divide, sing about, examine, and make pictures of apples, until one boy (probably in desperation) drew a horse to eat all the apples up.[83]

Parker agreed heartily with the Herbartians that a plan of correlation was needed but vehemently opposed the particular one they had proposed. Frank later recalled Parker's resistance to their scheme as prophetic:

---

[80] Emerson E. White, "Isolation and Unification as Bases of Courses of Study," *Second Yearbook of the National Herbart Society for the Scientific Study of Teaching* (Bloomington, Ill.: Pantagraph Printing, 1896), p. 16.

[81] Charles McMurry, *The Elements of General Method* (1st. ed. rev.; New York: The Macmillan Co., 1903), pp. 173–74.

[82] Charles DeGarmo, "The Principles upon Which the Co-ordination of Studies Should Proceed," *Journal of Proceedings and Addresses of the National Educational Association* (1895), p. 91.

[83] F. Louis Soldan, "What is a Fad?" *American Education*, V (Dec., 1901), pp. 201–07.

We had a battle royal on that question at the Denver N.E.A. meeting in 1894. Over and over again at that meeting he declared that the *child* should be made the center, not some study. As I look back on it now, he was searching for the problem or project plan of work, where you find your starting point for both curriculum and method within the child rather than within some branch of knowledge. In that tendency he was a long way in advance of the rest of us.[84]

Whatever was to be the fate of the particular doctrine of correlation the Herbartians advanced, they did succeed in creating an awareness in the minds of educators of the time of the need to promote unity in the child's mind. They alerted the teacher to the value of watching closely the process by which the child assimilates knowledge and of arranging the presentation of content so that logical, intellectual inter-relationships would stand out.

As we follow this discussion, and all other discussions of the Herbartians, whether of correlation, culture epochs, apperception, or the steps of the recitation, we become aware of a climate of thought and an approach to the curriculum that is different from anything that had gone on before. These men were not discussing content as such, nor even methods of instruction. Rather, they were discussing the process of selecting and ordering content in relation to the act of its assimilation by the child. To a profession that had been accustomed to think that the curriculum was the facts and generalizations as given in a textbook and that method was a way of teaching them, it was new and bewildering to talk of making the curriculum by means of the daily recitation. The range of attention had been widened, and many topics were being brought into focus against the background of the new theory that had not been thought of in the new way before.

Teaching careers

By 1895, Charles and Frank McMurry had each begun what was to prove a long and influential career in the training of teachers. Charles at Illinois State Normal University from 1892 to 1899, then at Northern Illinois State Normal until 1915, and at George Peabody College for Teachers until 1929, always worked directly with young teachers, close to what we have noted he liked to call "the smelting point" of education. He taught courses in basic and special methods, and supervised practice according to these methods.[85] He wrote some

[84] Frank M. McMurry, "Some Recollections of the Past Forty Years of Education," *Peabody Journal of Education*, IV (May, 1927), p. 331.

[85] Charles taught, for example, a course in pedagogy, part of the description of

thirty volumes in all, addressing himself principally to the teacher working with children in the instructional process. He revised his basic book on the method of selecting and organizing content, which we have already examined,[86] and got out a series of books on special methods, covering the whole range of content with each one elaborating the basic method in one subject matter area.[87] He worked out a sample course of study for all eight grades, as a guide to the method.[88] He and Frank collaborated on a book about the recitation, the ground plan for their approach in the classroom.[89] His books on projects in the twenties[90] were really descriptions of the older "type studies," used as foci in correlating the subjects. In spite of this extensive literature, Charles never felt that the central problem of unity and clarity in the curriculum had been adequately solved. Twice in his career, he stopped to indict the profession for this failure, holding their penchant for "fads" responsible for their distraction from a needed concern for system and order.[91]

---

which reads, "observations of illustrative lessons with children, the making of lesson plans according to the Formal Steps, and a discussion of some fundamental school problems," Northern Illinois State Normal School, *Announcements* (1907), p. 18.

[86] *Elements of General Method* (1st. ed. rev.; New York: The Macmillan Co., 1903). The original work, published in 1890, was enlarged slightly in 1892, the material on the formal steps was dropped from the reprintings in 1893, and a complete revision was issued in 1903.

[87] *Special Method for Literature and History of the Common Schools* (Bloomington, Ill.: Public School Publishing Co., 1894), 1st. ed. rev., 1903; *Special Method in Geography for Third and Fourth Grades* (Bloomington, Ill.: Public School Publishing Co., 1895), 1st. ed. rev., 1903; *Special Method in Natural Science for the First Four Grades of the Common School* (Bloomington, Ill.: Public School Publishing Co., 1896) 1st. ed. rev., 1904; *Special Method in the Reading of the Complete English Classics in the Grades* (Bloomington, Ill.: Public School Publishing Co., 1894) 1st. ed. rev., 1903; *Special Method in Primary Reading* (New York: The Macmillan Co., 1903) 1st. ed. rev., 1908; *Special Method in Language in the Eight Grades* (New York: The Macmillan Co., 1905) 1st. ed. rev., 1916; *Special Method in Arithmetic* (New York: The Macmillan Co., 1905).

[88] *A Course of Study for the Eight Grades of the Common School* (Bloomington, Ill.: Public School Publishing Co., 1895) 1st. ed. rev., v. i and v. ii, 1906.

[89] Charles and Frank McMurry, *The Method of the Recitation* (New York: The Macmillan Co., 1897), 1st. ed. rev., 1903.

[90] *Teaching by Projects: A Basis for Purposeful Study* (New York: The Macmillan Co., (1920) and *Practical Teaching: Large Projects in Geography*, Bk. I (Richmond, Virginia: Johnson Publishing Co., 1925).

[91] *Conflicting Principles in Teaching and How to Adjust Them* (Boston: Houghton Mifflin Co., 1914) and *How to Organize the Cirriculum* (New York: The Macmillan Co., 1923).

Frank taught at a graduate school, Teachers College, Columbia University, until retirement, preparing the critic teachers, supervisors, and principals who would later train and supervise the teachers. He judged that these educators needed a theoretical grasp of the basic method of selecting content more than they did detailed knowledge in each subject. Frank began immediately, in 1899, to teach a course in General Method, stressing the ends in education and the means for their attainment, the relative worth of studies, correlation, and interest.[92] At the same time, he offered a course in the curriculum of the elementary school for graduate students interested in research and investigation. The description of this course read as follows:

> The outline of study in each common-school subject will be determined by careful examination of the published curricula of the best schools of the country, by consultation with the heads of departments in the college, and by extensive discussion.[93]

Such a course, together with a growing number of related courses, continued to be taught by Frank and the staff until well into the twenties.

AN ASSESSMENT

Trends

The point of attack chosen by the Herbartians was more technical than theoretical. The Herbartian system was especially well designed for supervision and teacher training, to which the leading Herbartians devoted their attention. Instructions for the different phases of selecting the curriculum were so well formulated by Herbartian pedagogy that they could quite easily be used as teaching materials.[94] They were so

[92] Teachers College, Columbia University, *Announcement* (New York, 1899), p. 6. By 1907 the content of this course had been absorbed by later courses in the curriculum. Courses in special methods were taught from the beginning in separate subject matter departments.

[93] Teachers College, Columbia University, *Announcement* (New York, 1899), p. 7. The comparative study of curricula with which Frank began this course became in 1905 an experimental study of the curriculum, stressing feasible eliminations. Course content continued to change in response to developing conceptions of the curriculum.

[94] Kilpatrick, assessing years later the advantage the more explicit doctrine had for becoming widely known, commented, "Colonel Parker led a more vital movement, but Herbartianism had a better stated theory and so was easier spread." William H. Kilpatrick, "The Contribution of John Dewey to Education," *The Philosophy of John Dewey*, edited by Paul A. Schilpp (Evanston: Northwestern University, 1939), p. 465.

thoroughly detailed that with little help the teacher could almost follow the line of thought and evaluate himself.[95] The overall framework for the Herbartian curriculum was provided by the course of study. Details were elaborated in terms of the steps of the recitation, the type studies, and the special methods of organizing content in each subject. Even the Herbartian psychology consisted of an explicit terminology which could be formulated conveniently for college instruction.[96]

As a result, we can expect the profession was very busy making courses of study in the period from 1900 to 1910.[97] We are not surprised that in these ten years the formal recitation was a common classroom phenomenon.[98] Increased effort was soon to be put on detailed and systematic teaching plans. Not only did books on special

[95] Vivian T. Thayer has a good discussion of the fact that the transiency of teachers in this period, and the greatly increased demand for them, led to a real need for some formulation of the curriculum on which the poorly trained and inefficient might lean. See *The Passing of the Recitation* (Boston: D. C. Heath, 1928), pp. 14–17. Sarah Brooks of St. Paul once made a shrewd remark on this point. Mr. DeGarmo had said, she warned, "that mathematics is the formal quantitative study of inorganic nature. How is that to help us? . . . We must simplify our statements if we are to have the help of the teachers in the solution of these great problems regarding the curriculum." *First Yearbook of the National Herbart Society for the Scientific Study of Teaching*, Suppl. I (Bloomington, Ill.: Pantagraph Printing and Stationery Co., 1895), p. 148.

[96] Junius L. Meriam discovered that by 1900 psychology was accepted as important for teacher training and by 1905 the three principles of teaching which were recognized by most teachers as psychological were the process of proceeding from known to unknown, association, and apperception. *Normal School Education and Efficiency in Teaching* (Teachers College Contributions to Education, No. 1 [New York: Teachers College, Columbia University, 1905]), p. 44.

[97] A cursory count of elementary courses of study published before 1910 found in the Course of Study Collection in the Curriculum Division of the Library at Teachers College, Columbia University (approximately sixty-five cities and thirty-five states are represented), shows that the total number of cities and states making courses of study had practically tripled from 1900 to 1910. (Twenty-two cities before 1900 and forty-four new ones between 1900–1910; ten states before 1900 and twenty-four new ones between 1900–1910). The oldest course of study found was that of Boston's in 1869. With very few exceptions, those cities and states making courses of study before 1900 had revised them by 1910. Dorothy McMurry says she found "not a single detailed, carefully articulated course of study for the eight grades or even for the larger part of those grades" from 1880–1890. Dorothy McMurry, *Herbartian Contributions to History Instruction in American Elementary Schools* (New York: Teachers College, Columbia University, Bureau of Publications, 1946), p. 147. What courses of study existed were usually thin leaflets, containing either a graded topical outline or recommendations of pages to be assigned from certain texts. The courses of study after 1900 show a strong Herbartian influence, featuring type studies, correlation, home geography, local nature study, heroic biography, and pioneer stories.

[98] In the period between 1900 and 1910 "every good teacher was supposed to

methods begin to be in demand, but authors began to include in the texts themselves helpful hints to the teacher on correlation, presentation, application, and other Herbartian techniques. Standard courses in special methods in the different subject matter areas began to appear in teacher training, and the number of supervisors in these different subject matter areas greatly increased. The expansion of programs of teacher training as well as the increasing numbers of supervisors in the schools were no doubt partly due to the ease with which a technical approach can be acquired. Thus in a variety of ways the Herbartians began to accustom an ever-widening group of teachers to selecting the curriculum in a more orderly and methodical manner.

The McMurrys' contributions

It is tempting to look back from a vantage point at the end of the story and put an unerring finger on the particular efforts the Herbartians made which seem to bear closest resemblance to emphases which were prominent later. There are interesting parallels, however, and six of them in particular seem worth commenting on and will serve to summarize and assess the influence of the Herbartians on the developing stream of ideas about curriculum making.

To begin, the Herbartians probably did more than any one else to fix professional attention on a technique or method of curriculum making. As Kilpatrick commented many years later:

> Among the formative influences of the period under consideration none is more pronounced perhaps than Herbartianism as it was brought to this country . . . a body of educational thought as simple in conception as it was attractive in theory. Moreover it worked. Attacking squarely as this movement did, so much of what then prevailed, it brought conscious attention to almost the whole range of theory regarding the educative process.[99]

By giving names and terms to the elements of teaching, the Herbartians made it possible for the profession to think about, discuss,

---

have a lesson plan for each class period, and the five formal steps were much in evidence." William H. Kilpatrick, "Dewey's Influence on Education," *The Philosophy of John Dewey*, edited by Paul A. Schilpp (Evanston: Northwestern University, 1939), p. 465. Frank McMurry, appraising many years later the role of the formal steps, said that "they were an organization of classroom method and, to a considerable degree of the method of curriculum making." Frank M. McMurry, "Some Recollections of the Past Forty Years of Education," *Peabody Journal of Education*, IV (May, 1927), p. 329.

[99] William H. Kilpatrick, "Tendencies in Educational Philosophy," *Twenty-five Years of American Education*, edited by Isaac L. Kandel (New York: The Macmillan Co., 1924), pp. 60–61.

and study these elements, and begin to theorize. As Dewey said later, when their influence was judged to be waning:

> Herbart's great service lay in taking the work of teaching out of the region of routine and accident. He brought it into the sphere of conscious method; it became a conscious business with a definite aim and procedure, instead of being a compound of casual inspiration and subservience to tradition. Moreover, everything in teaching and discipline could be specified, instead of our having to be content with vague and more or less mystic generalities about ultimate ideals and speculative spiritual symbols.[100]

Their interest in technique dovetailed well with the pressure on the schools to include new content in the curriculum. As educators became more skillful at talking and thinking about making the curriculum, they were freer to consider proposals for content change since they had better ideas of how to set about making changes. The fact that they could think more clearly about the method of change also probably tempted them to consider changes, on the theory that knowledge of how to do something often inclines a person to do it. The push for change in content in the curriculum, coming as it did from several sources, served also to stimulate professional interest in techniques of curriculum making. Wider offerings, for example, raised the question of how teachers were to interest all children in them.

Second, the Herbartians preached a gospel[101] of the moral aim of education so timely that the whole future cast of thought about the curriculum was affected. The idea had been in the air for some time that the purpose of education should be the moral development of the child. The Herbartians expanded this to mean that the content of the curriculum should be chosen so that the child would learn to act morally (the best ideas lead to the best actions). The moral aim for education might have found embodiment only in pioneer efforts made by people who were not professional educators,[102] but the espousal

---

[100] John Dewey, *Democracy and Education: An Introduction to the Philosophy of Education* (New York: The Macmillan Co., 1916), p. 83.

[101] This word is used deliberately here. Charles McMurry, it should be remembered, had thought seriously of the ministry as a career. Some of his writings about the moral aim of education and many of the addresses given to the National Herbart Society by its members have almost an evangelical tone. See, for example, the apostrophe of W. P. Burris of Bluffton, Indiana, at the first meeting of the Herbart Society in 1895. "Herbartian pedagogy," he said, "is to be the angel to roll away the stone from the sepulchre of formalism." Frank McMurry's reference to his enthusiasm for Herbartian ideas as an "educational conversion" is interesting here.

[102] The thesis that the reforming progressive spirit of the times was reflected

41

of the idea by a group like the Herbartians gave it the needed language for discussion and a guarantee of continuous professional attention. The Herbartians were the first educators to organize for the purpose of bringing about specific improvements in American school practice. Unlike the founders of the American Institute of Instruction which was functioning in New England well before the Civil War, the Herbartians were not content with the promulgation of ideas but dealt with the actual problems that arise when new ideas are taken seriously. They were not only the first to found a permanent association but a successful first. The founders of the group were among the contemporary educational elite, and the organizing work was thoroughgoing. Any doctrines they considered would get respectful attention. When one of their ideas coincided with a growing cultural trend toward viewing education as a means of improving the life of an emerging nation, that idea was assured a future vitality and importance.

Later, morality itself was not to be challenged as an educational aim as much as the conservative nature of the morality of which the Herbartians approved. To men like the McMurrys, members of pioneer families who had achieved middle-class status by hard work and denial, the stable, essentialist view of the universe offered them by German idealism seemed attractive. The morality derived from this view was social, in contrast to the more individual view of morality as a direct responsibility to God (with which they were familiar).[103] This social view of morality was not unappealing, but the strictly submissive character of German social morality did repel the more independent Americans. They preferred to view social morality more in terms of the responsibilities pioneers felt to each other in establishing a new way of life. They thought of social morality as rooted in that consensus of social values in which they had been reared in the rural Middle West. Only DeGarmo, who had studied economics and political science in Germany and had been in contact with the ferment of ideas there in the eighties, saw the need to reexamine this assumed value consensus in terms of the demands of a rising proletariat in a growing indus- trialized nation. But however much educators came to differ from the

in and supported by all varieties of schools and educators is discussed by Lawrence A. Cremin in *The Transformation of the School* (New York: Alfred A. Knopf, 1961).

[103] See pages 55–56 of this study for Frank McMurry's description of the difficulty American teachers had with the whole notion of social morality at the Herbart Society's meeting in Milwaukee in 1897.

Herbartians on the content of morality, their original focus on the moral aim remained an important one.

Third, the Herbartians were the first systematic efficiency experts in education whose ideas received national attention. There had always been a native American interest in efficiency, but it was usually local and personal, not methodical and systematic. The Herbartian passion for economy of time and effort was closely linked to their interest in technique and method in curriculum making. It seemed as though these two interests fed each other. Only a technical approach would enable them to make any real progress in efficiency, and only real savings of time and energy justified studying and improving technique.

Charles McMurry, for example, discussed the idea of efficiency in some detail in *Elements of General Method*. The integration of knowledge, whether by correlation or other means, would save time for the learner since he would not first have to learn content and then have to learn how to integrate it. If this integration were matched to the stages of child growth, by means of the culture epochs for example, time and effort would both be saved since the child would not be trying to learn something at the wrong time. Integration of knowledge also avoided learning the same thing in two places, such as reading skills in both a reading class and in a geography class. The whole emphasis on apperception with its assumption of the active nature of each learning mind led to efficiency since each mind properly guided would do the best job of assimilating new ideas to fit existing ones.

There were even traces of efficiency in the notion that the integration of knowledge would lead to an integrated character whose ethical action would not be in conflict with itself. Or that integrated knowledge, as opposed to fragmentary and disorganized knowledge, would be more useful in practical affairs, especially since the type studies selected were usually of a practical nature, such as dams and factories.

Fourth, the Herbartians in calling professional attention to the "smelting process . . . where new, uncomprehended knowledge meets this tumult of the child's mind incident to getting it under control,"[104] helped to bring the children and the teachers out into the center of the educational stage, as dramatis personae of the play, relegating the theorist

---

[104] Charles A. McMurry, *Conflicting Principles in Teaching* (Boston: Houghton Mifflin Co., 1914), p. 258. Charles expressed this concern succinctly when he said, "If the teacher, at the close of her description, could have the mental state of each child photographed on the blackboard of her schoolroom, she would be in mental distress."

and the administrator to the wings in the role of supporting cast.[105] The growing importance of the practice school, the close analysis of lessons there, the elevation of teacher preparation to the level of university study, the new interest in the child's mind, and the theorizing about the relationship of that mind to knowledge—especially the importance given to the individual child's background of experience and the teacher's skill in bringing it to his mind—all tended to give a new importance to the actual ongoing classroom process, foreshadowing a more complete absorption by the curriculum maker in this process in the future.

Fifth, the Herbartians, sharing with W. T. Harris an innate respect for the structure of knowledge, began to search out those intellectual elements belonging to each formalized subject matter which they thought lay within the study of either a practical problem or a social or natural phenomenon. For example, the study of Minneapolis Falls revealed to them the presence of certain formal elements of method and concept belonging uniquely to a subject, whether it be geology or arithmetic or literature. The Herbartians insisted that the child should learn to think with each of these elements just as the geologist, mathematician, or poet would. Although they approved of the synthesis of knowledge represented by coal mining, for example, or an ear of corn, they were adamant against what they called the jumbling of the subjects which should help the child to think about coal mining and corn. Charles McMurry never felt that this emphasis on essential intellectual elements was taken seriously enough. Just before his move to Peabody, he wrote dryly that the great body of educational leaders "have not taught a complete lesson with a class of live children for years."[106] If they had,

[105] Charles's statement on these points was characteristically direct and pointed. Teachers, he said, must have "power to modify the course in regard to the selection and emphasis of topics, and especially in all the details of executing plans." Furthermore, there needs to be developed in teachers, first "a strong progressive spirit and willingness to entertain new ideas coupled with an expansive energy in meeting new situations, and second . . . a strong flexibility and power of adaptation by which the effective combination of old and new can be made." *Course of Study in the Eight Grades* (1st ed., rev.; New York: The Macmillan Co., 1906), II, pp. 18–21.

[106] Charles A. McMurry, *Conflicting Principles in Teaching* (Boston: Houghton Mifflin Co., 1914), p. 243. He himself had not only continued to do just this, but his search for the essential elements and structure of each subject may have jeopardized his professional reputation. Charles McKenny, a colleague, hearing an educational leader deprecate Charles McMurry by saying, "McMurry is one of the best-trained men in American education but his contributions are of an elementary nature and scarcely any of them is worthy of his standing," reminded

he went on, they would have realized that what the teacher needs is help with the fundamental thought-lines of each subject, the warp and woof, so to speak, of organized knowledge. In 1914, he wrote:

> Our recent writers on education have done little to help us upon this vital and very difficult point [how many and what concrete data are needed to organize a topic so as fully to clarify a definite concept or general notion]. They have given us no end of general psychological advice about the concrete and the abstract . . . but they never apply these principles themselves to a particular topic. . . . It seems as if they had come to the brink of a chasm and then retreated without descending into its depths.[107]

Frank McMurry, as late as 1923 in a critique of a yearbook on the social studies,[108] took the writers of the yearbook mildly to task for ignoring the fact that the subject matter content itself makes certain demands on the organization of the curriculum. He suggested that the student, armed with adequate information and practice in using it, must develop a consciousness of the right method of thinking in each subject. Curriculum makers must not neglect the question of how children should study the facts and their application. He illustrated his point with examples of teaching which would emphasize intellectual method in geography:

> Children were having a lively discussion of the Sahara Desert. . . . The teacher interrupted them by saying, "Suppose that we summarize here. What do you do when you summarize? . . . I shall let you suggest the proper times to stop for a summary. How will you know when such a time comes?" . . . In studying a map . . . you should have the habit of estimating the distances you are talking about according to the scale. . . . How far is it from Algiers to Timbuctoo?[109]

Although the ensuing emphasis on activity analysis drew attention away from the Herbartians' concern with the structure of the subjects, it reappeared in curriculum thought during the twenties.

the speaker that, "most of the higher-ups in education . . . are writing for the select few . . . the limited circle of the initiated," rather than [like McMurry for] the rank and file of the teachers of the country who, after all, are most in need of their help." Charles McKenny, "The McMurrys in American Education," *Peabody Journal of Education*, V (March, 1928), p. 267.

[107] Charles A. McMurry, *Conflicting Principles in Teaching* (Boston: Houghton Mifflin Co., 1914), pp. 171–72.

[108] National Society for the Study of Education, "Social Studies in the Elementary and Secondary School," *Twenty-second Yearbook*, Part 2 (Bloomington, Ill.: Public School Publishing Co.), 1923.

[109] National Society for the Study of Education, "Social Studies in the Elementary and Secondary School," *Twenty-second Yearbook*, Part 2 (Bloomington, Ill.: Public School Publishing Co.), pp. 302–03.

Finally, the Herbartians promoted, in the modern sense of the word, pedagogy as a university discipline.[110] They were fired by the intellectual solidity of the German tradition, in which the pedagogy taught was well-articulated with philosophy and psychology and in which the theorist himself tested his ideas in the university's own practice school. These young men, whose careers were opening before them, began to help lay the intellectual foundations for the study of education, creating the subject matter for an American theoretical and technical study of pedagogy. They were major contributors in fashioning the first professional curriculum in teacher education and its books and teaching methods in the various school subjects of study.[111] Influenced by the German example, they tended to relate pedagogy to the liberal arts of the medieval world which were about to be challenged by the modern sciences as foundational university disciplines. Developments in the physical and social sciences, then under way, were to change the face of knowledge. But the Herbartians established without question the place of pedagogy in the university and its need to be firmly rooted in the intellectual soil of the time.

In sum, the McMurrys as representative Herbartians can be called the pioneers in the curriculum field, the initiators, or pattern-setters. They compelled the profession to consider both the curriculum and how it is made, with such scope and range as to lead to fruitful effort by later theorists.

[110] As Dorothy McMurry put it, the Herbartians "probably put on a much more extensive and better organized advertising campaign than had been placed at the service of any previous educational scheme." *Herbartian Contributions to History Instruction in American Elementary Schools* (New York: Teachers College, Columbia University, Bureau of Publications, 1946), p. 49.

[111] See Harold Rugg, *The Teacher of Teachers* (New York: Harper, 1952), pp. 28–51 for an interesting discussion of this point.

3

John Dewey

DEWEY'S INTRODUCTION TO EDUCATION

We have seen that the Herbartian movement in the late nineties was not to be ignored by professional educators. It demanded either champions or critics, and it certainly did not lack the former. As to the latter, one of its most friendly and searching analysts was the young philosopher, John Dewey. We may well wonder why Dewey became interested in Herbartian ideas. The metaphysical base of Herbartian pedagogy would surely interest a philosopher, but other American philosophers did not seem to find Herbart's metaphysics as absorbing as did Dewey. Neither was Dewey an educator turned philosopher. Although he did many of the same things that helped establish the McMurrys firmly as lifetime professional educators,[1] Dewey from the outset kept largely to a philosophical point of view rather than a technical one. The key to understanding his interest seems to lie both in the nature of his theory and in the manner of his introduction to education. Given his basic philosophical position, he would probably have been drawn to education even though he had had little experience as an educator. At the same time, by a series of happy coincidences, Dewey early gained more direct insight into and competence about the details of educational practice than his relative professional inexperience and predominantly philosophical interests would otherwise have afforded him.

One such coincidence was the nature of his responsibilities for

[1] Like them, after he finished his undergraduate studies, he taught several years in village schools. Like them he went on to advanced study, attending the first of the American graduate schools, Johns Hopkins, instead of going abroad. Like them he came in contact with the University of Michigan (as a professor, not a student), a place where the academic climate had been for some time particularly favorable toward public education.

writing and teaching at Michigan where contact between the University and the public schools had long been a planned feature. We can appreciate the setting in which he worked at Michigan from the following description:

> The university formed a part of the state school system, and the high schools of the state were regularly visited by members of the university faculty. Dewey's interest in general education was stimulated by these visits as well as by his membership in the Schoolmasters Club of Michigan, formed in order to bring secondary and college educators closer through conferences and committees. He lectured frequently at teachers' institutes and various conventions on his studies of the learning process.[2]

A second coincidence was the fact that Dewey was the father of three small children while his basic ideas on education were being formed. What he had learned from William James about the importance of native tendencies led him to pay attention to their appearance in his own children.[3] His fatherly concern that his children attend good schools also had something to do with his later founding of a laboratory school at the University of Chicago.[4]

A third such coincidence was the fact that he was ushered into the American world of philosophical speculation by William T. Harris, a strong Hegelian, who was striving to embody Hegelian doctrine in the educational practice of the St. Louis public schools.[5]

---

[2] Neil McCluskey, *Public Schools and Moral Education* (New York: Columbia University Press, 1958), p. 191. In this period, Dewey contributed several articles to reviews on practical teaching problems in high school and higher education, health, the teaching of ethics, etc. In 1886 he wrote *Psychology*, a work in which, according to McCluskey, he tried to "drive in tandem Hegel's philosophy and G. Stanley Hall's evolutionary psychology." Institute topics were "attention," "imagination," "thinking," all related to teaching and study. William James, whose work Dewey admired, was also interested in teachers and teaching.

[3] Jane M. Dewey (ed.), "Biography of John Dewey," *The Philosophy of John Dewey*, ed. Paul Arthur Schilpp (Evanston: Northwestern University, 1939), p. 27. In his biography Dewey credits G. Stanley Hall, with whom he studied at Johns Hopkins, with alerting him to the importance of the new experimental psychology.

[4] Harold Rugg recalled that "in answer to a question about it, Mr. Dewey said that he joined in its organization mainly on account of the children (his own)." Harold Rugg, *Foundations for American Education* (Yonkers-on-Hudson, New York: World Book Co., 1947), p. 103. According to Dewey's biography, he did so to "release his children from the intellectual boredom of his own school days." Jane Dewey, p. 27. See A. Gordon Melvin, *Education: A History* (New York: The John Day Co., 1946), p. 323, for a slightly different interpretation.

[5] Dewey had sent Harris an essay on philosophy asking him whether Harris felt its author should "go professionally into philosophy." Harris had encouraged him and published it. Dewey shortly moved away from Hegel, but

A fourth occurrence was the failure of the most creative and vital public school figure of the day, Colonel Parker,[6] to forge a systematic theory for his own original school practice. To a philosopher like Dewey who admired Parker's unique approach to education, this combination might have been very stimulating.

Attention to the growth of Dewey's general philosophical thought gives us more direct clues to his interest in education than do the circumstances by which he came in contact with the profession of education. The inadequacy of his public schooling (he thought the schools a bore) was only a part of a greater set of incongruities which he began to perceive in the culture. Among these were the divisions and separations of a New England cultural heritage, the disorganized character of the modern world, and the distintegrative individualism of the day. A variety of influences gave form to these intellectual stirrings on Dewey's part. Hegel's synthesis of reality, Comte's faith in science as a regulative method of organized social life, and above all William James's restoration of the old, Greek biological conception of the psyche, all acted to draw into harmony in Dewey's mind elements of humanism, evolutionary biology, and experimental psychology.[7] He formulated a philosophy which gave both unity and creativity to living. He conceived of life as a process of intelligent adaptation to and control of the environment for personal and social ends. He thought of education as an integral part of that process, not something which serves life as a separate function. Something of this feeling may have been in Kilpatrick's mind when he said once that Dewey's philosophy:

> required its own incarnation in order to be itself and to get itself adequately studied and criticized. And such an incarnation within the ongoing life of any personality would *ipso facto* be an educative experience which would of necessity change that person. In this way, philosophy and

---

it may be more than coincidence that he moved away from Harris's kind of education, in the direction of a variety of his own.

[6] Dewey called him the "father of the progressive educational movement." John Dewey, "How Much Freedom in New Schools?" *New Republic*, LXIII (July 9, 1930), p. 204.

[7] Dewey himself gives an excellent account of the sources of his thought in an essay "From Absolutism to Experimentalism," *Contemporary American Philosophers*, eds. George P. Adams and William P. Montague (New York: The Macmillan Co., 1930), pp. 13–27. For a more extended treatment see Morton White, *The Origins of Dewey's Instrumentalism* (New York: Columbia University Press, 1943). For the educational aspects of his development an excellent source is Melvin C. Baker, *Foundations of John Dewey's Educational Theory* (New York: King's Crown Press, Columbia University, 1955), Chap. VI.

education early became for Dewey two complementary phases of one ongoing intellectual process, each phase exhibiting and connecting the other.[8]

CRITIQUE OF THE HERBARTIANS

Psychological aspect

In the early nineties, Dewey's interests moved steadily toward the formulation of a philosophical and psychological base for educational theory, which would be more adequate to his assessment of the cultural climate of America. He perceived that he shared an interest with the Herbartians in the relationship of education to philosophy and psychology. Their method of making the curriculum was based on such a foundation. It was not their reliance on a foundation that Dewey criticized, but the particular kind of foundation they had chosen. As a result, in the two important papers he presented before the Herbart Society during their first few years of existence, one in 1895 and the other in 1897, he recognized the usefulness of their attention to method in the curriculum but criticized their underlying psychology and metaphysics. These papers provided the Society with just that nice combination of judicious approval and searching criticism which invigorates but does not destroy. The members of the Society seem to have valued his ideas, for the Society itself thrived, and we shall find considerable evidence that the members modified many of their doctrines as the result of Dewey's suggestions.

Although the Society itself in its first years was busy applying Herbartian methods of organizing content to the American problem of a crowded curriculum, Dewey recalled the members to the more general consideration of a proper psychological and philosophical basis for pedagogy. He hoped to save American Herbartians from the uncritical use of any method of solving their problems that happened to present itself. It was his thesis that only methods which were in harmony with American character and values should be adopted by American Herbartians. Accordingly, he began his discussion of Herbartian doctrines with the topic of interest. It was the major psychological tenet of the theory, involving notions about the nature of mind, of ideas, and of the process of thought.

[8] William H. Kilpatrick, "Dewey's Influence on Education," *The Philosophy of John Dewey*, ed. Paul Arthur Schilpp (Evanston: Northwestern University, 1939), p. 452.

In his first paper,[9] after giving a lengthy and careful analysis of Kant's and Herbart's views on interest, Dewey tried to show how the Herbartian doctrine of interest overestimated the importance of ideas.[10] He suggested that Herbart, in trying too vigorously to get rid of faculty psychology (with which endeavor Dewey was in accord), had relied over-heavily on the ideas themselves as motives for the will. Granting that ideas are a basic guide to conduct, Dewey pointed out that since ideas do not in themselves motivate conduct, Herbart had had to find something which would. Unwilling to rely on any native factor, he had resorted to the feelings that result from the interaction of the ideas themselves, i.e. interest. This theory was logical enough, but it did not explain how to prevent this purely interactive pleasure from attaching itself to wrong ideas as well as right.

As a means of avoiding this dilemma, Dewey recommended that the individual human agent be restored as the link between knowledge and conduct. Recognizing that the individual's native impulses are the basic motivating force in conduct, Dewey pointed out that these impulses are so defined by objects and ideas that human purpose results. Dewey described purpose as an ends-means relationship. Purpose, he said, might be either immediate, as in the young child, for whom the activity is the end; or it might be mediate, as in the older person, for whom means and ends are somewhat separated in time. Ideas then become interesting to the mind that holds them, because they are useful in the satisfaction of its purpose.[11]

Dewey tried to show the Herbartians that, while they were relying

---

[9] John Dewey, "Interest as Related to Will," *First Yearbook of the National Herbart Society for the Scientific Study of Teaching*, Supplement II (Bloomington, Ill.: Pantagraph Printing and Stationery Co., 1895), pp. 209–246.

[10] Dewey accused Kant of ruling out feeling, as a proper motivating force for directing conduct, in favor of an elevated reverence for the moral law. This was merely eliminating feelings and then smuggling one in again in order to give moving power of some kind to ideas.

[11] The Herbartians' neglect of the human agent had always been a source of friction between them and Superintendent Harris. He contended that man, as an absolutely free will, could act freely at any moment, a conception which threatened the Herbartian's reliance on the right ideas to lead the will captive. Dewey put man as actor back in the moral context in the future by calling attention to the centrality of human purpose. Harris was immensely pleased with the address, recognizing that Dewey's emphasis on human agency gave real meaning to any talk about the actualizing of aims. Perhaps Dewey's use of a quotation from Hegel helped, "The aim [universal aim of Hegel] is empty without its actualizing in an agent." Harris, as an idealist, would not subscribe to Dewey's ideas on the relative nature of knowledge, however.

on ideas to form the mind and thus the character, he was relying on ideas as instruments to be used in the realization of human purpose. He charged them with taking a fixed view of knowledge, while he advocated a relative view. He contended that for the Herbartians interest *was* the outcome rather than, as he believed, being *in* the outcome. The Herbartians assumed the existence of a fixed body of knowledge that was both indispensable and potentially interesting to all human beings. Dewey insisted that ideas were interesting to the extent that they were instrumental to the purposes of the minds that held them.

In his next paper, Dewey would point out the need to root this satisfaction of human purpose firmly in the democratic social context if it were to lead to moral conduct of the same kind. Now he contented himself with approving those aspects of the Herbartian doctrine of interest which stressed its active nature and its attachment to ideas for intrinsic, not extrinsic reasons.[12]

Even though the paper was a frontal attack on Herbartian psychology, it was well received and fully discussed by the members. Copies were soon exhausted, and it had to be reprinted. Dewey made some additions to the second edition which seem to show that the Herbartians were not very upset by the psychological comments and were quite eager for more educational implications. Reference was made by Dewey to:

> . . . excision and re-writing as a result of a sufficient advance in mutual understanding since the first edition of psychological matters, permitting fuller treatment of the more distinctly emotional aspects.[13]

[12] According to Kilpatrick, Dewey had pointed out to them a common error, that "the self is the kind of thing that has to be moved from the outside; that left to itself, it would stand inert." William H. Kilpatrick, "Dewey's Influence on Education," *The Philosophy of John Dewey*, ed. Paul Arthur Schilpp (Evanston: Northwestern University, 1939), p. 457. Dewey's criticism of the Herbartian psychology was much sharper than that of their pedagogy. In the main, he approved of their educational practices and called them "sound educational sense." John Dewey, "Interest as Related to Will," *First Yearbook of the National Herbart Society for the Scientific Study of Teaching*, Supplement II (Bloomington, Ill.: Pantagraph Printing and Stationery Co., 1895), p. 238. He found three points of contact with them on educational matters: (1) their belief that interest ensued from the stirring-up of ideas and their action on each other, resulting in pleasure, (2) their conviction that interest attached itself to objects for their own sakes and not for extrinsic reasons, and (3) their reliance on interest to strengthen the right ideas and the corresponding interrelationships and so help to direct conduct.

[13] John Dewey, "Interest as Related to Will," *First Yearbook of the National Herbart Society for the Scientific Study of Teaching*, Supplement II (2nd ed.; Chicago: University of Chicago Press, 1895), p. 1.

Philosophical aspect

By the time Dewey was ready to give his second paper to the Herbart Society in 1897,[14] his laboratory school at the University of Chicago had been going a year, and he could begin to draw on his experiences there for examples to illustrate his views.[15] In speaking on *Ethical Principles Underlying Education,* he addressed himself to the major philosophical doctrine of the Herbartians—the moral aim of education. Dewey felt that the current interpretation of the nature of morality had ignored its necessarily social character:

> Our conceptions of moral education have been too narrow, too formal, and too pathological. We have associated the term ethical with certain special acts which are labeled virtues and are set off from the mass of other acts, and are still more divorced from the habitual images and motives of the children performing them. Moral instruction is thus associated with teaching about these particular virtues, or with instilling certain sentiments in regard to them. The moral has been conceived in too goody-goody a way. . . . Ultimate moral motives and forces are nothing more or less than social intelligence—the power of observing and comprehending social situations,—and social power—trained capacities of control —at work in the service of social interest and aims. There is no fact which throws light upon the constitution of society, there is no power whose training adds to social resourcefulness which is not ethical in its bearing.[16]

He went on to suggest that the kind of social intelligence which should be sought was intimately related to the particular kind of society in which it would function. The Herbartian view of the moral aim, he commented, was closely related to the cultural values of the society

---

[14] John Dewey, "Ethical Principles Underlying Education," *Third Yearbook of the National Herbart Society for the Scientific Study of Teaching* (Chicago: University of Chicago Press, 1897), pp. 7–34.

[15] Although one of the reasons Dewey established his school was for the sake of the education of his own children, it served to test his educational theories. "An emotional dissatisfaction with pure theorizing made him feel the need of practical experience to check and develop purely theoretical ideas. . . . This inspired a desire for an experimental school which should combine psychological principles of learning with the principle of cooperative association which he derived from his moral studies." Jane M. Dewey (ed.), "Biography of John Dewey," *The Philosophy of John Dewey,* ed. Paul Arthur Schilpp (Evanston: Northwestern University, 1939), p. 27. See Lawrence A. Cremin, *The Transformation of the School* (New York: Alfred A. Knopf, 1961), pp. 135–36, for a good discussion of the founding of the school.

[16] John Dewey, "Ethical Principles Underlying Education," *Third Yearbook of the National Herbart Society for the Scientific Study of Teaching* (Chicago: University of Chicago Press, 1897), pp. 25–26.

that produced it. He had made the point before in his analysis of Herbartian psychology:

> Herbartianism seems to me essentially a schoolmaster's psychology, not the psychology of a child. It is the natural expression of a nature laying great emphasis upon authority and upon the formation of individual character in distinct and recognized subordination to the ethical demands made in war and in civil administration by that authority. It is not the psychology of a nation which professes to believe that every individual has within him the principle of authority, and that order means co-ordination, not subordination.[17]

Dewey then proceeded to show by a series of contrasts how present practice in the school interpreted the moral aim narrowly and how this interpretation should be broadened to encompass a wider social morality. Was the teacher relied upon too much as the model of moral behavior? Then a wider social attachment should be sought, which would have a more permanent effect on the development of the child's character. Did educating a child for the future have a vitiating effect on his judgment, since a child's vision of the future is necessarily dim? Then he should be asked to judge and respond morally in the present which is real to him. Was emulation an inadequate motive for schooling since, in intellectual and artistic matters, the law is cooperation and participation? Then the child should create products for all to receive and use, cultivating reciprocity as well as positive, personal achievement. Was education for citizenship a limited aim since the child potentially is also a family member, a worker, and a community leader as well as follower? Then he should engage in a wider social life in school, as a member of a typical embryonic community. Were moral ideas—i.e. ideas about morality—furnished by improving literature and maxims, different from moral ideas—i.e. *moving* ideas—which guide conduct? Then these ideas must be acquired in a vital way if they are to furnish the motive power. Did a heavy reliance on the correction of wrong behavior imply a pathological situation? Then the social climate of the school should be such that the child is forming

[17] John Dewey, "Interest as Related to Will," *First Yearbook of the National Herbart Society for the Scientific Study of Teaching*, Supplement II (Bloomington, Ill.: Pantagraph Printing and Stationery Co., 1895), p. 241. Francis Parker had made the same point when he referred to the fact that nature study, with its devotion to a search for truth, had been considered "the horrible spectre of those who would hold the human mind in subjection both in church and state." John Dewey, "Interest as Related to Will," *First Yearbook of the National Herbart Society for the Scientific Study of Teaching*, Supplement II (2nd ed.; Chicago: University of Chicago Press, 1895), p. 157.

habits of positive service and learning to judge his behavior by such a standard.

Dewey concluded with an indication of the meaning for the curriculum of his view of the moral aim. The content of the curriculum, he stated, should consist of the conscious experience of man, as classified according to some "one dominant typical aim or process of social life." For example, the study of geography should comprise that content and those motives which are relevant to the interaction of the social life of man with nature. The study of history should include that content and those motives that are relevant to the past as a projected present, revealing methods of historical progress, etc. Thus each study should present that content and those motives which will reveal to the child one aspect of the total conscious individual and social experience of man.

According to Dewey, the "widening and deepening of the child's imagination of social relations, ideals, and means," describes the sequence of this content, moving as it does always in the direction of the sure possession by the adult of the intellectual resources of the culture.[18] He felt that three varieties of activities constituted the resources of the curriculum: (1) the life of the school as a social institution, that is the school as an embryonic community; (2) the methods of learning and doing work, that is, construction, production, creation, sharing, judging, and expression; and (3) the school studies, that is, the modes of personal experiencing by the child of history, geography, mathematics, or science.

Dewey proposed that the organization of the curriculum be such that the child's personal experience would reveal to him the basic and typical aspects of social life. For example, type phases of history studied, such as Rome, should show the child the working of the forces of political life. The life of primitive man should reveal to him the effects on social life of the introduction of tools into a culture. Dewey also gave examples of content which failed to reveal social process, culture epochs which were not related to the present, and biography which was not embedded in the community life it summed up and directed.

Dewey's challenge to the traditional, idealistic basis for morals was not lost on his hearers. Frank McMurry gives us a vivid account of it:

[18] This process was referred to by Dewey as the progressive reorganization of subject matter, in which the child's personal experience with the material of history and geography, for example, merges into an intellectual grasp of them as disciplines which make and test knowledge in unique ways.

Many persons present (over six hundred at that discussion) maintained that it [morality] was a purely individual matter. The dispute [aggressive to the point of bitter] finally centered on the question, "Was Robinson Crusoe non-moral?" and several times speakers asserted that, even though Crusoe was the only man on the island, he was grossly immoral if he tore the wings and legs off of a fly while it was still living. Morality, in short, concerned only one's self in relation to God. That was the first discussion of the social point of view in Education that I remember in this country, and this brief account suggests how utterly strange it was even to the better class of teachers.[19]

Dewey as yet was still groping for the formulation of education as social policy, which was to be so brilliantly embodied in *Democracy and Education*. But his statement of the way in which ideas are instrumental in the satisfaction of man's individual and social purposes probably compelled his hearers to reexamine their notions of the moral aim. Orthodox Herbartians had always contended that the moral aim was a social one, but to them it meant doing one's social duty within a traditional framework of values. In contrast, Dewey meant intelligence to be used as a critical and creative social force rather than as a conforming one. The subtlety of this difference was probably lost on many Herbartians, for in the next few years the Society was to hear a number of addresses on the social function of geography, education for citizenship, etc., whose contents were quite un-Deweyan. But Dewey had succeeded in raising questions about the social character of morals, which American educators would continue to ponder.

THE CURRICULUM OF THE LABORATORY SCHOOL

In the next few years, members of the Society reflected upon these criticisms by Dewey. Those who were interested visited his school to see his ideas in action.[20] Many could later read the excellent account of the details of practice there, as given principally in the *Elementary School Record*.[21] Its nine issues came out monthly during 1900. Each of the first eight described one aspect of the school's operation, such

---

[19] Frank M. McMurry, "Some Recollections of the Past Forty Years of Education," *Peabody Journal of Education*, IV (May, 1927), pp. 331–32.

[20] It would be surprising if Charles McMurry were not one of them. He was on leave from Illinois State Normal University to the University of Chicago, 1897–98.

[21] *Elementary School Record*, edited by John Dewey (Chicago: University of Chicago Press, 1900).

as science, history, music, etc., and the last issue discussed the curriculum.[22]

What the Herbartians could glean from the *Record* and other sources that would interpret the school to them probably consisted of (1) a description of the use of man's occupations as the core of the curriculum; (2) the sequence of the curriculum as developed according to the stages of child growth; and (3) the way in which the activities took deliberate advantage of child purpose, child activity, and child sociability.[23]

The use of the occupations

In the first stage, younger children in the school played at typical occupations, such as growing, cooking, and weaving, with as much realism as possible, simplifying the facts but never falsifying them. For example, they visited a farm and later "played" grocery store.

In the next stage, the children "played" at origins, as illustrated in primitive life. They attempted to recapitulate primitive life as a whole but in a childlike social setting. An ends-means relationship began to show itself as they reconstructed the social life of other times and places. For example, they traced the development of textiles by early man, carding the wool and spinning and weaving it. In this stage, the child was supplied with extra materials and activities in which he could practice his growing powers in language and mathematics.

In the third stage, the older child began to be able to lend reflective attention to the meaning of the social forces and processes implicit in the earlier study of occupations and to be able to isolate them and use them speculatively as means of building further knowledge. For example, broad social themes were studied, such as the early growth and settlement of Chicago, or the European backgrounds of Colonial America.

Sequence

As we can infer from the above, three stages of child growth were described quite broadly with no sharp break-off points between them.

[22] *The Child and the Curriculum* (Chicago: The University of Chicago Press, 1902) expands this last essay. It is important not to confuse what we know now about the school, based on the excellent and authoritative report of it made by Mayhew and Edwards in 1936, with the knowledge of it available to educators in 1900.

[23] What follows is based principally on the material found in the *Elementary School Record*.

In the first, the child's thoughts were considered to be the living meaning that saturates whatever he does. He *uses* number, he considers art as part of his life, etc. His imagination is the carrying medium for the facts and ideas as they pass through his thoughts and emotions. The school tries merely to keep his images moving. He is conscious of what he does but not as a process. He will remember playing miller but not the process of sifting flour. The key here is his absorption in activity.

In the second stage, the child consciously begins to relate means and ends, demanding activities that will test his efficiency. Formal work that is well connected with constructive and expressive work is enjoyed. The end may be the reconstruction of a primitive culture, and the sub-ends the working out again of their problems. The key is the logic of action or of meeting a practical difficulty.

In the third stage, the child is capable of reflective attention. He senses questions, doubts, and problems, and begins consciously to formulate the means to resolve them. For example, a child who was formerly occupied with making cameras is now interested in the principles of light. The key here is the logic of speculation.

REORGANIZATION OF THE HERBART SOCIETY

Although in the next few years the Herbart Society continued to meet and discuss, they tended to work over the same topics, and by 1899 the Society's meetings were definitely languishing. Yet no one really wanted to see the organization disappear. The scholarly quality of its discussions and the contacts made possible between men of common concerns were too valuable to lose. The Herbartian doctrines had been slowly recognized for what they were, a systematic, orderly way of organizing the curriculum, badly needed by the schools. As such they had been endorsed, even when they had been criticized and reconstructed. Many were asking if this methodical approach to the curriculum might prove to be the beginning step in a wider search for order, a more scientific kind of thinking about education. The proposal that the Society might prosper again under the name The National Society for the Scientific Study of Education was eagerly received.[24] Thus christened, the Society received a fresh impetus from which it

[24] Later the word "scientific" was dropped from the title, a rather untimely move, since they were to plunge into "scientific" matters shortly.

never faltered, becoming in later years a most important influence on the curriculum.

DEWEY'S TEACHING CAREER

As head of the departments of philosophy, pedagogy, and psychology at the University of Chicago during the years from 1896 to 1904, Dewey directed the training of a number of teachers. His chief influence was not in teacher preparation, however, but in the development of educational theory for the whole profession. Under the pressure of a regular schedule of classes in pedagogy and the daily contact with a laboratory school, operating in intimate relationship with the educational department of a university (a familiar Herbartian pattern in Germany), Dewey formulated the basic tenets of a pedagogical theory that was marked by its devotion to the practical consequences of good theory. His removal to Columbia University in 1904 marked the end of this period of direct contact with educational reality for Dewey. Having thought his way through to a position on the educational situation and having suggested needed action, he turned from the active, technical preparation of teachers to a more thorough and profound expression of his educational philosophy. Although he continued to evaluate and comment on important educational movements,[25] his major contribution was the unification of his theoretical insights on the meaning of education. His writings were especially influential[26]

[25] From 1905 to 1914 he taught at Teachers College, Columbia University, a course called Social Life and the School Curriculum. In it he stressed, "modern social movements: humanism, development of science, industrialism, democracy, etc. which have shaped the curriculum: social demands at present." See Teachers College, Columbia University, *Announcements* (New York, 1905), p. 52. The discontinuance of this course coincided with the offering of courses in educational sociology by the Department of Education. A course on the "application of sociology and social psychology to criticism and reconstruction of school methods designed to achieve ends of American democracy," offered for the first time in 1910, marked the first of a number of related courses to be offered by the Department of Educational Sociology at Teachers College, in 1918. *Announcements*, 1910, p. 48.

[26] Among the more important were: *School and Society* (Chicago: University of Chicago Press, 1900); *Psychology and Social Practice* (Chicago: University of Chicago Press, 1901); *The Educational Situation* (Chicago: University of Chicago Press, 1902); *The Child and the Curriculum* (Chicago: University of Chicago Press, 1902); *Moral Principles in Education* (Boston: Houghton Mifflin, 1909); *How We Think* (Boston: Houghton Mifflin, 1910); *Interest and Effort in Education* (Boston: Houghton Mifflin, 1913); *Schools of Tomorrow* (with Evelyn Dewey) (New York: E. P. Dutton and Co., 1915); *Democracy and Education*

although he also had a direct effect on students taking his courses.[27]

It is interesting to see how Dewey conceived of the curriculum as he taught about it in courses in pedagogy at the University of Chicago. He defined the curriculum as content, discussing theories for its selection, and he defined method as form, elaborating theories for interaction.[28] From a report of another course of lectures, he apparently used interaction to mean something similar to apperception:

> We might say that there are three points of view. First, there is the natural point of view of the child, then there is the scientific point of view or that of highly specialized knowledge, and when the teacher combines the two he has a third view.[29]

He gave the curriculum a dynamic cast by defining it as "that portion of the experience of the race which has been selected for reconstruction by the individual or group."[30] He showed attention not only to the method of curriculum selection and organization but also to the relationship of the child to knowledge. Both of these concerns he shared with the Herbartians.

CHALLENGES TO THE PROFESSION

One of Dewey's most important contributions in these years was to assess the educational situation and to formulate four challenges to the educational profession, particularly to those members who had concerned themselves with the problem of new content in the curriculum. Dewey did not categorize his challenges, and they can only be inferred from material scattered throughout a number of magazine articles and monographs. Considered together, the four comprise an interrelated program, each one of which represents one special way of getting hold of the whole program.

(New York: The Macmillan Co., 1916). A number of articles appeared in the *New Republic, Elementary School Journal,* and other magazines, and Dewey made several addresses before the National Educational Association.

[27] Among those influenced directly were important figures in curriculum such as W. W. Charters and Junius L. Meriam.

[28] John Dewey, *Pedagogy: Philosophy of Education; Syllabus* (Chicago: University of Chicago Press, 1898), p. 3.

[29] John Dewey, "The Method of the Recitation," A partial report of a course of lectures given at the University of Chicago (Oshkosh, Wis., 1899), p. 23. (Privately printed for the use of classes in theory at Oshkosh Normal School).

[30] John Dewey, "The Method of the Recitation," A partial report of a course of lectures given at the University of Chicago (Oshkosh, Wis., 1899), p. 53.

First, Dewey expected that the basic intellectual resources of the culture would be enlarged and transformed by coming technological changes. He anticipated that scholars would guide this reworking of knowledge in the direction of the unity and continuity a democratic culture required. That is, the older studies representing the symbols of intellectual life would be brought into harmony with the newer studies representing the present and direct enrichment of social life. Knowledge would be thought of as the method by which man enriched and improved his associative life.[31]

Second, Dewey reiterated the special opportunity the school had to help create a social harmony in which this newly developing knowledge would and could be used. He insisted that the way in which knowledge functioned in the life of the child would condition the latter's future use of it as an adult. As a result, he recommended that the school organize its curriculum around two concepts: (1) that knowing is experimental, and (2) that knowledge is instrumental to individual and social purpose.[32]

Third, Dewey reminded educators that the way in which the school is organized inevitably conditions the results achieved. He saw a fundamental contradiction between the school conditions of his time (graded school, time segments, emphasis on acquisition of isolated bits of knowledge, etc.) and the intent to develop moral character in a child whose growth is continuous and not cut into yearly fragments. To "bring order and power, initiative and intelligence" into the child's experience, educators must rework the basic school organization to permit the continuity and breadth which his development demands.[33]

[31] Dewey discusses this point in several sources, among which are the following: "Pedagogy as a University Discipline," *University Record*, I (Sept. 25, 1896), pp. 361–63; "The Situation as Regards the Course of Study," *Addresses and Journal of Proceedings of the National Education Association* (1901), pp. 332–48; *The Educational Situation* (Chicago: The University of Chicago Press, 1902); "Shortening the Years of Elementary Schooling: A Discussion," *School Review* VXI (Jan. 1903), pp. 17–20.

[32] Material on this point may be found in the following sources: *School and Society* (Chicago: The University of Chicago Press, 1900); *Elementary School Record* (Chicago: The University of Chicago Press, 1900); "The Relation of Theory to Practice in Education," *Third Yearbook of the National Society for the Scientific Study of Education, Part I* (Chicago: The University of Chicago Press, 1904), pp. 9–30; *The Child and the Curriculum* (Chicago: The University of Chicago Press, 1902).

[33] See especially *The Educational Situation*, and the *First Yearbook of the National Herbart Society for the Scientific Study of Education*, Suppl. II, pp. 244–45.

Fourth, the relationship of the teacher to the institutional organization of the school would need to be such that the continuity of development in the child could be properly directed. Dewey felt that current institutional relationships in schools based decisions about content and method on factors other than the needs of the child's growth. Decisions were made about the curriculum by an external authority above the teacher in a hierarchy, rather than according to the internal authority of truth about the child's growth. The latter is best known, Dewey felt, by the teacher who works directly with the child. Dewey recommended reworking the institutional relationships to permit a maximum of teacher control.[34]

AN ASSESSMENT

Common concerns

We have noticed a number of common concerns on the part of Dewey and the McMurrys during this period, although the proposals made by each show some differences, and the last word was not said by either one at this time. All of them helped to focus attention on the curriculum, and they agreed on the need for system and order in selecting content and method. They all based their particular system on a psychology and a philosophy. Attention to the process by which the child acquires knowledge was common to all, and all worked for a greater unity in this process, although a unity of a different kind. All accepted the aim of education as a moral one and the importance of knowledge as a guide in moral development, although Dewey's insistence that moral aims were social aims called attention to their disagreement on the nature of the moral aim. All cast the teacher in an active role in relation to the curriculum and tried to make teachers sensitive to the need for change. All wished to free the child from dull, mechanical, rote learning, and to capitalize on his vitality, activity, and drive, although they had different rationales for this recommendation.

Many years later, Kilpatrick, who knew both John Dewey and the Herbartians, was to make two assessments which may serve to show their common focus and also to point to their differences:

[34] The best early statement of this position is to be found in "Democracy in Education," *Elementary School Teacher*, IV (Dec., 1903), pp. 193–204. The point was to be further developed in *Democracy and Education* (New York: The Macmillan Co., 1916).

In the end it appears clear that the service rendered by the Herbartian movement was not to contribute a permanent deposit of educational theory—no single item of their doctrines remains as they taught it—but rather to stimulate thought. . . . To settle the disputes thus raised resort was had to new materials. . . . In the utilization of new materials, as is later indicated, education here made significant advance.[35]

On another occasion he commented:

It would of course be foolish to credit John Dewey with all the change, but it is not foolish, nay it is the solid truth, to say that he more than any other one person is responsible for changing the tone and temper of American education within the past three decades. . . . This does not mean that there is unanimity of opinion, and still less that the particular "occupations" work of the Dewey School is now standardized. Far from it. But the underlying doctrines, education as a process of living, the active child, interest . . . moral education, inherent subject matter—these are now practically for everybody—even critics of Dewey—the standard expectations of primary education.[36]

Dewey's contribution

Although Dewey shared with the Herbartians a concern for rationally conceived content and method, he transformed this common problem by placing it within a new philosophical and psychological framework. By so doing he gave the profession an enlarged vision of the potential of education in American culture. He foresaw the transformation of social life that would occur in America in the coming fifty years. He identified as the major source of this imminent cultural growth the coming technological changes to be brought about by science. He hoped that intelligent social action would guide both changes so that they would contribute toward the widest possible social welfare. He awaited a complete reworking of the intellectual resources of humanity to accompany the transformed cultural life. He urged that the school assume a major role in this cultural change by teaching an instrumental view of knowledge and an experimental method of knowing. He expected that the experimental temper and progressive spirit of the American culture would foster such social and educational action.

Dewey considered that this experimental and progressive spirit rep-

[35] William H. Kilpatrick, "Tendencies in Educational Philosophy," *Twenty-five Years of American Education*, edited by Isaac L. Kandel (New York: The Macmillan Co., 1924), pp. 60–61.
[36] William H. Kilpatrick, "The Contribution of John Dewey to Education," *The Philosophy of John Dewey*, edited by Paul A. Schilpp (Evanston: Northwestern University, 1939), pp. 464–65.

resented a cultural attitude native to America. He contended that America was fundamentally a future-oriented society whose glories lay in what it aspired to accomplish, not in what it could maintain from the past. Recently members of a pioneer society, Americans still retained an inventive and experimental attitude toward custom and belief. Formed from many national sources, they were at heart interracial and international, rather than narrowly national. America had too much industrial potential to need to rely upon a budding nationalism to give her international power. Egalitarian in temper, Americans were in practice classless and divisionless, and they would resist any tendency to develop class antagonisms. Such a social climate was strengthened by, and in turn gave particular importance to, science as a form of intellectual control over the forces of man and nature in the interests of man's welfare.

By a major effort of thought, Dewey had succeeded in freeing himself from a conflict between a native cultural habit of action that was experimental and progressive, and a view of the intellectual resources and purposes of the culture that was essentially conservative and a priori. In general, his hearers had not achieved this freedom. Their convictions on the value of the traditional content in the school curriculum, for example, were too firmly entrenched to be easily dislodged. For them, the rationale for the existence of knowledge did not lie in technological change but in the essential nature of the truth of the universe. Yet their native ways of acting tended to be experimental and progressive. Thus the philosophical harmony between knowledge and action, which was largely implicit in Dewey's writings of this period, and which would be made explicit in later years, may not at the time have made much direct impact on the minds of his contemporaries. But the very implicitness of this harmony made many of the specific suggestions Dewey offered seem sufficiently convincing to his contemporaries who had been formed in the same experimental and cultural atmosphere as he had. Many of the details of practice which he suggested were basically in harmony with the native social sympathy and invention of those who heard them described.[37]

[37] Charles McMurry shows in his revision of *Elements of General Method* in 1903 the incorporation of a number of Dewey's suggestions for the improvement of practice. Such passages as the discussion of interest on pages 115–16 and 157, the recommendation of motor activities on pages 115–20, and his treatment of the value of the practical application of knowledge on page 194 give evidence of the influence of Dewey's ideas. The change is in the direction of a more colorful, active, and practical classroom. Yet Charles, in adding these passages,

This does not mean that the Herbartians relinquished their view of knowledge as essentially something to be acquired. It means rather that for the Herbartians as for later theorists,[38] Dewey's contributions to educational thought made at this period (and comprehensively stated in *Democracy and Education* fifteen years later) were to serve as a wellspring of suggestion and promise whenever social invention and creativity seemed desirable.

---

did not modify in any important way his original view of method. As early as 1890, before Dewey's ideas had begun to be widely known, Charles had written, "The child itself should have something to do, some aim set up to be reached, a problem to be solved, a series of objects, places or words to develop—not simply something to learn by heart." *How to Conduct the Recitation*, p. 12. Charles intended that child interest, motor activity, and the practical application of knowledge should be used by the teacher to promote the child's assimilation of knowledge. Dewey thought more in terms of the child's discovery and evaluation of knowledge than of his mere acquisition of it.

[38] This is particularly true of those who organized "progressive" schools, which departed radically from the traditional school forms.

4   Bobbitt and Charters

BOBBITT

The efficiency movement in education

Although it would be some ten years after the impact of Herbartian ideas was felt that attention to the curriculum would take a new and significant direction, the intervening time was a busy one. Many in the profession spent it learning how to select and organize the content of the curriculum according to Herbartian ideas. They hoped that the latter would effectively solve the problem of overcrowding in the curriculum. Yet the insistent pressure for the inclusion of new content did not abate, and the Herbartian theory, although enthusiastically tried, seemed a somewhat academic way to meet the difficulty.[1] In the culture at large, the next decade was to be one of vigorous national economic growth, accompanied by significant developments in industrial technology and management. Educational leaders were to seek an appropriate orientation for the newly conscious educational profession within this expanding society. Reflecting a wider interest on the part of the rest of the culture in the economical use of time and resources, the rallying cry for those in the profession who tried to deal with a crowded and disjointed curriculum came gradually to be "efficiency in education."

The trend toward efficiency in education began in about 1900 and reached its active phase by 1910. We may consider as part of this emphasis the invention and adoption of methods for measuring aspects of education, often called the measurement movement, as well as the new psychological theorizing of Edward L. Thorndike and others. These efforts to streamline the educational enterprise reached a peak in the publication by the National Society for the Study of Education

[1] Samuel C. Parker, *A Textbook in the History of Modern Elementary Education* (Boston: Ginn and Co., 1912), has a good account of this pp. 421–29.

of four landmark reports on minimum essentials, from 1914 to 1918.[2] The concept of efficiency later became so well internalized in educational thinking that many of the practices first introduced in this early period were considered standard operating procedures by the middle twenties.[3]

Points attacked. The emphasis on efficiency during this period stimulated students of the curriculum to reexamine old content and methods and to evaluate the new. For purposes of this study, these efforts to improve the curriculum have been classified in the following categories, depending on the point with which the student of the problem began: (1) content, (2) outcomes, (3) expectations, (4) methods, and (5) supervision.

First, the search for the most desirable and useful content had been going on for some time. Herbert Spencer had posed the question much earlier in his famous essay entitled "What Knowledge Is of Most Worth?",[4] and Charles Eliot had asked it several times from 1888 to 1892.[5] The Herbartians continued to raise it during the nineties. They had been sharply critical of the failure of the Committee of Ten to deal with it,[6] and had been openly approving of the stand taken on it by the Committee of Fifteen.[7] The burden of their own efforts had been directed toward establishing certain content as the most desirable be-

---

[2] National Society for the Study of Education, "Minimum Essentials in Elementary-School Subjects." *Fourteenth Yearbook*, Part I (Chicago: University of Chicago Press, 1915); "Second Report of the Committee on Minimal Essentials," *Sixteenth Yearbook*, Part I (Chicago: University of Chicago Press, 1917); "Third Report of the Committee on Economy of Time in Education," *Seventeenth Yearbook*, Part I (Bloomington, Ill.: Public School Publishing Co., 1918); "Fourth Report of the Committee on Economy of Time in Education," *Eighteenth Yearbook*, Part II (Bloomington, Ill.: Public School Publishing Co., 1919).

[3] National Society for the Study of Education, "The Foundations and Technique of Curriculum-Construction," *Twenty-sixth Yearbook*, Part I (Bloomington, Ill.: Public School Publishing Co., 1926), pp. 129–30.

[4] Herbert Spencer, *Education* (New York: D. Appleton and Co., 1861).

[5] Charles Eliot, "Can School Programs Be Shortened and Enriched?" Referred to in "Shortening and Enriching the Grammar School Course," National Educational Association, *Journal of Addresses and Proceedings* (1892), p. 625.

[6] The Herbartians felt that the Committee of Ten had sidestepped the question of the relative worth of the studies by reemphasizing their disciplinary values. President James Baker of the University of Colorado expressed the dissatisfaction of many with the committee action when he said, "It is a theory that makes education formal and does not consider the nature and value of the content." National Educational Association, Committee of Ten on Secondary School Studies, *Report*, United States Bureau of Education (Washington, D.C. Government Printing Office, 1893), p. 57.

[7] Charles DeGarmo's comment on the Committee Report was typical. It

cause it developed the child morally. They had been supported by Dewey in this emphasis on the moral value of content even though he had been critical of a morality too narrowly conceived.

It was yet to be made clear whether cultural knowledge, practical knowledge, or both were to be considered as most useful in fitting the child for the "demands of civilization." This debate had begun as early as the eighties when educators faced the problem of an overcrowded curriculum. The curriculum of the academies and of the increasing number of industrial and technical schools had given the term "practical" a distinctly vocational meaning, that of preparation for the "life of work." At the same time, the term "cultural" had never lost its older flavor of class bias.[8] Whether a common school curriculum could harmonize two such different sets of content as the "cultural" and the "practical" was still an issue which a Committee on the Culture Element in Education, appointed by the National Education Association in 1903, kept alive.[9] A potential compromise in the shape of a third meaning was emerging, coalescing around a general feeling that education should train for the "work of life," that is, should bring about a gradual improvement in the general cultural level. In any event, the question of what content was of most value was still not resolved.

Second, both the Herbartians and Dewey had given attention to the educational outcomes, or the content actually learned by the child, despite their differences over what the nature of these outcomes should be. The doctrine of apperception, so basic to Herbartian theory, demanded such attention.

Third, members of the child study movement had emphasized differ-

---

"substitutes the demands of civilization for the former psychological demand of mental discipline as a guide to the estimates of educational value." National Herbart Society for the Scientific Study of Teaching, *First Yearbook*, Part I (Bloomington, Ill.: Pantagraph Printing and Stationery Co., 1895), p. 11.

[8] A good discussion of this point may be found in Oscar Handlin, *John Dewey's Challenge to Education* (New York: Harper, 1959), pp. 38–39.

[9] The dissatisfaction Baker had felt with the solution on the course of study proposed by the Committee of Ten had expressed itself in a proposal that a new committee be appointed, "to inquire into the contemporary judgment as to the culture elements in education and the time that should be devoted to the combined school and college course." In 1903, the Committee on the Culture Element in Education was appointed with Baker as its chairman. National Educational Association, *Proceedings* (1903), p. 306. This protest committee eventually became the famous Committee on Economy of Time. A tracing of the confusion in conception between cultural and practical knowledge may be found in Arthur B. Mays, "The Concept of Vocational Education in the Thinking of the General Educator, 1845–1945," *University of Illinois Bulletin*, No. 62 (1946).

ences in rate of growth in children and had urged teachers to adjust accordingly their expectations in regard to outcomes.

Fourth, the Herbartians had made teachers conscious of instructional improvement by their emphasis on general and special methods of selecting, organizing, and presenting content. Their approach had given new importance to the job of the supervisor by affirming that instruction in the different subjects would be improved by the use of these better methods. The conflict in influence of the special supervisor and the administrative officer of the school began to be sharper, and the whole question of the means of instructional improvement began to be studied and pondered.

Fifth, since the days of the early school committees, the community had supervised the schools by keeping a regular eye on the quality of instruction, as part of a generally developing social concern. This kind of supervision had become more systematic in the late nineties and had led to efforts on the part of some school men themselves to look at the efficiency of the total instructional program of their school in a more regular way. For example, Superintendent Maxwell of New York City published in 1904, in his annual report, age-grade statistics showing that 39 per cent of the elementary school pupils in New York City were retarded.[10] This reminder warned the teaching staff that the supervisory officer of the school meant to give the improvement of the instructional program a schoolwide focus.

Refinement in technique. Parallel to this general theoretical approach to a more efficient curriculum ran the search for more exact and reliable knowledge on which to make judgments on content and method. Educators needed a better way than that of armchair speculation to decide what knowledge was of most worth. They looked for a means of telling what the child had actually learned that would be more exact than the teacher's estimate. They hoped to find out how to make more specific and valid the gross differences in expectations arising from ages and stages of growth. They wished to discover some means of comparing the rival claims of different methods of teaching which would be more reliable than the logic of the proponents of each new method.

Instances of this search occurred with increasing frequency. For

---

[10] Cited in Hollis L. Caswell, *City School Surveys* (New York: Bureau of Publications, Teachers College, Columbia University, 1929), p. 92. Caswell also calls our attention to the fact that four committees on the classification and progress of children were appointed by the National Educational Association between 1904 and 1911.

example, President Eliot claimed that the time given by teachers to instruction in literature was outrageously great in relation to the amount of literature actually read by the children.[11] Joseph Rice, who tested thirty-three thousand school children in spelling, claimed that their ability to spell was not significantly related to the amount of time they spent studying spelling.[12] Earlier, George Fisher in England had used a standard model of handwriting, which he had contrived on the basis of his own judgment, to "rate" samples of children's handwriting, giving them numbers on a scale according to the degree to which their writing approximated the model.[13]

Contributions of psychology. The brake on all these efforts to make education more efficient had been the lack of knowledge of the statistical methods which would have permitted exact quantitative standards to replace individual judgment. These methods had been in existence since the work of Galton in 1875, but it was 1890 before James McKeen Cattell at Columbia University began to make original contributions in this area and to train a generation of psychologists in their use.[14] Scholars also had lacked the theory of the controlled experiment developed by Wundt in Germany, although knowledge of it had been slowly trickling into university scholarship in America as the result of the efforts of a number who had studied abroad. Edward Lee Thorndike was to combine statistical methods and the idea of the controlled experiment with a conception of mind as the total response of the organism (an idea of William James) to forge an original psychological theory which would give the efficiency movement the psychological base it needed.[15]

[11] He timed someone reading aloud all the books read in a typical grammar school during the first six years. It took the reader forty-six hours to read aloud the material Eliot estimated it took the teacher two years to teach.

[12] Joseph Rice, "The Futility of the Spelling Grind," *Forum,* XXIII (April, 1897), pp. 163–72.

[13] His work was discovered by Thorndike and reported in the National Society for the Study of Education, "The Measurement of Educational Products," *Seventeenth Yearbook,* Part II (Bloomington, Ill.: Public School Publishing Co., 1918), p. 9.

[14] Newton Edwards and Herman Richey, *The School in the American Social Order* (Boston: Houghton Mifflin, 1947), p. 797.

[15] Thorndike began his experiments on animal psychology while studying with William James at Harvard. Cattell was sufficiently impressed with Thorndike's work while he was a fellow at Columbia University to be instrumental in bringing Thorndike there later as a professor. An excellent source on Thorndike's contribution to the measurement movement is Geraldine M. Joncich (ed.), "Science, Psychology, and Education" (unpublished doctoral dissertation, Teachers College, Columbia University, 1961).

In brief, Thorndike's theory suggested that outcomes, however small and detailed, signified the organism's total response to a stimulus. If rewarded, this response tended to be repeated. Thus an arrangement of the conditions which provided the stimulus would affect the response, or the outcome. The influential aspect of the theory, for our purposes, was largely the conceptualization of outcomes as specific acts which could be identified and of the conditions leading to these outcomes as susceptible of being recognized and deliberately provided for. The theory marked a shift away from thinking of outcomes in terms of moral development, broad generalizations, sensitivity to problems, or any of the other more generalized goals so dear to former educational thought. In contrast, Thorndike suggested that only as outcomes were conceived of in terms of specific, total behavioral responses were they reliable indications of learning. This is not to say that such responses were not moral or intellectual and could not be judged as desirable or undesirable. A dishonest act was not any more acceptable because it showed the total response of the organism. But the dishonest act itself was what had been learned, and no amount of wishful thinking about the influence of uplifting literary selections on character could disguise the fact that, when put in a position to do so, the child cheated. Thorndike insisted that what the child actually did in response to stimulus showed what he had learned. Such responses could be submitted to a whole series of mathematical processes. They could be judged for probability, compared, tabulated, ordered, and correlated. The results would give the educators an improved basis for determining the effectiveness of teaching and learning.

Whatever the long term limitations of Thorndike's theory, it gave a tremendous boost to the movement for efficiency. The rapidity with which this emphasis on behavioral outcomes and their accurate determination spread is a tribute to the real need the theory filled. Beginning, in 1901, with a child study course which tested mental functions and the progress of children in the experimental schools at Teachers College, Columbia University, Thorndike taught a generation of educators his views on educational products. In 1902, he began to teach a course in educational statistics, and his book *An Introduction to the Theory of Mental and Social Measurements*, published in 1904, became the bible of the scientific educators of the next decade. His differences, in 1903, over the details of a theory of transfer of training with Charles Judd,[16]

[16] Judd, who had studied with Wundt at Leipzig in 1896, was to translate Wundt's *Outline of Psychology* in 1907. Judd was directing a psychological

who was influential in the measurement movement, merely strengthened the growing conviction on the part of educators that attention to outcomes susceptible of measurement would improve the efficiency of teaching and learning.

The flood of specific scales, tests, and tabulations which were to be so widely used in judging outcomes began with the development by Thorndike of a Handwriting Scale in 1908.[17] Many who had not studied with Thorndike were enlightened on the nature of the movement by becoming familiar with the specific scales and tests in use. Like the formulations of the Herbartians, these technical instruments strengthened the American reliance on "tools," intellectual as well as practical, which was becoming habitual to them as members of a developing technology.[18]

Influence of Committee on Culture. As the measurement movement got well under way, its effect upon the languishing Committee on the Culture Element in Education was galvanic. Since 1900, the Committee had

---

laboratory at Yale at the time. His major influence was felt as head of the Department of Education at the University of Chicago from 1909 to 1938. The following comment on Judd's work by Harold Rugg is illuminating: "Judd believed in having a small, highly selected body of students who would work with meticulous care at the laboratory analysis of human behavior. He had returned from Leipzig imbued with two of Wundt's lifelong interests. The first was the exact instrumental analysis of human behavior. This led him to develop the famous psychological laboratory at the School of Education, from which he and his students, from 1910 to 1930, reported a score of objective investigations. Judd, in contradistinction to Thorndike's lifelong measurement of the *products* of education, fixed his study on the *processes* of education." The second interest Rugg attributed to Judd was the psychology of social forces. Harold Rugg, *Foundations for American Education* (Yonkers-on-Hudson, New York: World Book Co., 1947), p. 722.

[17] National Society for the Study of Education, "The Measurement of Educational Products," *Seventeenth Yearbook*, Part II (Bloomington, Ill.: Public School Publishing Co., 1918), p. 12. According to Leonard Ayres, this scale was based on the equal difference theorem of Cattell.

[18] Lyman Bryson first commented on this when he said: "It is a caricature, of course, but it is expressive of the essential truth to say that in one kind of society, or at one stage, when a man wants to know how something is done, he must find somebody who knows the art; in a developed technology he looks for a book. In other societies a person who knows how to do something guards his knowledge and sells his services; in an explicit technology he is as likely to sell his knowledge. Europeans have not failed to notice that Americans think anybody can learn anything and have assumed that this innocent confidence had something to do with American character, or conditions or lack of traditional institutions." *The Next America* (New York: Harper, 1952), p. 42.

It was somehow appropriate that the science of education, like biology and the other physical sciences when young, should spend its infancy, while awaiting the growth of the disciplines which would eventually support and feed it, in inventory, survey, and rearrangement.

continued to debate in a desultory way about the growing conflict over the use of school time between those who felt that the cultural studies were paramount and others who wished that schooling were more "practical." In 1908, Baker had circularized some eighty university presidents, professors of education, superintendents, principals, sociologists, and business men, on whether the teaching of "real culture" need suffer the growing encroachments made by the demands of the industrial element for training. He had reported a consensus that a reasonable attention to efficiency and economy of time, the elimination of nonessentials, and a reduction of methods and theories to some degree of order would "save the scholar" and avoid the necessity of erecting an industrial system of education to parallel the cultural system.[19] This conclusion seems quite vague, but, by 1912, the Committee had changed its name to the Committee on Economy of Time and had formulated a definite plan of action. After a conference with "experts" actually administering public education, professors of graduate courses in education, and directors of educational research, the Committee announced its plan to sponsor "a number of well-directed fundamental studies of problems related to the general problem of economy."[20] Some six studies were announced on minimum essentials, eleven others on a variety of aspects, and some twenty-eight schools were reported at work. The Committee's report deplored the currently diffused and confused studies of education, and favored studying "our educational aims as related to our civic needs —the time, means, and methods in view of results." Such aims were basically humanistic, but, the report continued, "there is much waste . . . and 'culture' has been made the chief excuse of it."[22] The remedy for this waste was to vitalize "culture" by relating it to the life of the present day. In short, the culture studies were to be saved by making them socially useful,[23] and the new measurement movement would provide the means of determining the socially useful.

This concept of social utility was a triumphant fusion of the moral aim of the Herbartians with the new technique of the measurement

---

[19] National Education Association, *Addresses and Proceedings* (1908), pp. 466–78.

[20] National Education Association, *Addresses and Proceedings* (1913), p. 218.

[21] United States Bureau of Education, Bulletin 1913, No. 38, p. 62.

[22] United States Bureau of Education, Bulletin 1913, No. 38, p. 11.

[23] Henry Suzzallo, on the Committee, had opined that moral ideas could become of practical value when two classes in a community waged unfair war on each other and their differences needed to be compromised and that, furthermore, a good character was a business asset.

movement. Moral behavior was interpreted as that behavior which would make a difference in social life. The measurement movement would enable the educator to discover the detailed, specific bits of behavior which constituted this difference, as well as more exact information on ways by which these bits of behavior could be taught or learned. Whether what was learned would be socially useful as society was then constituted or socially useful in reconstructing society was a question the answer to which was postponed. The criterion of social usefulness was vague enough to cover both contingencies.[24]

Effect on survey movement. Although superintendents were slower to perceive the usefulness of measurement techniques as a means of getting teachers to improve instruction, by 1912 school administrators had shown enough interest in measurement to mark the beginnings of what was to be a movement toward instructional improvement. New York City, for example, established in 1912 a Bureau of Research to conduct a continuous built-in survey of the school system, using the new measurement techniques.[25] During the next decade, a definite survey movement was to develop from such beginnings and was to use the measurement approach with increasing frequency.

Group of leaders. The group of educators identified by the profession as "scientific" is as large as that of the Herbartians, and the many important figures it contains makes it difficult to select representatives from their number who particularly influenced thought on the curriculum. We have already noted Edward L. Thorndike, formulator of a psychological base for measurement, and Charles H. Judd, who made the department of education at the University of Chicago a major center for the quantitative study of education. But the group contained also the urbane and witty William C. Bagley, Professor of Education at Teachers College, Columbia University, a trenchant critic in polished

[24] The four yearbooks of the National Society which resulted from the work of the committee showed a variety of measurement efforts. There were some five or six studies of the social use of school subjects, ranging from a prediction of the number of children who would need to attain a certain skill on the Ayres Handwriting Scale, based on a study of the vocational distribution of the fathers of elementary school children, to interviews designed to discover what bankers thought a citizen should know about banking. There were a number of tabulations of current practice, such as vocabulary lists taken from readers or library books recommended by fifty cities. Reports of tests and scales measuring pupil achievement were few, as were studies of methods. The contents were provocative but rather scattered, showing few central threads.

[25] National Society for the Study of Education, "The Measurement of Educational Products," *Seventeenth Yearbook*, Part II (Bloomington, Ill.: Public School Publishing Co., 1918), p. 13.

prose; George D. Strayer, who helped introduce measurement into administration; pioneers like Stuart A. Courtis, tester of arithmetic in public schools, and Ernest Horn, who as Director of the University Elementary School at Iowa conducted social use investigations of spelling; Junius L. Meriam, Professor of Education at the University of Missouri and uncompromising school experimenter; Milo B. Hillegas and others. All these leaders had in common a real intent to modernize and streamline the educational enterprise. Their contemporaries, Franklin Bobbitt and Werrett W. Charters, did more than share this concern. Both men succeeded in enabling the profession to think about the curriculum and in particular about methods of making it in a fresh and seminal way. For this reason, they have been selected as especially good scientific educators with whom to continue our study of the developing curriculum field.

Enough has been said to show how absorbed the profession would shortly be in using real life as a criterion for weeding out useless content and tightening up method, basing its inquiries on statistical techniques being developed in this period. The adequacy of this purely surface attack on the curriculum was challenged however when in 1913 Franklin Bobbitt encouraged educators to think about the curriculum in a quite different way from those which had gone before. The Herbartian habit of relying on psychology and philosophy to criticize and improve the curriculum was ignored by Bobbitt. Using analogy and metaphor he proposed not only a different kind of curriculum from the existing one but, more important, a new way of formulating the curriculum itself. As a result, he succeded in freeing critical and evaluative thought from the confines of the curriculum as it was, and he enabled the profession to regard the problem of the curriculum in an entirely new light.[26]

Bobbitt's background

Philippine experience. One of the first steps Bobbitt took which had a bearing on the later development of his thought was, immediately after

[26] An earlier attempt at thinking about method had been made by the champions of the culture epoch theory, who tried to find in the correspondence between child development and racial evolution a method for making the curriculum. Although the correspondence was too inexact to be reliable and the theory went out of favor, it was an early example of the use of analogy in conceptualizing the curriculum. Students of the genetic movement in child study, which developed in the first part of the century, kept the approach alive and may well have contributed to the interest which launched the wave of progressive schools after 1915.

earning an AB from Indiana University in 1901, to go as an instructor to the Philippine Normal School in Manila, "in response to a call for teachers there."[27] During the first few years of our occupation of the Islands after the Spanish American War, American authorities had tried to hasten the modernization of the pretechnological culture there, which appeared to them to be needlessly primitive and costly in life and suffering. Being American, they worked especially hard on establishing the right kind of schools to hasten this acculturation. Bobbitt, together with six other Americans who had been teaching and supervising for several years in the Islands, preparing teachers for the new schools, and who were reasonably familiar with their potentialities and drawbacks, were chosen to help. They were asked to draw up an overall elementary school curriculum for the Islands. As Bobbitt himself recalls:

It was a virgin field in which we were free to recommend almost anything by way of meeting the needs of the population. We had an opportunity to do a magnificent and original constructive piece of work.

And what did we do? We assembled upon a table in the committee-room copies of the American textbooks in reading, arithmetic, geography, United States history, and the other subjects with which we had been familiar in American schools. We also assembled such American courses of study as we could find; and without being conscious of it, we mobilized our American prejudices and preconceptions as to what an elementary-school course ought to be. On the basis of these things we made out a course of study for the traditional eight elementary grades. We provided the traditional amount of each subject for each grade, distributed them as in American schools, and recommended American textbooks for the work.

The thing was not adapted to the conditions within the islands. As a matter of fact, we did not try to adapt it to those conditions—though we honestly thought that we were doing the thing needed.

. . . Fortunately for the people, the Director of Education was better able to look at essential realities; he cut the course down to six grades, unceremoniously threw out irrelevant materials, and without regard for the time-hallowed sanctities brought bodily into the course a number of things then far more than now regarded as superficial and plebeian, such as shop-work, cooking, sewing, weaving, rug-making, etc. We were properly horrified.[28]

To Bobbitt, then unfamiliar with the point of view of the professional educator on socially useful knowledge, this experience was unsettling

[27] Letter to writer from Mrs. Franklin Bobbitt, June 9, 1957.
[28] Franklin Bobbitt, *The Curriculum* (Boston: Houghton Mifflin Co., 1918), pp. 282–84.

but curiously liberating. As he commented later, "We needed something that would shake us out of the grooves and which at the same time was violent enough to obliterate them, and set thought free."[29]

Work at Clark University. On his return to the United States in 1907, Bobbitt attended Clark University where he elaborated earlier growth studies he had made on Philippine children. For Bobbitt, whose traditional notions of curriculum content had already received the shock of contact with sociological reality, the choice of Clark for his graduate work was fortunate. If any American university during that period could have shown him how to base the curriculum on the needs of the developing child, it was Clark. Beginning in 1888, its President, G. Stanley Hall, had made Clark a center of study and research on the stages by which each child recapitulates the development of the race. The given nature of these stages was seen by the theorists as the pattern by which to select school content and activities. The older view that the child had to adapt himself to the content presented to him had shifted to a newer view that the content should fit the individual development of the child. That is, content was to be selected primarily as it was useful to the child at his particular stage of development.[30] The graduate work that Bobbitt did at Clark in adapting the course of study to the stages of normal growth in Philippine children brought into harmony his widening vision of the interrelationship of child, society, and the curriculum.

His first university post was Instructor in Educational Administration at the University of Chicago in 1909.[31] This was Judd's first year there also, and as a colleague Bobbitt was introduced to the exciting new world of educational measurement which was to influence his thinking so profoundly.[32]

The Gary experiment. He was also close to the Gary experiment in nearby Indiana, just two years old and already a center of speculative interest to theorists. William Wirt, a former student of Dewey's at Chicago, had tried to reconstruct the Gary schools according to Dewey's

[29] Franklin Bobbitt, *The Curriculum* (Boston: Houghton Mifflin Co., 1918), p. 284.

[30] An interesting discussion of this point may be found in Lawrence A. Cremin, *The Transformation of the School: Progressivism in American Education 1876–1957* (New York: Alfred A. Knopf, 1961), pp. 101–05.

[31] Since as yet there was no graduate field of educational administration, Bobbitt, with others, began to create it, working from the basis of their preparation in other fields. At that time, educational administration was a good choice for a man interested in overall decisions on curriculum.

[32] By 1915, Bobbitt had become a member of the Committee on Economy of Time.

notion of the school as an "embryonic community life, active with types of occupations that reflect the life of the larger society and permeated throughout with the spirit of art, history, and science."[33] In so doing, Wirt found himself involved in reworking the school organization (regulation of children's time and energies) and eventually the institutional organization (regulation of the teacher's roles and status), as Dewey had predicted anyone would who tried seriously to rework the curriculum. Typical of the changes at Gary were the platoon system, by which children were freed from permanent desks, and the individualized programs, by which they were freed from class recitations and the lockstep of the graded school. Supervision was transformed from a set of orders, percolating down through the system, to a relative autonomy of action in each functional part of the school (shops, laboratories, gardens, classrooms, etc.) and a coordination of them all through joint planning and attack on problems.[34]

At first, Bobbitt saw in Gary an example of what he and his colleagues should have done in the Philippines—use the school as a "lever of social progress."[35] But a closer look at the avoidance of usual wasteful practices in the school—such as an idle plant in summer, an idle child caught in the lockstep of the grades, and the unintentional sabotage by the teacher of the school's goals—caught Bobbitt's interest, and he began to think about the school organization itself as a means of carrying out educational purposes.[36]

Scientific management. His thinking received a fresh impetus in 1911 from the publication of a book by Frederick Winslow Taylor on scientific management in industry.[37] Attention to industrial efficiency was not new, but the wide popular interest in the idea on the part of college

[33] John Dewey, *The School and Society* (Chicago: University of Chicago Press, 1900), p. 44.

[34] William P. Burris, "The Public School System of Gary, Indiana," United States Bureau of Education, Bulletin 1914, No. 18.

[35] Franklin Bobbitt, "A City School as a Community Art and Musical Center," *Elementary School Teacher*, XII (Nov., 1911), pp. 119–26.

[36] Franklin Bobbitt, "The Elimination of Waste in Education," *Elementary School Teacher*, XII (Feb., 1912), pp. 259–71.

[37] Frederick W. Taylor, *The Principles of Scientific Management* (New York: Harper and Bros., 1911). A provocative discussion of the effect of scientific management on the newly emerging field of school administration during this same period may be found in Raymond E. Callahan, *Education and the Cult of Efficiency* (Chicago: University of Chicago Press, 1962). It is interesting to see how both curriculum theorists and administrators caught the contagion of industrial efficiency (often they were the same persons, initially) and to speculate how much they influenced each other.

professors and government officials made Taylor's account of it welcome. The theory was applied for the first time in 1912 to a university, and the school survey movement was soon launched.[38] The key to Taylor's theory was that the standards set for the finished product would provide quality control of the whole processing function. He substituted supervision by means of working directions covering the whole process of production for supervision through personal authority. His theory suggested to Bobbitt that the fundamental tasks of management were about the same whether carried on in schools or in factories, and the analogy set Bobbitt to thinking about education as an example of a process to be managed, similar to the processes found in industry.

Method of curriculum making

The analogy. Using industry as his controlling metaphor, Bobbitt began to think about the curriculum. If (he theorized) the school were a factory, the child the raw material, the ideal adult the finished product, the teacher an operative, the supervisor a foreman, and the superintendent a manager, then the curriculum could be thought of as whatever processing the raw material (the child) needed to change him into the finished product (the desired adult). The nature of this processing would be discoverable as truth, in the same way as whatever would properly temper a steel rail was true and whatever had traditionally been done to temper it might or might not be. The determination of such a curriculum or process could best be done by using the most thorough experimental and quantitative means at hand. Variations in the curriculum would result only as processes were discovered to be more nearly in accord with truth. They also would vary with the changes in standards set for the finished product by the consumer. The analogy led Bobbitt to select the mature adult as the consumer and the highest type of adult life as the standard for the finished product. If adult life was to be the measure of the process, then child life should be heeded only to the extent that attention to child nature was effective in improving the product. The whole process of the curriculum was to be controlled, not by human will, but by the truth or science which would produce the desired end product.

Bobbitt explained his analogy in the *Twelfth Yearbook of the National*

---

[38] Morris L. Cooke, an efficiency engineer, was asked to survey eight university departments of physics. Charles R. Kelley, "Toward an Interpretation of the New Movement of 1915 in Educational Administration" (Doctoral dissertation, Teachers College, Columbia University, 1961), p. 8.

80

Society for the Study of Education, calling it "Some General Principles of Management Applied to the Problems of City-School Systems." He listed eleven principles of management, but he gave over half his attention in the paper to the first two, judging them of crucial importance:

> Principle I. Definite qualitative and quantitative standards must be determined for the product.
>
> Principle II. Where the material that is acted upon by the labor processes passes through a number of progressive stages on its way from the raw material to the ultimate product, definite qualitative and quantitative standards must be determined for the product at each of these stages.[39]

We must remember that in talking about the product he was really talking about people. The key to the theory was this emphasis on a standard product, i.e. the ideal adult. This standard was to guide the supervisor, administrator, teacher, and even the student himself. It would be useful in evaluating method, rating teacher effectiveness and qualifications, guiding in-service training, and providing the working instructions or the daily lesson plans for the school.

The standards for this ideal adult should be set by the community, Bobbitt contended. It was the transportation world which determined the standards for steel rails, although any efficient steel mill had a good general knowledge of what was wanted. In the same way, the schools were merely society's agents charged with turning out a product as nearly standard as possible. Bobbitt admitted that standards for the ideal adult were somewhat controversial and had not yet been properly determined, but he insisted that until society was mobilized to indicate its standards clearly, the inquiry had to be started by someone. He suggested that the educators should be the ones to get it started. Further, the educators were the only ones qualified to determine the progressive stages for the product—such as the time to begin a study, how long it should be followed, and how well it should be done. We can see from just these specifications that, in order to implement Bobbitt's method of determining the process and the product, the educational measurement expert would certainly have his work cut out for him.

Bobbitt's own summary statement of the curriculum, or the process by which the standard product is produced, is the following:

[39] Franklin Bobbitt, "The Supervision of City Schools," *Twelfth Yearbook of the National Society for the Study of Education,* Part I (Chicago: University of Chicago Press, 1913), p. 11.

To summarize these matters: (1) As a foundation for all scientific direction and supervision of labor in the field of education, we need first to draw up in detail for each social or vocational class of students in our charge a list of all of the abilities and aspects of personality for the training of which the school is responsible.

(2) Next we need to determine scales of measurement in terms of which these many different aspects of the personality can be measured.

(3) We must determine the amount of training that is socially desirable for each of these different abilities and state these amounts in terms of the scales of measurement.

(4) We must have progressive standards of attainment for each stage of advance in the normal development of each ability in question. When these four sets of things are at hand for each differentiated social or vocational class, then we shall have for the first time a scientific curriculum for education worthy of our present age of science.[40]

The key to the operation of the process was the concept of "science" or "law." To the degree that everyone—teachers, supervisors, etc.— knew and acted on the best there was to be known about method, capacity, and attainment, the process would function smoothly and effectively. This put a high premium, of course, on the kind of work the educational measurement experts were doing. It also cast the role of the supervisor in a slightly different light. It meant that both teacher and supervisor were operating in terms of an objective set of realities. Their common problem would be to join forces in discovering and acting on these realities.

Social need. Judged in relation to the whole of Bobbitt's future work, this first essay served chiefly as an exercise enabling him to grasp the problem of the content of the curriculum by focusing on the end product, or the ideal adult, and on the process by which this end product is elaborated. In the beginning, Bobbitt found most absorbing the challenge of setting up measurable standards for this adult and for the stages by which he was produced. But as he began a decade-long study of these standards with his students in curriculum classes at the University of Chicago, he and they became aware of the need to know the particular culture in which this ideal adult would live. In his next book, *The Curriculum,* written in 1918, Bobbitt shows the results of his study of contemporary America. The intervening years had been those of war. As America had come of age industrially and interna-

[40] Franklin Bobbitt, "The Supervision of City Schools," *Twelfth Yearbook of the National Society for the Study of Education,* Part I (Chicago: University of Chicago Press, 1913), p. 49.

tionally, she had consolidated earlier social reform movements and at the same time acquired new social problems. These problems became the social setting for the ideal adult Bobbitt was seeking. The new social problems, as he saw them, all revolved around a central social phenomenon. Technological growth had created a social interdependence which required social cooperation for human welfare. As Bobbitt phrased it in his preface:

> Since the opening of the twentieth century, the evolution of our social order has been proceeding with great and ever-accelerating rapidity. Simple conditions have been growing complex. Small institutions have been growing large. Increased specialization has been multiplying human interdependencies and the consequent need of coordinating effort. Democracy is increasing within the Nation; and growing throughout the world. All classes are aspiring to a full human opportunity. Never before have civilization and humanization advanced so swiftly.[41]

The areas in which such social solidarity was needed were the familiar ones of the social reformer: industrial conflict, public health, consumption, international relations, civic improvement, conservation, monopolies, etc. The ideal human being who would live in a culture with both the potential and the problems of modern technological America should be equipped to make the most of his opportunity. In response to this evident social need, Bobbitt contended, education should develop in the adult the powers and abilities which would enable him to work for social cooperation. As Bobbitt put it:

> Education is now to develop a type of wisdom that can grow only out of participation in the living experiences of men, and never out of mere memorization of verbal statements of facts. It must, therefore, train thought and judgment in connection with actual life-situations, a task distinctly different from the cloistral activities of the past. It is also to develop the good-will, the spirit of service, the social valuations, sympathies, and attitudes of mind necessary for effective group-action where specialization has created endless interdependency. It has the function of training every citizen, man or woman, not for knowledge about citizenship, but for proficiency in citizenship; not for knowledge about hygiene, but for proficiency in maintaining robust health; not for a mere knowledge of abstract science, but for proficiency in the use of ideas in the control of practical situations. . . . We have been developing knowledge, not function; the power to reproduce facts, rather than the powers to think and feel and will and act in vital relation to the world's life. Now we must look to these latter things as well.[42]

[41] Franklin Bobbitt, *The Curriculum* (Boston: Houghton Mifflin Co., 1918), p. i.
[42] Franklin Bobbitt, *The Curriculum* (Boston: Houghton Mifflin Co., 1918), p. iv.

Activity analysis. Bobbitt's prescription for social action is hardly new. It is the old Herbartian emphasis on moral behavior, phrased in terms of the contemporary social setting, as Dewey had urged the educational theorist to do. One noticeable difference is that, since the needs of a changing culture furnish the requirements of the educated man, there is more attention given to these social needs than is usual. As we read on, however, we see that Bobbitt's grasp of the end product as the key has shifted the whole problem and given him a new way of looking at the curriculum. In the past, the theorist had said, in effect: let us teach that specific content in the social studies which will develop civic participation. Bobbitt had no quarrel with the teaching of civic participation by means of the social studies. What he did want to change was the starting point of the proposition. Instead of starting with an analysis of the subjects, or, like Spencer, with the knowledge that will best prepare man for his life activities, Bobbitt suggested starting with an analysis of the life activities themselves. His mind had been freed to do this since he was guided by the analogy he had drawn between the educative process and the process by which a steel rail is made. Further, he saw the need to clothe the life activities of the ideal man in the specific details of his particular society at his particular moment. For example, he contended that a study of the activities of the ideal man would disclose the particulars of his civic participation. We could know if he votes, takes part in civil affairs, knows the facts about his city, protects himself against political fallacies, and understands statistical tables, persistently, honorably, generously. From these particulars of his activities could be deduced the "abilities, habits, appreciations, and forms of knowledge"[43] he had needed in order to carry out these civic activities. The latter abilities, analyzed completely so that they were "numerous, definite and particularized," would then become the objectives of the curriculum. In addition, Bobbitt gave the curriculum itself the same moving nature as the life activities for which the child was being prepared. The curriculum thus would be "that series of things which children and youth must do and experience by way of developing abilities to do the things well that make up the affairs of adult life; and to be in all respects what adults should be."[44]

Notice that because Bobbitt thought about the curriculum as es-

[43] Franklin Bobbitt, *The Curriculum* (Boston: Houghton Mifflin Co., 1918), p. 42.
[44] Franklin Bobbitt, *The Curriculum* (Boston: Houghton Mifflin Co., 1918), p. 42.

sentially a process, like the process of casting and tempering a steel rail, he was freed from all former allegiance to any particular subject matter or method. He could thus be eclectic without fearing confusion, because his conception of the process was controlled always by the end point. Yet he saw the process as more than a series of activities since he was sensitive to the experimental character of activities for human beings. It was not a question of merely habituating children to the right activities. Bobbitt sensed that children, unlike steel rails, interact humanly with anything they do. They reflect, dislike, enjoy, and sabotage. A child does more than plant trees on Arbor Day; he feels, thinks about, and judges the activity of planting. The problem, as Bobbitt saw it, was to arrange the child's activities so that his potential abilities would properly unfold. And so Bobbitt insisted upon the dimension of experience as essential to the process by which the child is turned into the ideal adult.

Definition of curriculum. If Bobbitt was to think about "that series of things which children and youth must do and experience by way of developing abilities to do the things well that make up the affairs of adult life," he was also obliged to consider the child's activities and experiences as a whole, only a part of which went on in school. Bobbitt's thinking led him precisely to this conclusion:

> The curriculum may, therefore, be defined in two ways: (1) it is the entire range of experiences, both undirected and directed, concerned in unfolding the abilities of the individual; or (2) it is the series of consciously directed training experiences that the schools use for completing and perfecting the unfoldment. Our profession uses the term usually in the latter sense. But as education is coming more and more to be seen as a thing of experiences, and as the work-and-play-experiences of the general community life are being more and more utilized, the line of demarcation between directed and undirected experience is rapidly disappearing. Education must be concerned with both, even though it does not direct both.[45]

Bobbitt then suggested a division of labor on the curriculum objectives. "The curriculum of the schools will aim at those objectives that are not sufficiently attained as a result of the general undirected experience," he asserted. These objectives would be discovered as the individual made mistakes in his life activities. "The curriculum of the directed training is to be discovered in the shortcomings of individuals

---

[45] Franklin Bobbitt, *The Curriculum* (Boston: Houghton Mifflin Co., 1918), p. 43.

after they have had all that can be given by the undirected training," he concluded.[46]

Further, he used the early childhood experiences of the ideal man as the pattern for the most desirable early experiences for all. In so doing, he ran into the old rift between the cultural and the practical. He had to decide whether to select the ideal man from among, as he phrased it, the "bankers, bishops, or judges" or from among the "hard-handed laborers upon our streets, or in our mines and factories?" He solved the conflict by a compromise, making man's common social functions his central point of reference. First, he pointed out the value conflict itself:

> Current discussion of education reveals the presence in the field of two antagnostic schools of educational thought. On the one hand are those who look primarily to the subjective results; the enriched mind, quickened appreciations, refined sensibilities, discipline, culture. To them the end of education is the *ability to live* rather than the practical *ability to produce*. . . . On the other hand there are those who hold that education is to look primarily and consciously to efficient practical action in a practical world. The individual is educated who can perform efficiently the labors of his calling; who can effectively cooperate with his fellows in social and civic affairs; who can keep his bodily powers at a high level of efficiency; who is prepared to participate in proper range of desirable leisure occupations; who can effectively bring his children to full-orbed manhood and womanhood; and who can carry on all his social relations with his fellows in an agreeable and effective manner.[47]

He went on to identify it as a pseudo conflict, suggesting that the ability to live and the ability to produce were both valid ends in education and could exist in a harmonious relationship. He concluded:

> We have here simply to do with two levels of functioning, two levels of educational experiences, both of which are essential to fullness of growth, efficiency of action, and completeness of character. Both are good, both are necessary; one precedes the other. One is experience upon the play-level; the other experience upon the work-level. . . . One is the luxuriation of the subjective life which has a value for objective experience even though one be not conscious of the values at the time. The other looks to the conscious shaping and control of the objective world; but requires for maximum effectiveness the background of subjective life provided by the other.[48]

[46] Franklin Bobbitt, *The Curriculum* (Boston: Houghton Mifflin Co., 1918), p. 45.

[47] Franklin Bobbitt, *The Curriculum* (Boston: Houghton Mifflin Co., 1918), p. 3.

[48] Franklin Bobbitt, *The Curriculum* (Boston: Houghton Mifflin Co., 1918), p. 6.

86

For experience on the play-level, he used the professional man as his model. After quoting a passage from William James showing that the developmental conditions of the accomplished gentleman permit him to taste of the "essence of every side of human life, being sailor, hunter, athlete, scholar, fighter, talker, dandy, man of affairs, etc. all in one," he went on to say:

> One has to examine the activities of men among those social classes where from childhood into adulthood the play-impulses have had full opportunity to function; where they have not been stifled by adverse conditions and barren opportunity. It is best revealed by men and women of the leisure classes and of independent means. . . . They are instantly recognized to be larger men and women than those who have been held within the narrow grooves of serious vocational, civic, and family duty. . . . The professional men stand poised, erect, full-statured, physically flexible, buoyant with energy. Intellectually, they are rich in stores of the world's wisdom and their mental horizon and outlook are as wide as the world itself.[49]

The model for experience on the work-level was the modern industrial worker in scientific industry. Bobbitt felt that the analysis of each occupation into tasks and factors would result in the development of the controlling science which should dominate the consciousness of the worker. "He must think each factor in terms of the science of that factor. His planning consists of putting his science-ideas to work," Bobbitt contended.[50] This controlling science had its counterpart in childish work experiences in which the student planned the actual practical performance of a task, deciding on the result and the processes to be used, and testing in imagination each step in the series. Although the student must be protected from the crushing and injuring effect of failure by the intervention of the adult, he must not be robbed of what Bobbitt calls the antecedent performance, in which he thinks through the process to the end result.[51] In this way, the student could

[49] Franklin Bobbitt, *The Curriculum* (Boston: Houghton Mifflin Co., 1918), pp. 221–22.
[50] Franklin Bobbitt, *The Curriculum* (Boston: Houghton Mifflin Co., 1918), p. 72.
[51] At this point, Bobbitt discusses the project method, giving as examples school corn clubs, antimosquito campaigns, sewing, and shop projects. He approves of projects if "knowing and doing" are properly blended as he recommends. Franklin Bobbitt, *The Curriculum* (Boston: Houghton Mifflin Co., 1918), p. 31. Stevenson credits Bobbitt with first borrowing the idea of projects from vocational education and applying it to the curriculum. See John Alford Stevenson, "The Project Method of Teaching" (University of Illinois Graduate School, 1921), p. 30.

begin to master the relationships between ends and means, which should govern his later work experience.

Social implications. Bobbitt's definition of the curriculum process required educators to take a stand on social values at a time when an older assumption of a commonly accepted value core was breaking up in the face of important, cultural cleavages. Bobbitt succeeded in side-stepping this issue by assuming that the value crisis was more superficial than profound, and that science would help man understand the nature of the conflict and make rational choices.

Bobbitt was quite clear-sighted about the value conflicts of his day. In discussing the search for standards for a good bricklayer, for instance, he said:

> Men do not agree as to the characteristics of the most desirable types of work. The employers of the bricklayers will be inclined to use maximum productiveness as the criterion of superior work; and unquestioning obedience to orders and contentment with any kind of hours, wages, and working conditions as proper mental attitudes. The employees will judge otherwise as to some of the factors. . . . The correction of grammatical or spelling errors, for example, has no important economic results. Property distributions are not affected. Men do not, therefore, greatly care what the list of grammatical or spelling weaknesses may be that are to be corrected by the training in our schools. . . . But in the occupational field, property is affected. An undesirable occupational condition very frequently gives increased profits to one group and does harm to a second. . . .[52]

He saw that his new method of curriculum formulation would require the selection of ideal adult activities according to some criterion. Among the choices were the maintenance of the status quo or a deliberate molding of the future in a certain direction. Bobbitt chose the latter and defined the direction in terms of the greatest good to the greatest number. He relied on science as a means of settling possible disagreements over the nature of this greatest good. Using the scientific method of curriculum making, educators would accumulate a body of representative knowledge about social behavior which would permit control of the future. Bobbitt felt that, in the hands of democratic men, this control would be rightly exercised for the welfare of all. As Bobbitt pointed out in discussing the public pressures constantly put upon the schools to remedy obvious social flaws:

[52] Franklin Bobbitt, *The Curriculum* (Boston: Houghton Mifflin Co., 1918), p. 65.

Scientific management demands *prevision—accurate prevision*. It demands understanding that sees all factors in true and balanced relation without any distortion due to claims or oppositions of special interests. This means that scientific survey and analysis of human needs must be the method of discovering the objectives of the training that is demanded not by individuals, but by the conditions of society.[53]

In the beginning, a list of social shortcomings could be assembled on which all right-thinking men already agreed. "A program can be scientific without being complete," he commented. And, in the long run, he hoped that such agreements would grow. Activity analysis, he felt, showed the need for the development of a large-group consciousness, which would provide the climate of social cooperation necessary to bring bricklayer and employer to see the need to act in their common interest—the economic health of the nation.

Procedures. Bobbitt's formulation relied on a "controlling science" which could be used in the supervision of a school system. In order that such a science be sufficiently explicit to the people guided by it, he recommended that each superintendent and his staff "cooperatively draw up a concise summary of the curriculum principles to be kept in mind in connection with each subject."[54] The idea that the teacher might play a more active role in selecting and organizing the curriculum was not a new one. There was a precedent for such participation which Bobbitt's method attempted to rationalize. For example, as early as 1902, we find Superintendent Louis Soldan asking the teachers to help make the course of study for the St. Louis public school system. Eight teachers worked with principals and supervisors on improving a course of study draft, which was originally prepared by Soldan. He then circularized over one thousand teachers for suggestions and changes in this tentative course and asked that a revisory committee be set up by grades to incorporate these recommendations.[55] In 1904, under the sponsorship of the Chicago Principals Association, a group of specially selected teachers tried out a new course of study in the Chicago schools and recommended improvements in it.[56] After 1910, the year of an

[53] Franklin Bobbitt, *The Curriculum* (Boston: Houghton Mifflin Co., 1918), pp. 69–70.

[54] Franklin Bobbitt, *The Curriculum* (Boston: Houghton Mifflin Co., 1918), p. 288. Bobbitt himself began work on the formulation of a set of principles of this kind, and he later incorporated them in a book, *How to Make a Curriculum* (Boston: Houghton Mifflin Co., 1924).

[55] *Course of Study for the St. Louis Public Schools*, 1902, p. 2.

[56] *Course of Study for the Chicago Public Schools*, 1904, p. 3.

epic fight for greater control of the National Education Association (then in the hands of an "old guard" of university presidents and school superintendents who had literally made the Association in its early years), the classroom teacher began to assert a growing prestige.[57] In a number of course of study revisions, touched off by the measurement movement which gained momentum about this time, teachers were asked to gather data directly from the classroom. For example, in 1916, Frank Ballou, active in the investigation of arithmetic achievement and Director of the Department of Educational Investigation and Measurement of the Boston Public Schools, asked selected teachers who had been working on measurement to serve on committees to set up aims, minimum essentials, and suggestions for testing, all of which would be incorporated into a new course of study.[58]

CHARTERS

Charters's background

Teacher training experience. Although we have no way of knowing, we can guess that Bobbitt, in his book *The Curriculum,* formulated a method that W. W. Charters had been reaching toward for years. Although his early experiences differed from Bobbitt's, both men were enthusiastic proponents of the method of curriculum formulation we have just examined. Charters was not an administrator like Bobbitt but a teacher of teachers like the McMurrys. Just out of college in 1898, he became principal of the Hamilton Model School in connection with McMasters in Toronto. He moved on to a Ph.D. in Methods of History Teaching at the University of Chicago, studying under Dewey, whom he acknowledged to have influenced him deeply. As an Instructor in Education and Supervisor of Practice Teaching at the Minnesota State Normal School in Winona, he continued to prepare teachers. In 1907, he became a Professor of Theory of Teaching at the University of Missouri where he came into contact with what he himself called later a "significant laboratory school." Called the University Elementary School, it had been established there in 1904 by Junius L. Meriam, a former student of Dewey's at Teachers College, Columbia University.[59]

---

[57] Mildred S. Fenner, *National Education Association: History* (Washington, D. C.: National Education Association, 1945), pp. 30–34.

[58] *Course of Study for the Boston Public Schools*, 1916, p. 8.

[59] Harold Rugg called him "one of the first of the new doctors in 'education' at Teachers College." *Foundations for American Education* (Yonkers-on-Hudson, New York: World Book Co., 1947), p. 558.

Meriam was attempting to embody in practice Dewey's emphasis on the child. Child activities such as observation on field trips and excursions, play, stories, both constructive and expressive handwork, together with much discussion, constituted the curriculum of the University Elementary School. Charters found Meriam's method of selecting and organizing the curriculum thought-provoking, and observation of the school's practice led him to make some rather searching criticisms of Meriam's apparent neglect of content. For example, he wondered whether the improvement of the normal activities of children would, as Meriam contended, best prepare them for adulthood. He felt that the traditional school subjects were being neglected.[60] He questioned whether children didn't need a number of learnings that the "free flow" of activities in Meriam's school might not happen to provide.[61] Charters's own favorite selection from the ideas of Dewey was the emphasis on the social character of education. If subject matter were created originally to satisfy social needs, as Dewey had suggested, it was surely evident that such needs were continuing. Charters wondered whether these needs could safely be ignored or whether there was some subject matter that must be taught to satisfy them.

Charters's first book, *Methods of Teaching*,[62] written in 1909 shortly after his acquaintance with Meriam's school, was a good example of that blend of ideas gleaned from both Dewey and the Herbartians that was so typical of the writings of the first decade of the century. The book included an excellent section on correlation and apperception and gave particular attention to Dewey's analysis of the act of thought. Charters was also eclectic in his choice of teaching methods. The theme of the book, as well as of another one written for rural teachers on method,[63] was that: "Children then should be assisted in school not only to do what they want to do, but also to want to do what is best

[60] Rugg credits Ernest Horn, who was Meriam's assistant during the beginning years of the experimental school, with saying that "its extreme freedom—'license' I think he called it—made a lifelong conservative out of him." Harold Rugg, *Foundations for American Education* (Yonkers-on-Hudson, New York: World Book Co., 1947), p. 559.

[61] Charters commented later that although the graduates of the school were able to keep abreast of others who had studied the conventional curriculum, teachers had often smuggled in grammar or arithmetic anyway, and parents had felt a very heavy strain in helping their children to catch up. *Curriculum Construction* (New York: The Macmillan Co., 1923), pp. 149–50.

[62] *Methods of Teaching: Developed from a Functional Standpoint* (Chicago: Row, Peterson and Co., 1909).

[63] *Teaching the Common Branches: A Textbook for Teachers of Rural and Graded Schools* (Boston: Houghton Mifflin Co., 1913).

for them to do."[64] Charters thought Charles McMurry underestimated the usefulness of mediate interest as a means of heightening motivation. The practical situation was precisely the one in which the child felt the strongest need. If a boy did not like arithmetic but did like horses, Charters felt that the teacher should use the boy's interest in horses to motivate the arithmetic. Thus he wove his procedure for selecting and organizing content around the twin themes of socially useful knowledge and child motivation. The primacy for Charters of certain social needs and the subject matter which would fulfill them can be seen from these words:

> All subject matter has been created and preserved by the race to satisfy needs and solve problems, and . . . in the schools such parts of this subject matter as satisfy the most fundamental needs are taught. . . . To complete a practical description of this conception as applied to teaching it has been found necessary to discuss the methods of arousing the appropriate needs and the conditions under which they are found present, and to investigate the methods pursued by experience both in satisfying these needs, to the aid of which subject matter is invoked, and in securing the maximum degree of such satisfaction.[65]

Some of the elements of the method of curriculum making which he was later to formulate are already apparent in this book. For example, he contended that any knowledge which has survived in the struggle for intellectual existence has done so because it has continued to meet a recurring human need. This notion of the persistence of need was to be basic to Charter's activity analysis. He was to regard man's current activities as essentially methods of solving persistent needs. In the activity, he was to discern not only the need but the knowledge that had had survival value in the satisfaction of this need. In this book, Charters also attributed the structure of an organized subject to the function for which the subject was organized. His thesis was that facts had always been organized according to their method of use. As he made this analysis of knowledge and method, he came very close to the point of looking directly at them both as they functioned in adult activities in society.

Work on economy of time. Not yet ready to think his ideas through

---

[64] *Teaching the Common Branches: A Textbook for Teachers of Rural and Graded Schools* (Boston: Houghton Mifflin Co., 1913), p. 323. Faced, like the McMurrys, with classes in teacher training, Charters was inclined to couch his theory in fairly simple and direct language which was doubtless a boon to the teacher.

[65] Charters, *Methods of Teaching: Developed from a Functional Standpoint* (Chicago: Row, Peterson and Co., 1909), p. 3.

to their final form, Charters began to do some work on the problem of arousing a feeling of need in the child. He chose grammar, a subject for which he felt that the child would easily recognize a need. He focused on the errors children made, reasoning that their correction would be motivating and would also be economical of both the child's time and effort. His study appeared in the Sixteenth Yearbook of the Committee on Economy of Time.[66] Charters's emphasis in this study, the child's use of grammar as a source of information on what to teach, took him ahead another step toward activity analysis.

Job analysis

Introduction. Job analysis in industry, first clearly formulated by Taylor and others as early as 1910, had become a large-scale undertaking by the early twenties. In 1919, Charters was appointed the Director of a Research Bureau for Retail Training at the Carnegie Institute of Technology in Pittsburgh. We can only guess whether it was this appointment, Bobbitt's book on the curriculum, or some other event that marked the turning point in Charters's thought. Whatever the influence, Charters began at this time a labor on which he would spend the major portion of his professional life—the job analysis of a host of adult occupations and the construction of curricula and teaching methods in them.[67] Shortly afterwards, he enunciated a method of

[66] As we have seen, Bobbitt also used this idea of the pathology of the subject to distinguish between the directed curriculum and the undirected curriculum. Both men were to abandon the notion later.

[67] Among these occupations were pharmaceuticals, radio education, veterinary medicine, recreation leadership, secretarial duties, leadership in industry, and women's activities (for the Stephens College curriculum, on which Charters was a consultant). As Director of the Bureau of Educational Research at Ohio State for the fourteen years until his retirement, he supervised and inspired many more job analyses in the occupations.

Speaking candidly on this part of his professional work some years later, he said: "The building of curricula by the functional analysis method has been carried farther than elsewhere in the field of the vocations. . . . On the one hand, the trades are relatively simple in their operations, and are relatively superficial, so far as the theory underlying practice is involved in the use of good methods. In order to be a satisfactory plumber or carpenter, one does not need to have a great mass of so-called 'fundamental' information on which to base his practice. . . . On the other hand, the support given to vocational education through the Smith-Hughes Act . . . shows itself in at least two ways. First, some funds are provided by the Federal Board for research into curriculum-organization; and second, many of the Smith Hughes officials situated both in Washington and in the outlying states have sufficient leisure and clerical assistance to make it possible for them to work out courses of study on the functional basis." National Society for the Study of Education "The Foundations and Technique of Curriculum

curriculum formulation which was very similar to the one already outlined by Bobbitt.

The problem of content. Charters essayed a complete, full-scale exposition of his ideas on curriculum making in a book called *Curriculum Construction.*[68] His emphasis differs from that of Bobbitt because of a different initial approach to the problem. As we have noted, it was through the improvement of teaching that Charters became interested in the curriculum, not, like Bobbitt, through the improvement of the management of education. Bobbitt's concept of experience implied the function of knowledge, but he failed to spell out exactly what that function was. Charters understood too well the teacher's notion that the curriculum was content to fail to give explicit attention to knowledge in his method of curriculum formulation. True to the temper of his educational era, Charters wanted knowledge to be useful for living. What is more, he wanted the learner to be stimulated to acquire knowledge because he had perceived its usefulness. As a result, Charters analyzed the life activities for their knowledge content, not for needed human abilities as did Bobbitt. He was seeking some way by which the new method could deal with knowledge.

He found it in an idea he got from Dewey, that knowledge is really method, and that method is really knowledge.[69] As he explained it:

> All the content of the curriculum is methodic. Everything taught or discovered, recorded or achieved, has been a method. . . . Loyalty, for instance, originally was and still is being developed as a means of attaining group solidarity. . . . In like manner facts are methods of control. In spelling, for instance, it is a fact that *pencil* is spelled p-e-n-c-i-l, but this combination of letters is meaningless except as it is a means of putting on paper some characters which will describe, or bring to the writer's mind, or help the reader to understand, the object of value for which it stands. . . . Even the fact *Bombay is in India* is a statement by which to locate a city.[70]

Having established a convincing connection between activity and knowledge, he went on to point out that: "the problem of the schools

---

Construction," *Twenty-sixth Yearbook*, Part I (Bloomington, Ill.: Public School Publishing Co., 1926), p. 365.

[68] Werrett W. Charters, *Curriculum Construction* (New York: The Macmillan Co., 1923).

[69] He acknowledged the great help Boyd Bode had given him with this formulation.

[70] Werrett W. Charters, *Curriculum Construction* (New York: The Macmillan Co., 1923), pp. 74–75.

is theoretically quite simple. The best methods of realizing ideals and performing activities must be collected."[71] These methods would be collected from analysis of the life activities of men in society. Since these activities were nothing more than methods of meeting recurrent needs which embody relevant facts, the analysis of these methods, i.e. activities, would give the facts which are integral to the activity.

Organization of content. Charters was prepared for the rediscovery of much of the old content by this collecting process. It was to be rediscovered, however, within a new conceptualization—its social usefulness. Charters thought that this form was the most appropriate one anyhow. Knowledge formulated in this way was easier for the ordinary person to apply to his problems, and he would also be more motivated to learn it. Charters called this new form for content the "primary subjects" and warned that their slow discovery would mean a period of confusion for students of the curriculum, during which adjustments would have to be made. As he said:

> We find it possible to eliminate the obviously useless from the subjects by a partial reorganization and thereby to perform a useful service, but to secure an objective basis for a complete reorganization we must carry through an analysis of life activities. The absence of such an analysis undermines the validity of any comparisons between what the curriculum is and what it ought to be.[72]

He pointed out that some content is not directly and openly recognized as method when the activity is analyzed but that such content is nevertheless involved. He described the value of this content by saying:

> These are service subjects which are important not because they are directly useful in the performance of activities, but because they are derived from material which has practical service value. They are necessary to a complete understanding of the primary material.[73]

For example, the English "used" by a machinist is "necessary to understand" his work, and the chemistry involved in food preparation "explains why" certain procedures are recommended to the cook. Charters called this kind of knowledge the "connective tissue" which holds together the "primary method."

Charters's emphasis on life activities in place of subject matter

[71] Werrett W. Charters, *Curriculum Construction* (New York: The Macmillan Co., 1923), p. 79.

[72] Warrett W. Charters, *Curriculum Construction* (New York: The Macmillan Co., 1923), p. 151.

[73] Werrett W. Charters, *Curriculum Construction* (New York: The Macmillan Co., 1923), p. 105.

constituted no real challenge to the knowledge included in the conventional curriculum. Much of the old content would still be found functioning in the activity. The major change would be the appearance of new organizing centers for this content.

Curriculum pattern. We have noticed that Bobbitt, as an administrator, give little attention to the pattern into which the curriculum was to fall in the daily life of the school. He seemed to have accepted the traditional subjects as the essential form of the curriculum and have based the sequence of experiences and activities on a vaguely assumed, developmental growth in the child. Although Charters's interest in teaching led him to work more vigorously on the problem of pattern, he made no original contribution here either. Rather he accepted as useful the wide variety of experimentation which had been going on in the selection and organization of conventional subject matter. He seemed to regard the question of the best design or pattern as incidental to the method of curriculum making itself. Once the basic "method-knowledge" was identified, he felt, then any of a variety of conventional devices would be useful organizing centers for the presentation of this knowledge. His own predilection in later years was for a pattern of instruction very similar to the steps involved in carrying out the activity. Such a pattern is strongly reminiscent of Pestalozzi's work on an alphabet of the subjects. Charters, speaking in the late twenties about the trend in teaching of vocational skills toward giving the student an "alphabet" of operations in the skill (some thirty-eight operations in sheet metal working, for example) with which he could then make any necessary combinations for any new job, commented:

> This modification of teaching procedure is significant. It indicates a return to methods which were discarded twenty-five years ago by the theorists in education. Under the criticism that to learn the elements without a recognition of their uses destroyed interest, educators ceased teaching the alphabet and taught interesting sentences. Music teachers no longer began musical instruction with the scales; instead, they introduced their pupils to tunes. It was felt that the so-called "logical" method produced less interest in the student than did those methods in which the student used his material immediately. Now we find these thoughtful professional men reverting to the discarded method. They feel that, if the elements are taught, combinations can be easily learned; and we may assume that interest in the process will be developed from the interest that the pupils have in the vocation. This is a very interesting change in present procedure by a return to earlier procedures.[74]

[74] National Society for the Study of Education, "The Foundations and Technique of Curriculum Construction," *Twenty-sixth Yearbook*, Part I (Bloomington,

But in 1923, reflecting on teaching and its relationship to the new method of curriculum making, he contented himself with discussing and evaluating a number of curriculum patterns then in use: (1) the project method, which he concluded is valuable *if* its content is that of life projects, which it frequently is not; (2) the conventionally organized subjects, whose usefulness he recognized; and (3) "incidental" teaching, the usefulness of which, he decided, was neither limited by nor recommended by activity analysis. He concluded that, if a choice must be made between school subjects and projects, "any efficient system of instruction would include both methods of attack, until on scientific grounds it should be demonstrated that one is superior to the other."[75] He went on to say that, once the most important elements of the school subject had been determined by activity analysis:

school projects must be so selected that they will give drill and instruction on each of the items so as properly to prepare the student to use them in the broader range of life activities. School projects cannot be selected haphazard. They are controlled by two factors: on the one hand they must parallel life activities, and on the other hand they must include the items of the subjects in their proper proportions.[76]

Procedure of curriculum making. It may clarify matters to give Charters's procedure of curriculum making. Comments by the writer of this study on some of Charters's steps are given in brackets.[77]

First, determine the major objectives of education by a study of the life of man in its social setting. [Typical objectives are citizenship, morality, and social efficiency. These who offer instruction shall determine the objectives after a "sagacious and sensitive interpretation of the spirit of the generation."][78]

Second, analyze these objectives into ideals and activities and continue the analysis to the level of working units. [Ideals are to be selected by a faculty by vote of its members, not lightly nor arbitrarily, but after serious study of social demand. There is room in a democracy for differences of values.

Ill.: Public School Publishing Co., 1926), p. 371. The educational profession has continued to be interested in task analysis. See Robert M. Gagné, "Military Training and Principles of Learning," *American Psychologist*, XVII (Feb., 1962), pp. 83–91.

[75] Werrett W. Charters, *Curriculum Construction* (New York: The Macmillan Co., 1923), p. 150.

[76] Werrett W. Charters, *Curriculum Construction* (New York: The Macmillan Co., 1923), p. 151.

[77] Werrett W. Charters, *Curriculum Construction* (New York: The Macmillan Co., 1923), p. 102 gives Charters's procedure.

[78] Werrett W. Charters, *Curriculum Construction* (New York: The Macmillan Co., 1923), p. 94.

Activities are to be derived from objective studies of the physical and mental activities of men in society. These studies must be made scientifically and the conclusions may be shared by all. The analysis must be thorough enough to result in a complete series of small, detailed steps for each activity. "The perfect analysis is one which is carried to the point where the student can learn without assistance. If it is put into the form of a book, the ideal text is one which teaches itself. In it the material is so expertly presented that the student understands everything, can follow it through to its end, incorporate it in his experience, and use it in his life of action."][79]

Third, arrange these in the order of importance. [Objective measurement is the only reliable means to be used. Expert opinion may be a useful temporary measure.]

Fourth, raise to positions of higher order in this list those ideals and activities which are high in value for children but low in value for adults. [Examples are dramatization, games, fairy stories, and obedience.]

Fifth, determine the number of the most important items of the resulting list which can be handled in the time allotted to school education, after deducting those which are better learned outside of school.

Sixth, collect the best practices of the race in handling these ideals and activities. [Such collections should include empirical studies of adults in action, as well as studies of children's activities.]

Seventh, arrange the material so obtained in proper instructional order, according to the psychological nature of children. [Items four to seven depend heavily on the collection of empirical evidence.]

Charters continued to emphasize the practice of having teachers participate in curriculum making. He suggested that the determination of ideals be the responsibility of the staff of each school. He had included ideals in his theory in order to avoid the subjective character of the pure, individual satisfaction of need. They seem to be extraneous to the method of curriculum formulation he advocated but necessary to his theory of knowledge. At any rate, they were to be determined, and he suggested that they be chosen by a consensus of each faculty of each school.

In addition, a plan was given for faculty reorganization of the course of study. A steering committee, directed by a person "for whom the whole project is the major duty"[80] and composed of a representative teacher from each subject, was to get a consensus from the staff on

[79] Werrett W. Charters, *Curriculum Construction* (New York: The Macmillan Co., 1923), p. 60.
[80] Werrett W. Charters, *Curriculum Construction* (New York: The Macmillan Co., 1923), p. 156.

ideals and was to coordinate the work of the subject committees which were to determine objectives for the subjects, that would be in harmony with the ideals. The teachers were then to carry out the findings of the committees and report their experiences for review and revision. This was a basic pattern of operation that was already becoming standard at the time Charters described it.

AN ASSESSMENT

Meeting Dewey's challenges

Of Dewey's four basic challenges to the profession—a reworking of knowledge, curriculum organization, school organization, and institutional organization—Bobbitt and Charters made their major contribution to two. First, they expressed the need they felt for a basic reorganization of knowledge around social activities. Bobbitt called attention to some work already done in this area which the schools might take advantage of—such as occupational studies, economic geography, industrial and economic history, sociology, anthropology, and the history of scientific discovery.[81] Developing scholarship in the social sciences was to give a theoretical foundation for such a reorganization.[82] The new concepts and theories were not to have real influence on the curriculum for another decade, however.

Second, they jarred the institutional organization of the schools to some extent. Their emphasis on the controlling science as a reference point for supervision gave the teacher more professional status. Theoretically the teacher, supervisor, and even the child could evaluate the process of the curriculum if the appropriate measurement techniques had been perfected. As Bobbitt once commented:

> These standards are not set up by the supervising principal himself, nor are they set up by the teacher. The standards represent common aims toward which both must strive. The success of both depends upon the ends being attained. Principal and teacher are thus put upon a common level. Neither exercises arbitrary authority over the other.[83]

[81] Franklin Bobbitt, *The Curriculum* (Boston: Houghton Mifflin Co., 1918), pp. 92, 103, 109, 139, 161, 200.

[82] Dewey, in discussing the need for a new philosophical synthesis, had mentioned such social categories as communication and participation as possible new organizing centers for knowledge. "From Absolutism to Experimentalism," edited by George P. Adams and William P. Montague, *Contemporary American Philosophy,* (New York: The Macmillan Co., 1930), p. 26.

[83] Franklin Bobbitt, "The Supervision of City Schools," *Twelfth Yearbook of*

Thus the very suggestion that education might be evaluated on the basis of a "truth" which could be verified gave the teacher potential access to that truth. The role of the administrator and principal then became one of facilitating this process: helping teachers who are weak, eliminating the teachers who cannot be helped, and, in general, providing the needed incentives and material conditions. The supervisor also would be responsible for giving the teacher a set of generalized working plans, derived from the overall purposes of the school. The teacher was then left to "the direction of his inner technical knowledge as to standards and procedure."[84] Bobbitt was confident that the quality of instruction would not be impaired by the use of these generalized working plans. "So long as the teacher uses standard methods or better, and accomplishes standard results or better, there is no need of supervisory interference or supervisory direction," he declared.[85] The feeling grew among the students of the curriculum that the teacher and supervisor and administrator were all embarked on a common search for understanding.

In addition, the emphasis on a method of curriculum formulation foreshadowed the casting of teacher and administrator in a new set of institutional roles. The traditional prerogative of the superintendent to set school goals could be weakened by a method which derived educational objectives from an analysis of social needs. Such a method might be employed as effectively by intelligent teachers as by administrators. Power would shift subtly from persons in authority to those with technical skills.

Bobbitt and Charters were not very instructive in regard to a new curriculum organization to implement their method of curriculum formulation. Bobbitt was clear about his categories of social activities: occupational efficiency, citizenship, physical efficiency, leisure occupations, and social intercommunication. But he described the process itself which the child undergoes as a "series" of activities and experiences, and that was his most explicit statement of the way in which these bits of experience would be put together in a school program.

---

the National Society for the Study of Education, Part I (Chicago: University of Chicago Press, 1913), p. 27.

[84] Franklin Bobbitt, "The Supervision of City Schools," Twelfth Yearbook of the National Society for the Study of Education, Part I (Chicago: University of Chicago Press, 1913), p. 93.

[85] Franklin Bobbitt, "The Supervision of City Schools," Twelfth Yearbook of the National Society for the Study of Education, Part I (Chicago: University of Chicago Press, 1913), p. 93.

Although Charters addressed himself more directly to this problem, he tended to suggest only minor improvements in existing curricular organization, rather than a fundamental reworking of that organization. Apparently both theorists felt that their major task had been accomplished when they had answered the question of what to teach, and they were content to leave the problem of organization to others.

Joint contribution

The chief contribution of Bobbitt and Charters was to bring to professional awareness a new specialization—curriculum making or curriculum formulation, as it was variously called. These were new labels in education for a new kind of phenomenon, the method or process of curriculum making. Derived from an analogy with the process of industrial manufacture, the new method began, not with traditional subject matter, but with the life activities of the adult. Proceeding by gradual and precise steps, the curriculum maker who followed the process could formulate a curriculum. This was not a change in a former method but the introduction into professional thinking of the idea itself of a method of making the curriculum.

That Bobbitt himself was conscious of the revolution in curriculum thinking which this approach suggested is clear from the following passages. In the first, he described his initial perception in the Philippines of the need for a changed outlook:

> We needed *principles of curriculum-making*. We did not know that we should first determine objectives from a study of social needs. . . . We had not come to see that [education] is essentially a process of unfolding the potential abilities of a population, and in particularized relation to the social conditions. . . . A large portion of our profession appears to need something that will lift them out of the grooves of routine traditional thinking—or rather out of an imitation that is not thought—and which will so obliterate the grooves that their minds will be free to think out new problems.[86]

By 1918, he had realized what was lacking:

> At the present stage of developing courses of training it is more important that our profession agree upon a *method* of curriculum-discovery than that we agree upon the details of curriculum-content.[87]

[86] Franklin Bobbitt, *The Curriculum* (Boston: Houghton Mifflin Co., 1918), pp. 283–84.

[87] Franklin Bobbitt, *The Curriculum* (Boston: Houghton Mifflin Co., 1918), pp. 284–85.

And so he had offered the profession *his* method, hoping that they would be stimulated to try it, perhaps refine and improve it, or even suggest a better one. But, whatever the success of his method, he felt that he had taken a step in the right direction. "To know what to do is as important as to know how to do it," he commented.[88]

Once the method had been described, the profession would need instruction in its use. The answers to such questions as how one followed it, what its pitfalls were, and what some examples of it were, constituted a wealth of information which could be used as instructional content. Not only Bobbitt and Charters but many of their contemporaries[89] were able to fill several books and a number of magazine articles on the method, as well as to teach college courses in it.

Further, the way was prepared for the appearance of a new expert, the curriculum maker. Bobbitt and Charters had suggested what his know-how might be, and a sizeable block of this information was already in existence. It consisted of the real, technical expertness of those who had been making educational measurements for a decade. In addition, the expert at curriculum making should know how to derive curriculum objectives from the analysis of activities. He should be able to suggest grade placement and interest level for activities. He should be competent to direct committee action in setting up objectives or translating them into activities. As Charters had suggested, such a person might be expected to give full time to the direction of curriculum work.

Both men also turned the profession's attention strongly toward the culture, but in different ways. Charters called attention to the individual in society faced with persistently recurring problems. He suggested that education should show him how to solve them. By preparing the individual for his life activities, his education would help satisfy his needs within a social framework. Bobbitt called attention to a society whose problems confronted the individual. He suggested that education should prepare the individual to solve these social problems. By preparing the individual for his life activities, his education would, furthermore, get him ready to discharge his social functions and gain individual satisfaction. The first position accepted society as it was and emphasized the importance of the individual. The second position sought

[88] Franklin Bobbitt, *The Curriculum* (Boston: Houghton Mifflin Co., 1918), p. v.
[89] Among them were Frederick Gordon Bonser, Milo Burdette Hillegas, Herbert Bruner, Junius Meriam, Lois C. Mossman, L. Thomas Hopkins, and Ernest Horn.

to improve the society and located the individual in a social context. Both positions were to be espoused by later students of the curriculum.

How influential were the proposals made by Bobbitt and Charters on the developing stream of ideas about the curriculum? If the Herbartians inaugurated a comprehensive approach to the curriculum and Dewey gave this approach its philosophical tone and temper, what did Bobbitt and Charters do? They represent a group which sought, by the use of formula or method, to give the curriculum a dynamic dimension. Drawing an analogy with the steps in industrial manufacture, they spelled out a process which, if followed by the curriculum maker, would result in an evolving curriculum, reflecting changes in values and activities as these were taking place in the culture. Although the particular method they described was to be improved and even challenged, the habit of method which they suggested was to remain a permanent part of the curriculum maker's thought.

There was good reason for this to occur. The new method went far beyond previous efforts to improve the process by which content was selected and organized. Such tinkerings by the Herbartians had left unaltered the assumptions commonly held about desirable content. The new method represented a shift in focus, subtle but profound, from the content of the curriculum to the method of formulating that content. In this shift, method assumed priority over content. The whole question of the content of the curriculum became dependent on the method of curriculum formulation, rather than the method dependent on the content. Content became a variable and relative notion, rather than a fixed and immutable one. The effect of this shift would prove to be somewhat unexpected. Those, for example, who formerly determined content—such as the scholars in the established disciplines or individual, educational style-setters—would find their power to determine content challenged, not so much by new leadership as by the very notion of method in the minds of the whole profession. The notion of method would give fresh perspective to old orthodoxies and new prominence to some educators, especially classroom teachers, and its neutrality in a value crisis would prove troublesome. But as a notion it would persist, shaping subsequent thought on the curriculum.

5   Harold Rugg

THE EDUCATIONAL SITUATION

Introduction

It is tempting to ascribe the next decade of curriculum revision to
the influence exerted by Bobbitt and Charters. It is safer to say that
the programs inaugurated were harmonious with their ideas. It was
to be a decade of attention to the measurement of the socially useful.
It was also to be a decade of growing attention to the child, typified
by the wave of progressive schools. Above all, it was to be a time of
trial for the new method of curriculum making. It seems almost as
though there now ensued a period of testing and exploring alternatives
which would ultimately demand some pulling together of the resulting
developments. Harold Rugg's work in this decade epitomizes such a
period of reconnaissance ending in a final synthesis. In order to understand this period, however, we should review briefly a number of
developing trends which were to provide a significant background for
Rugg's contribution.

Courses of study

One such trend was the fresh wave of course of study making that
resulted from the trial of the new method of curriculum formulation.[1]
The earlier impetus to streamlining courses of study had been given

[1] According to Trillingham, the first systematic curriculum making and revision
began around 1920. Few school systems undertook the organization and administration of complete curriculum programs. Most of them worked on specific
problems, such as a course of study in a subject, or a special research study.
Clinton C. Trillingham, *The Organization and Administration of Curriculum
Programs* (Los Angeles, Cal.: University of Southern California Press, 1934),
p. 7. By 1926, practically all the schools surveyed for the *Twenty-sixth Yearbook
of the National Society for the Study of Education* reported curriculum revision.

by the measurement movement. This second major effort within a decade to improve the course of study could now rightly be called curriculum revision. A look at several examples of such curriculum revision programs should give us some idea of the method as it appeared in action.

In St. Louis, under the direction of Walter Cocking, the principals selected the objectives according to social needs, and the teachers, working in committees with full-time chairmen, listed suitable activities and later tried them out in practice. The teacher-chairmen were taught a short course in "curriculum-technique" by the director of the general curriculum program. The resulting curriculum was judged to be very well worked out, and its use was recommended to other school systems that were planning curriculum revision.[2]

In Detroit, curriculum making was a blend of scientific research and system coordination, very similar to Bobbitt's original formulation. Administration and supervision were two distinct divisions within the system. In a typical manner, curriculum revision began in Detroit with the identification of a city-wide problem, such as learning difficulties in spelling. The whole system was then mobilized to discover the "facts" relevant to the problem. The supervisory arm of the system did the necessary research to discover the best methods for teaching spelling, and city-wide plans were tried out, improved, and finally adopted. "The critical factors in cooperative, scientific curriculum-construction are, in our opinion, a conviction that education takes place in accordance with discoverable natural law, and the existence of machinery of cooperation. Detroit is fortunate in having both," curriculum specialists in Detroit concluded.[3]

In Denver, the teachers, working in committees, determined the objectives and selected the activities to realize them. Although the program stressed initial research and study by the teachers as well as freedom to hold differing views from those of the supervisors, the most desirable kind of curriculum activities were generally held to be those which endeavored to "show the pupil what and why he ought to study."[4]

[2] National Society for the Study of Education, "The Foundations and Technique of Curriculum-Construction," *Twenty-sixth Yearbook*, Part I (Bloomington, Ill.: Public School Publishing Co., 1926), p. 248.

[3] National Society for the Study of Education, "The Foundations and Technique of Curriculum-Construction," *Twenty-sixth Yearbook*, Part I (Bloomington, Ill.: Public School Publishing Co., 1926), p. 203.

[4] National Society for the Study of Education, "The Foundations and Technique of Curriculum-Construction," *Twenty-sixth Yearbook*, Part I (Bloomington, Ill.: Public School Publishing Co., 1926), p. 236.

Teacher participation was highly valued, but the rationale for the continuance of teacher committees after appropriate curriculum activities had been selected and embodied in a course of study was not clearly thought through.

In state programs such as those in Wisconsin, Missouri, and Connecticut, members of the state Departments of Public Instruction chose the objectives for the state, leaving the selection of activities to the teachers.[5]

As we might expect, the programs showed considerable variety. In all of them, however, objectives and activities were prominent. Teachers had become more active in curriculum revision, and the emphasis on social needs had been increasing.

Subjects

Another interesting trend which helps us understand events of the coming decade was the determined defense of the cultural subjects by their own specialists. Because of the equal status given even the newer subjects by the Committee of Ten, their champions had all tended in the beginning to make common cause against any suggestion that subjects were not the real core of the curriculum. While these specialists were meeting in annual round tables at the National Education Association as early as 1901, observers began to discern a slowly widening rift between those specialists who defended the disciplinary value of the subjects and those who thought the subjects should help raise the general cultural level of the nation. Two of the most aggressive groups were the teachers of English and the teachers of the social studies. The appointment in 1911 of a Committee on Articulation of High School and College brought the issue out into the open. Protest meetings of English teachers who objected to formal literary requirements for college entrance had motivated the appointment of this committee. Apparently the English teachers felt that functional English was urgently needed and objected to the iron control exercised over content by college entrance requirements.[6] Judd was on this committee, of which the purpose had broadened by 1913. Renamed the Commission on the Reorganization of Secondary Education, it was charged with formu-

[5] National Society for the Study of Education, "The Foundations and Technique of Curriculum-Construction," *Twenty-sixth Yearbook*, Part I (Bloomington, Ill.: Public School Publishing Co., 1926), Chap. viii.

[6] National Society for the Study of Education, "The Foundations and Technique of Curriculum-Construction," *Twenty-sixth Yearbook*, Part I (Bloomington, Ill.: Public School Publishing Co., 1926), pp. 43–45.

107

lating "statements of the valid aims, efficient methods, and kinds of material whereby each subject may best serve the needs of high-school pupils."[7] Of the various subject matter subcommittees appointed, the most active was the one on social studies.[8] James Harvey Robinson, as a member, urged the inclusion of content in the curriculum that would help children understand "the most vital problems of the present."[9] The report of the subcommittee on social studies in 1916[10] emphasized the need to relate the social studies to the pupil's present interests and to the vital problems of the day. Dewey was quoted as urging attention "to the needs of present growth . . . [as] the best possible guarantee of the learning needed in the future."[11]

When the Commission on Reorganization was first appointed, it had elected a Reviewing Committee whose members were drawn from all the subcommittees.[12] This group was charged with outlining "those fundamental principles that would be most helpful in directing secondary education."[13] It took three years in formulating them. After reviewing the work already done by the subcommittees and finding that the chief emphasis had been on social efficiency and personality development, it concluded that the key to education was to be found in life activities. Categorized according to major social functions, these activities were to be the seven cardinal objectives of secondary education: health, command of the fundamental processes, worthy home membership, vocation, citizenship, worthy use of leisure time, and

[7] National Education Association, Commission on the Reorganization of Secondary Education, *Preliminary Statements*, United States Bureau of Education, Bulletin 1913, No. 41 (Washington, D.C.: Government Printing Office, 1913), p. 8.

[8] Thomas Jones was head of the social studies subcommittee, James Hosic of English, William Kilpatrick of mathematics, Otis Caldwell of sciences.

[9] National Education Association, Commission on the Reorganization of Secondary Education, *Preliminary Statements*, United States Bureau of Education, Bulletin 1913, No. 41 (Washington, D.C.: Government Printing Office, 1913), p. 24.

[10] Some sixteen reports were issued by the subcommittees, appearing regularly from 1915 (civics) to 1922 (home economics).

[11] National Education Association, Commission on the Reorganization of Secondary Education, *The Social Studies*, United States Bureau of Education, Bulletin 1916, No. 28 (Washington, D.C.: Government Printing Office, 1916), p. 11.

[12] Clarence Kingsley was the head; James Hosic, Cheesman Herrick, William Kilpatrick, Otis Caldwell were among the some twenty members.

[13] National Education Association, Commission on the Reorganization of Secondary Education, *Cardinal Principles of Secondary Education*, United States Bureau of Education, Bulletin 1918, No. 35 (Washington, D.C.: Government Printing Office, 1918), p. 5.

ethical character.[14] The committee specified that principals, councils, and teachers' committees should work together to bring about a curriculum that would carry out these objectives and thus prepare the child for "complete and worthy living." The work of this committee can be considered as an adroit move to defend the place of the traditional subjects in the curriculum by identifying them as comprising the major source of useful social knowledge.

Another wing of specialists in subject matter inherited the older Herbartian notion of correlation as a help to the child in assimilating and applying knowledge. As early as 1909, a Committee of Eight of the American Historical Association had published extensive recommendations on the correlation of history with geography, literature, and art. By 1916, the term "social studies," representing a somewhat correlated approach to geography and history, was in use.[15] In 1922, Rugg and others founded the National Council for the Social Studies, established to enable teachers in the related fields of history, geography, and civics to talk together.[16] In this same period, specialists in the teaching of English had tried to bring English into closer relationship to the other subjects in the curriculum—another Herbartian idea. In 1929, the National Council of Teachers of English appointed a Curriculum Commission on Correlation to work on the problem. These efforts to preserve the conventional subjects by keeping their content as non-specialized as possible differed in origin from, but were not inharmonious with, the general streamlining that was going on in curriculum content in other ways. More important, as we have seen, such endeavors reminded the profession of the role of the scholar in preserving cultural values.

The superintendent

The new curriculum approach had had another stimulating effect. By 1923, the members of the powerful Department of Superintendence had begun to sense that the superintendent's traditional role as the educational leader of the school system was being challenged by the

[14] National Education Association, Commission on the Reorganization of Secondary Education, *Cardinal Principles of Secondary Education,* United States Bureau of Education, Bulletin 1918 No. 35 (Washington, D.C.: Government Printing Office, 1918), p. 5.

[15] The Commission on the Reorganization of Secondary Education was among the first to use it.

[16] Harold Rugg, *Foundations for American Education* (Yonkers-on-Hudson, New York: World Book Co., 1947), p. 575.

new specialists in curriculum making.[17] To clarify their leadership function, the Department had issued its first yearbook on the status of the superintendent, following it in 1924 with one on the elementary school curriculum.[18] By 1926, they had organized a nationwide Cooperative Plan of Curriculum Revision which outlined the superintendent's indispensable role in unifying the nation's approach to the curriculum. "Education is not a local matter but . . . there are national ideals to be worked for," they had stated,[19] and they had recommended the superintendent as the strategic person to take part in a national search for a common approach.

A school system might belong to this Cooperative Plan (at least three hundred did) if it contributed at least part of the time of one officer to work on the problem of curriculum revision in his own school system. In the yearbook, the curriculum was defined as what the pupil learns and experiences. The teacher was to guide these experiences according to a blueprint or course of study based on an organic study of the needs of the individual in the modern social world.[20] Such a blueprint must be constantly revised, they said, so that it would continue to be up to date, and it must be adapted in use to fit each individual teaching situation. They envisioned a future encyclopedia of curriculum literature as a further aid to unity. The acceptance by this influential group of curriculum making as an important educational task was of value to the growth of the idea of method in curriculum making.

College courses

The demands made on the colleges for the preparation of curriculum specialists furnish another example of change brought about by the

---

[17] Clarification of role was sought also by the principal. The Department of Elementary School Principals was organized in 1922, and four of their yearbooks in their first decade of existence were on the topic of supervision.

[18] "The Status of the Superintendent," *First Yearbook of the Department of Superintendence, National Education Association* (Washington, D. C.: National Education Association, 1923); "The Elementary School Curriculum," *Second Yearbook of the Department of Superintendence, National Education Association* (Washington, D. C.: National Education Association, 1924).

[19] "The Nation at Work on the Public School Curriculum," *Fourth Yearbook of the Department of Superintendence, National Education Association* (Washington, D. C.: National Education Association, 1926), p. 9.

[20] "The Nation at Work on the Public School Curriculum," *Yearbook of the Department of Superintendence, National Education Association* (Washington, D. C.: National Education Association, 1926), p. 46.

new curriculum approach. As early as 1916, the interest in minimum essentials in the curriculum had brought about a burst of specialized course offerings at Teachers College, Columbia University.[21] By 1922, these offerings were supported by the establishment of an Institute of Educational Research.[22] The scope of such an institute did not seem adequate to cover all of the new theory involved, and, in 1926, a Bureau of Curriculum Research was founded as well, for the purpose of studying and collecting outstanding curricula and curriculum making practices.[23] It had become evident also that the preparation of curriculum specialists had been going on as a matter of expedience for a decade. In the same year, a Department of Curriculum was established which brought together a number of previously isolated courses.[24] A specialized interest in the curriculum was still thought of as an educational sideline, however, because the courses in this department were designed for "superintendents of schools, principals, supervisors and heads of departments who are interested in the study and reconstruction of the curricula of elementary and secondary schools."[25] Among the offerings were two general courses: one emphasizing backgrounds for curriculum makers and the other instructing in the procedures of curriculum making itself.[26]

Progressive schools

In the period between 1915 and 1921, increasing numbers of progressive schools were established. Beginning as early as 1907,[27] this

[21] In 1916, a Department of Educational Experimentation, a Department of Education Statistics, and a Department of Educational Tests were all established.

[22] It had three arms: one in educational psychology under Edward Thorndike, one in school experimentation under Otis Caldwell, and one in field studies under George Strayer.

[23] Florence Stratemeyer and Herbert Bruner were its first directors. The kind of work done by the Bureau is typified by the report by Florence Stratemeyer on *The Effective Use of Curriculum Materials* (New York: Bureau of Publications, Teachers College, Columbia University, 1931).

[24] Some sixteen courses in eight other different departments were identified as courses in curriculum.

[25] Teachers College, Columbia University, *Announcements*, 1926, p. 41.

[26] Teachers College, Columbia University, *Announcements*, 1926, p. 42. One course description was of "a comprehensive view of basic considerations, historical, comparative, philosophical, sociological and experimental." Bonser, Reisner, Russell, Raup, Snedden, Gates, and Rugg taught it jointly. The other course was "administrative and educational procedures involved in determining pattern and content" for those who will be called upon to share in curriculum reconstruction.

[27] This was the year Marietta Johnson established the Organic School in Fairhope, Alabama.

111

movement reached its peak in the years just after the first World War.[28] There had been in existence since 1900 a number of influential laboratory schools connected with university departments of education, and some of them were quite experimental in both program and curriculum.[29] But the appearance in 1915 of Dewey's *Schools of Tomorrow,* a record of a number of promising, experimental efforts in a variety of schools, and in 1916 of Dewey's *Democracy and Education,* the matured statement of his educational philosophy, may have strengthened a growing movement to found a new kind of school that would reject educational tradition and strike out boldly in a new direction. An interesting number of the founders or directors of these schools do seem to have been influenced by Dewey's writings and teachings.[30] Rugg suggested once that attendance in itself at a progressive school may in some cases have been the source of an interest in experimentation.[31]

RUGG'S BACKGROUND

Early conflicts

One of the puzzles which a knowledge of Rugg's early years helps to solve is his abrupt transformation in the early twenties from an educational technician into a social critic. This shift is of real interest to us since it led him to become an active part of the curriculum movement in an especially significant way.

Evidences of a preparation for this change came in Rugg's early childhood. The influence of his family's social status during his boyhood on his later growth was not lost on Rugg when he came to make a

[28] Of the thirty-odd schools founded between 1910 and 1930, over half of them were established in the six years between 1915 and 1921.

[29] University of Chicago Laboratory School—1896 (Dewey was the director); Speyer School, Teachers College, Columbia University—1899 (Frank McMurry was the first principal); Francis Parker School, Chicago—1901 (staff trained by Parker); University Elementary School, University of Missouri—1904 (its director, Meriam, was Dewey's student); Experimental School, University of Iowa—1915 (Horn, a student of Meriam, was the principal).

[30] Traces of Dewey's influence can be found, for example, in accounts of the early beginnings of such schools as Oak Lane County Day School, Beaver County Day School, the Organic School at Fairhope, Walden School, the public schools in Gary, the University School in Missouri, and Lincoln School in New York City.

[31] He cited two cases—Perry Smith, Director of the North Shore Country Day School, Chicago; and Katharine Taylor, Director of Shady Hill, Cambridge, Massachusetts—both of whom were among the first children to attend the Francis W. Parker School. "Francis Wayland Parker and His Schools," *Yearbook of Education* (Yonkers-on-Hudson: World Book Co., 1957), p. 412.

personal assessment in after years. He recollected then that he had early felt a conflict between the desire to be conventionally successful in the emerging industrial world and a wish to vindicate the ideals of his New England forbears. Conscious of nine generations of them behind him, men like his great-great-grandfather Asa who fought at Concord, he had watched an independent-minded, carpenter father struggle against the ruthless action of a rigid economic order. His feelings about this unequal battle had worked themselves into decisions on schooling and even on his choice of profession. Commenting later on his two years of work after high school in a textile mill where he moved shortly from the weave room into the office, he said: "The new contact with accounting orders and sales revealed to me the discrepancy between the wages of the herd, the salary of the white-collared executive and the dividends of the owner."[32] Such early experiences carried a potential which might have turned him into either an "owner" or a crusader.

Rugg felt that the regimented curriculum of the public school had had no part in developing his insight into the culture. "Certainly the episodes of the twelve-grade mass school were replicas of the mass mind," he recalled.[33] Not once in school did he remember hearing of the industrial revolution. His unlettered father, whose refusal to join a carpenter's union cost him his job, had been the only one even to hint at the dislocations of technological change. Never did he remember reading a contemporary American writer or producing anything creative in school. Yet he lived just forty miles from Fitchburg, where Edward Bellamy had written *Looking Backward,* and thirty miles from Quincy "where Francis W. Parker . . . had only recently become a storm center of educational reform."[34]

Prodded to go on and make something of himself, he had graduated in 1908 from Dartmouth in civil engineering, transformed by college study into a technician whose chief pursuit was the "reduction of error." But the early stirrings to "understand" himself and his world continued to reassert themselves. His success as an engineer, where he discovered that the formulas he had learned in college actually did fit "railroad

[32] Harold Rugg, *That Men May Understand: An American in the Long Armistice* (New York: Doubleday, Doran and Co., 1941), p. 176.
[33] Harold Rugg, *That Men May Understand: An American in the Long Armistice* (New York: Doubleday, Doran and Co., 1941), p. 174.
[34] Harold Rugg, *That Men May Understand: An American in the Long Armistice* (New York: Doubleday, Doran and Co., 1941), p. 176.

spirals on sharp curves to the nice adjustments of speed,"[35] did not lead him into industry but merely served to send him back to school to teach engineering. With the intellectual "reach" that was to become characteristic of him all his life, he went on to study education itself, as well as psychology and sociology, in graduate school at the University of Illinois.[36]

Measurement movement

Rugg's graduate study at the University of Illinois was with William Bagley, Lotus Coffman, and Guy Whipple, all important figures in the measurement movement. These men momentarily stilled his feelings of disquiet with the social order by giving him a faith in science. Foremost among what Rugg himself later called the builders of the first foundations of education, they were themselves followers of the "conforming way." They believed that the welfare of the individual and the good of society were in harmony and that "education was the adjustment of the individual to his world."[37] They had found the key to social harmony in research. Rugg commented that he had merely changed "the job, the data with which I worked—not my fundamental outlook or interest. Society made me a technician, and the change from engineering to education left me still a technician. . . . I was only one of a very large band of intellectuals, outside the universities as well as inside, who with Lippmann and company were proclaiming salvation through fact-finding."[38]

---

[35] Harold Rugg, *That Men May Understand: An American in the Long Armistice* (New York: Doubleday, Doran and Co., 1941), p. 179.

[36] Part of his curiosity about education may have come from his brush in college with academic skepticism about the "new" education. As he commented later, "In 1910 the chief indoor sport among professors of the liberal arts was to spend the evening together laughing uproariously over the latest yarns— apocryphal they proved to be—of how Dewey was bringing up his children. . . . I know, for I was in those liberal arts professors' living rooms, looking and listening, a young engineer trying to discover what it was all about." Harold Rugg, *The Teacher of Teachers* (New York: Harper, 1952), p. 70. His decision to study sociology may have stemmed from his earlier sense of the industrial unrest that underlay the contemporary economic system.

[37] Rugg quotes this phrase from *The Meaning of Education* by Nicholas Murray Butler (New York: The Macmillan Co., 1898), and goes on to say, "My own graduate study of 'education' in Illinois (1911) began with the reading of this book. . . . It constituted generally the student's first 'Introduction to Education.'" Harold Rugg, *The Teacher of Teachers* (New York: Harper, 1952), p. 44. Rugg included Butler in the group he called builders of educational foundations.

[38] Harold Rugg, *That Men May Understand: An American in the Long Armistice* (New York: Doubleday, Doran and Co., 1941), pp. 181–82.

114

For a time, Rugg's search for an intellectual ballast to counteract what he called the "violent, cultural mind shifts of a dynamic and changing civilization"[39] remained quiescent. As he commented later:

> For some years after leaving college I lurched violently from one political and economic faith to another. . . . Higher education in those days . . . succeeded in doing little more than develop partisan loyalties and a vague discomfort on hearing the first strains of the national anthem. My citizenship enthusiasms during the next decade spent themselves on superficial differences between the major political parties and the reform of obvious social evils.[40]

In 1916, Rugg was appointed a professor of education at the University of Chicago, and Judd and Bobbitt became his colleagues. With them he plunged into the throes of the great fact-finding movement then in progress. He revealed himself to be both skillful and successful at measurement. In a short time, he published *Statistical Methods Applied to Education*, a handy manual on statistical formulas and graphic methods for "teachers of education . . . educational investigators generally and school officials interested in making the best use of statistical data and displaying the results to their supporting public in the most effective graphic form."[41] This book probably earned him a place on the Army's Committee on Classification of Personnel, enabling him to take part in the first tryout of the new intelligence tests on adults in 1917. Rugg found the work he did for them on officer personality ratings stimulating.[42] But it was his contact with another committee member, Arthur Upham Pope, who was in touch with avant-garde groups in artistic and social criticism, which somehow released the long-gathering pressure within Rugg.[43] This friendship seems to mark the beginning of a major shift in Rugg's thinking away from a technical approach to culture and toward a judgment on modern industrial civilization. This seemingly abrupt change in outlook was, as we have seen, merely long in brewing.

---

[39] Harold Rugg, *That Men May Understand: An American in the Long Armistice* (New York: Doubleday, Doran and Co., 1941), p. 178.
[40] Harold Rugg, *That Men May Understand: An American in the Long Armistice* (New York: Doubleday, Doran and Co., 1941), p. 178.
[41] Harold Rugg, *Statistical Methods Applied to Education* (Boston: Houghton Mifflin Co., 1917), pp. v–vi.
[42] Harold Rugg, "Is the Rating of Human Character Practicable?," *Journal of Educational Psychology*, 1921, 1922.
[43] Harold Rugg, *That Men May Understand: An American in the Long Armistice* (New York: Doubleday, Doran and Co., 1941), pp. 320–21, 169–70.

Intellectual shift

Rugg's shift of interest began quietly. In 1917, Teachers College, Columbia University, assisted financially by the General Education Board, established Lincoln School. It was intended to be a laboratory in which the current search by educational scientists for real-life content might be concentrated. Here, it was hoped, the experts at measurement might work together to eliminate useless content and discover materials that would fit the social needs, capacities, and interests of the individual child. Rugg, as its first Director of Research, in 1919, seems to have felt that the school had begun by overemphasizing the child. He said later that at first he:

> measured and charted the abilities of every child in the school, . . . built up the Lincoln School's first system of records and worked with the teachers at bringing up the achievement of a "child-centered" school not sufficiently concerned with "social needs."[44]

Even while he was busy measuring abilities, the ferment of his new insights was working, and New York proved to be a more stimulating place for him than Chicago had been. Contacts in Greenwich Village, for example, put him in touch with contemporary movements of artistic and social protest.[45] Scholarly social criticism was finding a voice in the New School for Social Research, formed in 1917 by such liberals as Charles A. Beard, James Harvey Robinson, and James McKeen Cattell.[46] Rugg met, heard, discussed, and read the books or listened to the lectures of the new scientists, social critics, poets, and writers. He saw performed the works of dancers and dramatists and viewed the creations of architects, sculptors, and painters. With them, he was startled and shocked by the social hysteria after the war. The Red Scare from 1919 to 1921 and the later charge that the critical and scholarly teaching of history was undermining patriotism served Rugg and his new circle of acquaintances as a cold reminder that all was not well in the culture.

In response to these experiences, Rugg began to meditate on his

[44] Harold Rugg, *That Men May Understand: An American in the Long Armistice* (New York: Doubleday, Doran and Co., 1941), p. 188.

[45] The writer Waldo Frank introduced Rugg to these groups. Rugg says Frank's influence was a very important one. Harold Rugg, "The Artist and the Great Transition," Waldo Frank, (ed.), *America and Alfred Stieglitz* (New York: Doubleday, Doran and Co., 1934), pp. 179–98.

[46] President Butler had dismissed Cattell and Henry Dana from Columbia University, presumably because of "critical" scholarship. Robinson and Beard had resigned at the same time.

role as an educator in a crucial moment of history. He gained permission from Otis Caldwell, the Director of Lincoln School, to be released from conventional research on mental abilities and to be freed to select for himself that part of the school's task on which he wanted to concentrate. He began to wade into a mass of scholarly material documenting a variety of emerging viewpoints on man and society. He was trying to get a panoramic view of the conditions and problems of modern civilization, a total picture of life as it had been and was being lived in America and the world. That the experience attracted him powerfully at the same time that it caused him qualms is apparent from a comment he made some years later:

> While I was rebellious at injustice and temperamentally for the underdog, nevertheless, if one had dug to the roots of my attitudes during this reading time he would have found there great uneasiness caused by the things I read. My first glimpse into the library of social criticism disturbed as much as excited me. Lacking historical and world perspective, I felt these questionings of monopoly and the inequalities in the distribution of the social income as attacks on my personal sense of security. I had always believed that the machinery of industrial civilization was essentially admirable and that capitalism was to be accepted on its proved merits and not really to be challenged. The Webb's *Decay of Capitalist Civilization*, to name a single example, was certainly not pleasant reading for one of my background. I had never been much concerned with the underlying forces at work in the industrial world. My mind had never endeavored to discover the basic economic and psychological determiners of the contemporary situation. And here was a questioning of the whole current industrial order, with proposals for its radical reconstruction![47]

Slowly but surely, Rugg's discomfort convinced him that a little knowledge of the culture, such as he had had, led inevitably to broad mind swings on a radical and conservative pendulum. He realized that he should have had a more comprehensive knowledge of civilization, which would have given him intellectual stability. As he could testify from personal experience, the young people of the nation were the ones who most needed such a broad background.

EFFORTS AT SYNTHESIS

Social studies series

Stimulated by a sense of the need for better curriculum materials in social studies, Rugg set out to write a series of volumes that would

[47] Harold Rugg, *That Men May Understand: An American in the Long Armistice* (New York: Doubleday, Doran and Co., 1941), p. 202.

117

present the youth in the American public schools with a "total word portrait of contemporary society" as sketched by scholars.[48] He tried out the first drafts on the young people in laboratory classes at Lincoln School. Used later in pamphlet form in a number of public schools, the material eventually appeared in the form of an imposing series of fourteen basic volumes for grades three through nine. The collection began with story materials for the primary grades and ended with two volumes for the high school.

The research done for the series was worthy of someone with Rugg's investigative background. As he described it himself:

> Objective research was the keynote of the whole enterprise. Being without precedent and extensive beyond example, it required the collaboration of many minds, especially in technical studies. The technical investigations included twenty-five studies: three studies of existing curricula in history, geography and civics, of the procedure of national committees from 1892 to 1921 and of pupils' abilities and attainments; thirteen studies of what problems of contemporary life to teach, of the chief trends of civilization and of the central concepts and principles which educated minds use in thinking about them; three studies of the grade placement of curriculum materials and of the development of pupils' abilities; six studies of learning and of the organization of curricula.[49]

In addition, he tried to validate "scientifically" the concepts and generalizations he had selected, by using only factually documented materials, multiplying cases, and searching for unanimity. Although he found little use for them, wherever he could he used statistical methods to find averages, dispersion, and reliability.[50]

The series tried to incorporate the newly emerging, scholarly interpretation of the panorama of American civilization. The key concepts, by means of which young people could deal with the problems of contemporary civilization, were those which scholars were then forging. The focus of the study was on the identification and solution of current social issues, according to these concepts. The materials were

---

[48] He had early shown this comprehensive approach to knowledge. He told of himself that "as a junior in college I had published my somewhat absurd *Complete Outline of European History*. (I still flinch at the title, but it and my lectures did coach Dartmouth sophomores successfully through Eric's dreaded History I and History II!)." Harold Rugg, *That Men May Understand: An American in the Long Armistice* (New York: Doubleday, Doran and Co., 1941), pp. 48, 193.

[49] Harold Rugg, *That Men May Understand: An American in the Long Armistice* (New York: Doubleday, Doran and Co., 1941), p. 45.

[50] Harold Rugg, *That Men May Understand: An American in the Long Armistice* (New York: Doubleday, Doran and Co., 1941), p. 220.

organized around these issues in a "dramatic, vivid, compelling" way. As Rugg commented later:

> To understand civilization changing our young people must see it changing. The conditions and problems of today are but the product of the moving trends and factors of yesterday. Every area of the social order would have to be put both in its long-time and short-time historical setting.[51]

One of the chief means of illuminating these changes was the "case, dramatic episode, concrete situation." Rugg felt that the pageant of action, conflict, romance, conquest, and cooperation would build up in the "minds and spines of children a huge array of meanings, concepts, generalizations, insights, and attitudes."[52]

Working for the first time within a school for children, he was confronted with the problems of planning a school program and providing for learning and motivation.[53] As a teacher in Lincoln School, he had been aware of what was then labelled "progressive" practice, and he gave at least lip service to it in his writings by his lavish use of terms like creativity and growth. But a close examination of his program for a social studies curriculum proves it to be centered essentially in concepts enmeshed in words rather than in plans for activities which would develop child meaning and experience. However much he talked of "a program of guided living," or of "materials and activities," or of "creative child growth," he relied chiefly on the reading and discussion of a series of books to develop in the child the intellectual understanding needed to live in a modern industrial society. He tried to fit the contents of these books to the child's level of understanding by watching teachers and children use his materials in the classroom. He sought to analyze and understand how the children's meanings were growing, what new relationships they were seeing, what helped them to generalize and solve problems, whether their values were distorting their judgment. But he did not use these discoveries as the basis for a suggested series of activities and experiences that would foster insight,

[51] Harold Rugg, *That Men May Understand: An American in the Long Armistice* (New York: Doubleday, Doran and Co., 1941), p. 212.

[52] Harold Rugg, "Curriculum Making: Points of Emphasis," *Twenty-sixth Yearbook of the National Society for the Study of Education*, Part II (Bloomington, Ill.: Public School Publishing Co., 1926), p. 156.

[53] "I had never taught in the elementary school," he recalled, in commenting on his first exploratory drafts of the materials, "—and yet had to teach, to illustrate to the other teachers what I was talking about, improvising a good deal of it as I went along." Harold Rugg, *That Men May Understand: An American in the Long Armistice* (New York: Doubleday, Doran and Co., 1941), p. 205.

creativity, and improved child living. Rather he used them to improve the quality of the writing of the episodes and other learning exercises that the young people were to use in studying the world about them.[54] His definition of the ideal social studies curriculum as a "word portrait" of society was not a casual one.

As an intellectual framework, his material was good. He worked to develop techniques to improve intellectual insight in children. For example, he tried to present both sides of a controversy, to build good stereotypes, and to clarify "bad" concepts by presenting them as hypotheses that were not yet fully verified. His goal was to accustom young people to problem-solving, verification, weighing of evidence— "taking thought before they took sides."[55] Only thus, he reasoned, could they be ready to implement democracy as adults, and work to meet the great challenge of contemporary life as he described it a decade later:

> Can the Americans, scattered over a two-billion-acre continent, operate a technically efficient and sustained-yield economy and at the same time preserve the democratic principle?[56]

Criticism of curriculum making

Although Rugg gives evidence of having known the work of Bobbitt and Charters, we sense that he identified them with a movement with which he was impatient. Its very virtue, exclusive reliance on method, was for Rugg a fault. He was in accord with both men in their search for a content that was more sensitively related to the living culture of men, but their use of an analytical method to formulate this content seemed to Rugg too timid and value-neutral. He himself had no compunction about boldly wading in and seizing "good" content. The time-honored method of the scholar suited him as a way of arriving at a synthesis of all knowledge. Charters' view of method as knowledge might do no more than turn up some socially useful knowledge that would merely preserve the status quo, and Bobbitt's social analysis probably seemed to Rugg too much like Judd's formal "institutional"

[54] Harold Rugg, *That Men May Understand: An American in the Long Armistice* (New York: Doubleday, Doran and Co., 1941), p. 229. His own comment is illuminating. "As an engineer habituated to meet situations as problems and to design before building, I tended naturally to regard curriculum construction as a technological process, not an act of sentiment or evangelical faith." P. 216.

[55] Harold Rugg, *That Men May Understand: An American in the Long Armistice* (New York: Doubleday, Doran and Co., 1941), p. 244.

[56] Harold Rugg, *That Men May Understand: An American in the Long Armistice* (New York: Doubleday, Doran and Co., 1941), p. 313.

approach. Rugg felt that Judd emphasized a generalized social cooperation, without being willing to identify the particular social and psychological obstacles actually operating against that cooperation. Years
later, in an appraisal he made of the contribution of the movement
these men represented, he said:

> Slowly the measurers extended their techniques from an analysis of what
> is taught in the school to what should be taught, using primarily the
> criterion of social use. The general basic theory was that those facts, ideas
> and skills which are actually used by a considerable part of the general
> population were the ones to be taught in the schools.[57]

His assessment shows that he underestimated the method of activity
analysis. Charters' view of the method did tend to confine content to
the status quo. But Bobbitt had insisted that the analysis would disclose
the kind of individual needed by society—his qualities, abilities, attitudes, and concepts. Rugg also was interested in this individual, but
his own approach to curriculum shows his mistrust of the pragmatic
context of society itself as the source of value and insight. Rather Rugg
looked to the scholar whose intellectual "purchase" came from a
traditional *pou sto* outside the concerns of practical action.

Child-centered school

As we have noticed, Rugg's contacts in New York were with artists
as well as social critics. Conscious that they were "inventing forms,
designs, which were appropriate personal interpretations of living *in*
America," Rugg described these artists as "creative pioneers."[58] Out
of the living stuff of American experience they were forging styles which
were to express the unique American culture. Quite easily, Rugg could
find their educational counterpart in the progressive schools. As he
sought the widest possible view of culture and education, he could
easily conclude that these schools balanced the picture in favor of the
child.

Various as were the motives that impelled the founding of these
schools, most of what we hear about them does have the quality of an
authentic personal statement. Their founders, most of them gifted
teachers, seem deliberately to have cast out public school tradition as
too routine and mechanical and to have started afresh.[59] They sought

[57] Harold Rugg, *That Men May Understand: An American in the Long
Armistice* (New York: Doubleday, Doran and Co., 1941), p. 298.

[58] Harold Rugg, *That Men May Understand: An American in the Long
Armistice* (New York: Doubleday, Doran and Co., 1941), p. 341.

[59] Henry Harap says that the movement for modern educational change forked

to penetrate the nature of the child and interpret his spontaneous interests and purposes in order to develop new school forms more appropriate to them. In an attempt to communicate their insights, their descriptions of practice contain words such as "freedom," "self-expression," "complete living," and "harmonious development." We would expect Rugg to call their founders the artist-teachers and to find in these schools the perfect foil for the increasing emphasis on the social role of the school.

Rugg himself did not find progressive school practice very comfortable. Reminiscing, his comment was:

> One grave deficiency developed in them. Frequently in rebelling against the regimentation of children they went too far in the other direction, defining freedom as complete "absence of restraint." They took too literally the principle of Cizek and other artist-teachers; "Take off the lid!" In some cases liberty was extended to license. In their first years most of the new schools were too garrulous, noisy and not too clean. While they were active, alive and experimental, the fine balance of freedom and control which makes for child initiative, regard for order and for other personalities, were [sic] lacking in many of them. . . .

> I shall never forget Billy Mearns's halfway serious proposal to my psychological department at a faculty meeting at Lincoln in 1924. Devise, he said, a scale for G. Q. to go along with those for I. Q., E. Q., A. Q., and the like. "Give us a 'garrulous quotient', to measure the most dominant trait of our youngsters." . . .

> I was in and out of a dozen of the child-centered schools after 1915; they did seem to me to have failed to reach the balance between discipline and initiative which we are seeking today for the true "modern school."[60]

Yet these schools supplied the dynamic factor that Rugg missed in the scientific formulations. He ended by idealizing them so that they would reinforce his emphasis on creativity as a necessary antidote to the domination of the culture by the machine. When in 1927 he and Ann Shumaker wrote a description of progressive schools called *The*

---

in 1915 into two streams. One of them, fed by the publication of Dewey's *Democracy in Education,* was the experimental school, which started the educational enterprise anew. The other was course of study revision, fed by the appearance of the yearbooks of the National Society for the Study of Education. This stream accepted the basic framework of the school and tried to improve it. Henry Harap, *Curriculum Trends at Mid-Century* (Cincinnati: South-Western Publishing Co., 1953), p. 5.

[60] Harold Rugg, *That Men May Understand: An American in the Long Armistice* (New York: Doubleday, Doran and Co., 1941), pp. 305–06.

Child-Centered School, he selected creative self-expression as the central theme for the volume.[61]

Twenty-sixth Yearbook

Proposal. By 1924, Rugg felt that he had begun intellectually to "think around" the field of education. He had succeeded to his own satisfaction in conceptualizing it as a field, by trying to penetrate to its scholarly roots, both sociological and psychological. He knew that the new group of specialists who called themselves curriculum makers had tried to conceptualize it also, although they had confined themselves to the use of method in the analysis and synthesis of the educational task. Was it possible that they could be brought to see the limits of method—the need for solid stuff or scholarly content to give vitality, significance, and direction to their analysis of social activities and their selection of educational experiences? At any rate, Rugg thought it worth a try. He broached the matter to the Executive Board of the National Society for the Study of Education, a group which, as we have seen, had given the curriculum their major attention from the days of their founding as the Herbart Society. He suggested that, in view of the current widespread interest in the problem of the curriculum, the Society should try a yearbook on it with a fundamental approach. Rugg proposed that a committee be appointed to study the method by which the content of the curriculum should be selected and assembled, rather than the teaching of any particular content. He pointed out that there were then two current ways of using the method of curriculum formulation. If the curriculum maker was committed to a child-centered emphasis, he began with an analysis of the activities of the child. If he was committed to a society-centered emphasis, he began with an analysis of the activities of the adult. Was it possible that this divergence was more seeming than real and that, by following an old tradition in the Herbart Society of "true educational open forums," they might substitute study for controversy? Each group might be able to show that what the other group seemed to oppose they actually merely ignored or minimized in defense of a particular view. Might, Rugg asked, a series of round tables identify these differences as matters of communication and emphasis, thus leading to a closer philosophical unity?

[61] Harold Rugg and Ann Shumaker, *The Child-Centered School: An Appraisal of the New Education* (Yonkers-on-Hudson, N. Y.: World Book Co., 1928). The book did include four critical chapters on the lack of direction of these schools.

Setting. It was a persuasive proposal. As we have seen, curriculum making was in full swing in schools all over the country, and new curriculum programs were being worked on, most of them for the first time. Curriculum directors and specialists were in demand, and their activities in the schools had raised new questions about the traditional roles of principal and supervisor. Curriculum courses in colleges were expanding, and curriculum research bureaus were being established. Progressive school practice, so different from traditional practice, was disturbingly vital, forcing the profession either to ignore it or reconcile it with current doctrine.

Rugg's qualifications. Rugg was well-fitted to coordinate a yearbook of this kind. His work in educational measurement had given him a real command of its assumptions and techniques. He had taught in an outstanding progressive school. He was on the staff of Teachers College, Columbia University, which was among the leading schools in the preparation of curriculum specialists. He was in touch with scholarly developments in the social sciences, in a decade in which the curriculum maker talked often of education as a preparation for social life. He lacked only experience in the specialization itself—curriculum making.

Procedure. The Executive Board acceded to Rugg's proposal, and plans were made for a yearbook. Everyone agreed that a good first step would be an inventory of current practice. There had been a great deal of experimentation, and educators had been ingenious in adapting the new method to the realities of public schools. Details of this adaptation would be very interesting. It was decided that city and state school systems would be surveyed to find out whether they were revising their curricula and how it was being done. Several outstanding public and private schools would be asked to report their practices as examples of what could be done. Rugg offered to summarize the new ideas on curriculum construction and write an historical account of how curriculum making had begun and grown.

The hoped-for philosophical synthesis required special planning and a budget. It was decided that five round tables would be held over a period of two and one-half years, each one lasting one or two days. In order to get them started, eight members of the Yearbook Committee would be asked to prepare individual statements of what they conceived to be the issues and problems of curriculum making. These statements would be discussed by the whole Committee and used as a starting point in their search for a common point of view.

Membership. Who was to be on the Committee? Looking back twenty

124

years later, Rugg said he regretted its homogeneity. His later comment was:

I wish now that I had known enough in picking the committee to include several of the great leaders on the sociological, psychological and esthetic frontiers. Although Veblen was dying, Turner, Thomas, Boas, Robinson, Beard, and others were all vigorous, and I knew them. It might have been difficult, if not impossible, to secure a community of discourse and thought between them and the professors of education for whose scholarship they had little respect. I did the next best thing: I wove into the report the essence of the views of these students of the social frontier.[62]

Perhaps he had "known enough" at the time but was not quite sure he could bring it off. In the yearbook he said:

An ideal conference on the reconstruction of the school, therefore, would assemble a great variety of interests and experience; far wider, indeed, than we have been able to bring together. The group would comprise, in addition to technically trained students of education, disinterested students of contemporary civilization—analysts aloof from the academic formulae of education—the poet, the novelist, the dramatist, the architect, critics of economic, political, and cultural life, students of the development of society, specialists in contemporary industry, business, government, population, community, and international affairs. These would cooperate with students of the scientific study of child capacities, methods of learning, educational experimentation and measurement, school administration, and the documentation of materials. Such a range in personnel would produce, of course, a confusion of vocabularies and would necessitate a more prolonged exchange of views than it is feasible to provide for in the present instance.[63]

The Committee, as chosen, were all professors of education, and the twenty associated contributors were administrators and teachers. It became a full-dress educational conference sponsored by a society which had at last succeeded in establishing, as a professional expert, the professor of education whose special interest was in curriculum.

Survey of practice. The accomplishments in curriculum to date, as represented by the survey report, were indeed impressive. The yearbook disclosed that by 1926 curriculum making was a widespread educational phenomenon. As had been suspected, curriculum construction and the related problems of supervision had been so recently undertaken by

[62] Harold Rugg, *Foundations for American Education* (Yonkers-on-Hudson, New York: World Book Co., 1947), p. 636.
[63] National Society for the Study of Education, "The Foundations and Technique of Curriculum-Construction," *Twenty-sixth Yearbook*, Part II (Bloomington, Ill.: Public School Publishing Co., 1926), p. ix.

most schools[64] that practice was highly individual, and all felt a need for standards. The initiative toward curriculum revision seemed to have been taken almost wholly by schoolmen themselves.[65] The conventional machinery of revision had become a committee of teachers under the direction of administrative or supervisory officers.[66] Curriculum revision was usually done in subject matter areas and rarely, if ever, around any other focus.[67] Skill in organizing school systems for curriculum revision and in the use of the specialist seemed to be growing, and procedures were becoming more systematic.

The lore that had already accumulated around administrative procedures for curriculum making, as shown by the reports of practice, was well summarized by Rugg. Practice, he said, had shown that good administrative procedures required at least five conditions:

1. "The development of a research attitude toward the problem on the part of those in responsible charge," i.e. everyone.

2. The establishment of a "separate and autonomous Department of Curriculum-Construction, coordinate in budget, leadership and authority" with other departments. Such a department would be the nucleus for the direction of the instructional work of the school, at that time a major task of school administrators.

3. The employment by this department of "trained and experienced specialists in curriculum-making . . . under the direction of an executive officer" who should report to the superintendent. This officer should control the function of instruction.

4. The appointment of committees of teachers and principals to undertake the endless detail of curriculum-making; assembling and organizing materials, preparing and revising outlines, selecting books, phrasing objectives, illustrating teaching methods. In the absence of funds to hire technically trained people, teachers themselves must function as "specialists, clerks, statisticians, and educational psychologists."

[64] Almost all schools reported curriculum revision; 20 per cent continuous curriculum revision, 75 per cent during the previous five years. National Society for the Study of Education, "The Foundations and Technique of Curriculum-Construction," *Twenty-sixth Yearbook*, Part II (Bloomington, Ill.: Public School Publishing Co., 1926), p. 123.

[65] National Society for the Study of Education, "The Foundations and Technique of Curriculum-Construction," *Twenty-sixth Yearbook*, Part II (Bloomington, Ill.: Public School Publishing Co., 1926), p. 126.

[66] National Society for the Study of Education, "The Foundations and Technique of Curriculum-Construction," *Twenty-sixth Yearbook*, Part II (Bloomington, Ill.: Public School Publishing Co., 1926), p. 127.

[67] National Society for the Study of Education, "The Foundations and Technique of Curriculum-Construction," *Twenty-sixth Yearbook*, Part II (Bloomington, Ill.: Public School Publishing Co., 1926), p. 133.

5. The use of outside specialists to provide "proper perspective" on curriculum making. Free as they are from "entangling alliances with the existing program" they would avoid regarding topics, subjects, and grade materials as isolated units, and help keep the total curriculum problem in view.[68]

Agreement on recommended committee procedure was more tenuous. The central problem seemed to be the tendency for committees to parallel and duplicate the contents of a good text in the skill subjects, in an effort to produce some kind of "revision."

Philosophical synthesis. As the Committee began to meet as a whole to work on the philosophical synthesis, the discussions of the proposed issues raised additional ones, and the final composite list had eighteen items. On each of these, the Committee deliberated until it arrived at a joint statement of tentative agreement. In addition, nine members of the group prepared supplemental statements giving their divergencies from the agreement. The issues, agreements, and supplemental statements all appeared in the yearbook.[69] The Committee decided also that the contributions of John Dewey and the Herbartians to curriculum making had been fundamental enough to warrant inclusion in the yearbook of quotations from their basic writings. They wished thus to emphasize "the manner in which educational theory revolves around certain recurrent fundamental issues."[70]

Artfully, the Committee had been chosen to represent a wide variety of viewpoint, ranging, in Rugg's own words, "from Judd to Kilpatrick, from Bagley to Bonser." Deliberately and patiently, Rugg had set the stage so that the Committee's thinking would be polarized around the central issue—whether the child or society should be the basis around which to select the curriculum. The yearbook gives evidence of the success of the plan. Rugg's opening statement traced the historical roots of the current "lag" between society, the curriculum, and child growth. His summary called for the elimination of that "lag." A survey was made of two kinds of practices in curriculum making: those in public schools (largely society-centered) and those in private laboratory schools (largely child-centered). Issues and problems were clearly phrased in

[68] National Society for the Study of Education, "The Foundations and Technique of Curriculum-Construction," *Twenty-sixth Yearbook*, Part II (Bloomington, Ill.: Public School Publishing Co., 1926), pp. 439–42.

[69] Unlike the Herbartians, they did not include the discussions.

[70] National Society for the Study of Education, "The Foundations and Technique of Curriculum-Construction," *Twenty-sixth Yearbook*, Part II (Bloomington, Ill.: Public School Publishing Co., 1926), p. 8.

terms of the two approaches. Stuart Courtis burst out impatiently in his supplementary report, "It seems to me that the statements of the Committee make it quite clear that the center of emphasis in education is shifting from subject matter to children."[71] He proved his point with a long list of cullings from the General Statement. Charles Judd countered, rather bitingly, with the comment that "the mature individual [is] a product of social control by the group . . . [and] is in need of long, tedious guidance under the most attentive and sympathetic control in order to rescue him from the social incompetency which is characteristic of his infancy."[72] He too found support for his position in the yearbook and referred quite complacently to "the exhibition which the General Statement gives of so high a degree of concord among the members."[73]

Even the representative quotations from Dewey and the Herbartians were all carefully selected to highlight the issue of a child-centered versus a society-centered curriculum. As Charters summed it up succinctly, "I have nothing to add. . . . I approached the conference of the group with the hope that substantial agreement might be reached on one question—the controversial question of a child-centered curriculum . . . I believe that the curriculum must be based upon the needs, interests, and activities of both children and adults. Naturally therefore, I was delighted to find complete agreement among all members of this group on that point. When this fact became evident, I felt that, so far as I was concerned, the conference was a success."[74]

Although a new concept of the curriculum was emerging, no definition for it could be found of which all approved. The Committee rejected as out-of-date the statement that the curriculum is "formal subject matter (facts, processes, principles), set-out-to-be-learned without adequate relation to life."[75] Instead, the members agreed to describe it as "a suc-

[71] National Society for the Study of Education, "The Foundations and Technique of Curriculum-Construction," *Twenty-sixth Yearbook*, Part II (Bloomington, Ill.: Public School Publishing Co., 1926), p. 94.

[72] National Society for the Study of Education, "The Foundations and Technique of Curriculum-Construction," *Twenty-sixth Yearbook*, Part II (Bloomington, Ill.: Public School Publishing Co., 1926), pp. 113–14.

[73] National Society for the Study of Education, "The Foundations and Technique of Curriculum-Construction," *Twenty-sixth Yearbook*, Part II (Bloomington, Ill.: Public School Publishing Co., 1926), p. 117.

[74] National Society for the Study of Education, "The Foundations and Technique of Curriculum-Construction," *Twenty-sixth Yearbook*, Part II (Bloomington, Ill.: Public School Publishing Co., 1926), p. 71.

[75] National Society for the Study of Education, "The Foundations and Technique of Curriculum-Construction," *Twenty-sixth Yearbook*, Part II (Bloomington, Ill.: Public School Publishing Co., 1926), p. 17.

cession of experiences and enterprises having a maximum of lifelikeness for the learner . . . giving the learner that development most helpful in meeting and controlling life situations."[76] This view of the curriculum was said to be the result of the new emphasis on changed behavior as the true outcome of education, and the new conviction that only "traits learned in a natural, or lifelike setting, give promise of emerging definitely in appropriate conduct."[77]

Bobbitt insisted that this general curriculum was only a summation of the individual curriculum of the children. "Curriculum-making is mainly concerned with the making of the *individual curriculum* for the individual boy or girl, by himself, or herself, as guided by teacher and parents."[78] Kilpatrick confused matters by stating that the curriculum is only a phase of a larger working whole called "the educative process." A further reading discloses this educative process to be remarkably like the above agreed upon definition of the curriculum, leaving the reader right where he started.[79] Bagley's terse reference to the curriculum as the "large groups of elementary, or 'fundamental' materials" such as the basic language arts, the basic arts of computation and measurement, and geography and national history[80] seemed to contradict the "agreement" that it was a succession of experiences. Rugg's summary remained true to the definition agreed on and called the curriculum "the pupil activities and the materials of instruction that arouse them."[81] Yet, when we read the following footnote to Rugg's introduction to the yearbook, we feel that, allowing for the up-to-date character of its contents, his idea of the curriculum is at heart not very different from the one the Committee rejected, formal subject matter set-out-to-be-learned:

[76] National Society for the Study of Education, "The Foundations and Technique of Curriculum-Construction," *Twenty-sixth Yearbook*, Part II (Bloomington, Ill.: Public School Publishing Co., 1926), p. 18.

[77] National Society for the Study of Education, "The Foundations and Technique of Curriculum-Construction," *Twenty-sixth Yearbook*, Part II (Bloomington, Ill.: Public School Publishing Co., 1926), pp. 18–19.

[78] National Society for the Study of Education, "The Foundations and Technique of Curriculum-Construction," *Twenty-sixth Yearbook*, Part II (Bloomington, Ill.: Public School Publishing Co., 1926), p. 47.

[79] National Society for the Study of Education, "The Foundations and Technique of Curriculum-Construction," *Twenty-sixth Yearbook*, Part II (Bloomington, Ill.: Public School Publishing Co., 1926), p. 120.

[80] National Society for the Study of Education, "The Foundations and Technique of Curriculum-Construction," *Twenty-sixth Yearbook*, Part II (Bloomington, Ill.: Public School Publishing Co., 1926), p. 29.

[81] National Society for the Study of Education, "The Foundations and Technique of Curriculum-Construction," *Twenty-sixth Yearbook,* Part I (Bloomington, Ill.: Public School Publishing Co., 1926), p. 426.

Under proper conditions, of course, the true educational intermediary between the immature child and adult society is the teacher. If we had 750,000 teachers, (or even, say, 300,000) who, like William Rainey Harper, "could teach Hebrew as though it were a series of hair-breadth escapes," the *curriculum* itself would stand merely as a subordinate element in the educational scheme. The teacher would occupy the important place of guidance we have given to the materials of instruction. But under the current hampering conditions (better, of course, than in earlier decades and improving slowly) of inadequately trained teachers of large and numerous classes, heavy teaching programs, insufficient facilities and lack of educational perspective—I fear we tend to reverse the process and teach hair-breadth escapes as though they were Hebrew. Hence my allegiance to the curriculum rather than to the teacher as the effective educational intermediary between child and society.[82]

How successful was the attempt to arrive at unity? One unexpected result of the effort was a broader view of curriculum construction. The yearbook managed to herd under the wing of curriculum making some educational activities that had not been there before. For example, the progressive schools had not been regarded as pioneer curriculum makers either by themselves or by what had in a decade become the old guard in curriculum making. There is no evidence that Bobbitt, who first used the label curriculum formulation, considered as curriculum makers the Herbartians, Dewey, the various National Education Association committees, the commissions of investigation in the subject matter fields, the state legislatures, and the textbook publishers. Yet activities by all these individuals and groups were labelled by the *Twenty-sixth Yearbook* as curriculum making.

The Committee signed a joint statement, but it was a cautious and limited agreement, although issues were clarified as a result of the decisions. The statement succeeded in clothing the agreements in language general enough to justify a continued academic discussion of the real issues, but, as Rugg himself said, the general statement tended to "flatten out peaks of emphasis."[83] Kilpatrick, who claimed the "honor— or ignominy—of consistently deviating most from the present practice . . . [yielding] most in the effort at agreeing upon the next practicable steps . . . [and] making so great concessions [in the joint statement] as to cause him at times to wonder what of his own position was left,"

---

[82] National Society for the Study of Education, "The Foundations and Technique of Curriculum-Construction," *Twenty-sixth Yearbook,* Part I (Bloomington, Ill.: Public School Publishing Co., 1926), p. 3.

[83] National Society for the Study of Education, "The Foundations and Technique of Curriculum-Construction," *Twenty-sixth Yearbook,* Part II (Bloomington, Ill.: Public School Publishing Co., 1926), p. 147.

in the end provided the clue. "He would be but churlish," he said, "who ... would not join with the others in ... the most feasible next steps."[84]

Later developments suggested that Rugg's hope that their divergencies would prove to be more seeming than real became, after all, irrelevant. Collaboration on the general statement for the yearbook both identified the problem and, in the process, took most of the steam out of it. The very thoroughness with which the issue was explored probably finished its usefulness as a rallying point for doctrine. By the time the discussions were over, the antagonists knew their differences very well. They did not relinquish them as much as they relinquished their partisan value. The controversy between the claims of the child and society became a permanent one, unsettled, but valuable as a foundational problem and a stimulus to thought. The discussion served to clear the air and enable the profession to move on to equally urgent problems which had not yet been attempted. The participants themselves expressed their sense of relief by saying that they were willing to make concessions in the interests of "agreements which may serve as a working basis for the next practicable steps."[85]

Rugg's special contribution. It was probably due to Rugg's efforts that the yearbook was called *The Foundations and Technique of Curriculum-Construction.* The word "foundations" is an interesting one, used here. We have followed Rugg's increasing absorption in the developing social sciences. In the previous decade he had been equally engrossed in psychology. Somehow, the field of education alone never seemed to provide Rugg with enough ideas. We have compared the inventory stage in education during and before the war, in which Rugg was so active, to a similar stage in the natural sciences. Perhaps it is also characteristic of the early stages of a new field to seek relationships with other disciplines. We gather from hints here and there that Rugg, at least, thought these relationships would give the field of education more stature. The term "foundations" had been a favorite of William Kilpatrick, a colleague of Rugg's at Teachers College, Columbia University. Kilpatrick had used it as early as 1916 to entitle a course on method. To Rugg, the term suggested solidity and worth, both in breadth and depth. Taking advantage of the original yearbook statement which

[84] National Society for the Study of Education, "The Foundations and Technique of Curriculum-Construction," *Twenty-sixth Yearbook,* Part II (Bloomington, Ill.: Public School Publishing Co., 1926), pp. 119–20.

[85] National Society for the Study of Education, "The Foundations and Technique of Curriculum-Construction," *Twenty-sixth Yearbook,* Part II (Bloomington, Ill.: Public School Publishing Co., 1926), p. 12.

had announced the study of curriculum making to be a "fundamental" one, Rugg boldly centered the whole presentation of the yearbook around his own new social insights and his previous psychological ones, calling them the "foundations" of the curriculum.[86]

As an organizing metaphor he used the idea of social "lag" borrowed from the sociologist William Ogburn,[87] and applied by Rugg to the relationship of the curriculum to the culture. The thesis of social "lag" was that

> various parts of modern culture are not changing at the same rate, some parts are changing much more rapidly than others; and that since there is a correlation and interdependence of parts, a rapid change in one part of our culture requires readjustment through other changes in the various correlated parts of the culture.[88]

In the same kind of semijournalistic language that he had used earlier in the social science series, Rugg painted a vivid picture of the "lag" that had developed since 1776 between the curriculum, a "lazy giant" sleeping peacefully in complacent aloofness, and the culture, a dynamic, torrential current of technological transformation with its resultant staggering social cleavages.

His choice of metaphor was a happy one, recommending as it did that the curriculum be brought up-to-date. Americans, then as now, shrank from being considered old-fashioned. Rugg was able to arrange all the past history of work on the curriculum in terms of this lag, pointing to the contribution of some movements as especially helpful and to others as especially obstructive.[89] The note of division in the figure permitted him to mention all kinds of gaps. He dutifully recorded a "lag" between an outmoded curriculum and the child, but this analogy was somehow awkward, and he did little to develop it. On the value cleavages in the culture, he drew the following picture:

> The whole continent resounds with the impact of groups; in this respect it merely reflects the contemporary order in other countries. Suspicion,

[86] In doing this, he was adding sociology to the psychology and philosophy which were considered basic by the Herbartians and Dewey.

[87] Ogburn had been Rugg's colleague at the University of Chicago. The term was first used by Ogburn in his book *Social Change*, published in 1922. Later he was the central figure in the government-sponsored research on social trends and national resources. Especially important was the report called *Recent Social Trends*, published in 1933 by the federal government.

[88] William F. Ogburn, *Social Change: with Respect to Culture and Original Nature* (New York: B. W. Huebsch, Inc., 1922), pp. 200–01.

[89] He praised the laboratory schools and the measurement experts; he condemned textbook writers, subject matter committees, and the believers in mental discipline.

misunderstanding, friction, pervade the social life of people in many parts of the earth. Successive decades of American political and economic history have been characterized by the realignments of countries, sections, and groups. The contemporary order reveals this same division of our people into cliques. They exhibit distressing cleavages; for example, that of proletarian worker and capitalistic owner, of Protestant and Catholic; producer and middleman; black and white; industrialist and farmer.[90]

He saw another set of gaps yawning between the subjects of the patchwork curriculum, or the "assembly of parts," as Rugg called it. He even pointed out gaps in content within the subjects when they were organized "morphologically."[91]

The remedy for all these disunities, said Rugg, was a synthesis of knowledge, or a curriculum that was scholarly, up-to-date, functional, and compelling. Such a curriculum would provide the key of understanding for youth, helplessly facing a confused culture and obliged shortly to take a mature part in the solution of the problems. The curriculum would represent the drama of American life, and the child would have a ringside seat. As he watched the conditions and problems of what was essentially a complex civilization, presented with all the fire and dash of life itself, his mind and feelings would become involved, and he would experience a "vivid, propulsive understanding of American life." He would have a "thrilling, gripping experience" which would enlarge his sympathies and create in him the "desire both to live effectively and raise the level of the whole culture."[92]

The yearbook, under Rugg's editorship, became a tour de force by which he managed subtly to infuse curriculum making with the spirit of social criticism. There is little indication, however, that the critical tone was quickly caught by the profession. As Rugg himself said later, commenting on the lethargy about social problems of even progressive educators in the late twenties:

The socially minded nucleus of the Directors of the Progressive Education Association could not get the Board to pay vigorous attention to the

[90] National Society for the Study of Education, "The Foundations and Technique of Curriculum-Construction," *Twenty-sixth Yearbook*, Part I (Bloomington, Ill.: Public School Publishing Co., 1926), p. 5.

[91] Rugg used this term to describe subject matter content selected and organized by those "interested in classification, in naming parts and describing forms, rather than in developing an understanding of function and functioning." *Ibid.*, p. 22. He echoes here judgments on the curriculum made just before the advent of the Herbartians.

[92] Many of these passages are reminiscent of the enthusiastic tone of Charles McMurry's writings.

problem of building the secondary curriculum around the problems of the swiftly changing society. Constantly at Board meetings we warned of impending dangers to our society, unless a large minority of the people were quickly taught to understand what was happening. Not more than four or five of the score of Directors took seriously what with amused "tolerance," they called "Harold's annual crisis speech."[93]

Yet Rugg had made his point, and the large group of influential leaders in curriculum making who worked on the yearbook were perhaps to remember it when the depression struck.

AN ASSESSMENT

Trends

The yearbook reported the progress of several minor trends begun in the previous decade. First, measures to promote the economy of time had become institutionalized and routinized in school practice. The question, "In what subjects does the elementary course of study set up standards by age and grade?" was answered by most school systems with information on their testing program. As the author of the report commented:

These figures seem to the writer to prove that anything useful that is made available for schoolmen will be put to use. The simpler more objective tests have already become a part of routine classroom work. The larger cities apparently make a little more use of these newer tools than the smaller cities.[94]

Second, the educator's loyalty to change itself was now so well internalized that the Committee's endorsement of continuous curriculum revision was hardly needed. Rugg warned that the change motive had indeed become so compulsive that

it is most important that those who are constructing our school curriculum shall maintain an overview of the total situation; lacking that, their orientation will be biased, their emphasis misplaced. There is grave danger that they will continue to commit themselves uncritically to plans and movements—to take up the current modes only to discard them as unthinkingly as they adopted them.[95]

[93] Harold Rugg, *Foundations for American Education* (Yonkers-on-Hudson, N. Y.: World Book Co., 1947), p. 576.
[94] National Society for the Study of Education, "The Foundations and Techniques of Curriculum-Construction," *Twenty-sixth Yearbook*, Part I (Bloomington, Ill.: Public School Publishing Co., 1926), p. 130.
[95] National Society for the Study of Education, "The Foundations and Tech-

Third, the curriculum experts no longer "served" the research committees of the National Education Association as had the Herbartians. They now replaced these committees, acting as agents for solving curriculum questions and for raising issues relevant to curriculum formulation.

Meeting Dewey's challenges

Of Dewey's four challenges, Rugg seems to have met only the first, that of a needed reorganization of knowledge; but he worked on that in a very energetic way. His chief aim was to bring about a scholarly synthesis both of the cultural knowledge used in the curriculum and also of the supporting disciplines which lay back of the process of curriculum making itself. Lacking experience and interest in teaching itself, he gave the necessary but perfunctory attention to matters of curriculum organization, institutional organization, and school organization—the other three tasks Dewey had set. But he did help confirm the scholarly disciplines as a basic dimension of curriculum making.

Rugg's contribution

To begin, Rugg instigated and successfully carried out a large-scale synthesis and assessment of all previous efforts to devise a method of selecting and organizing content for a democratic school. The conference at which this synthesis was forged and the yearbook which reported it clarified the past and set tasks for the future. Rugg identified for the first time as curriculum makers many who had formerly not been so considered, and helped furnish a clear and widely distributed statement of the nature of curriculum making. In effect, he got the profession to set its seal of approval on the new specialization.

Second, by sheer personal force, Rugg managed to infuse curriculum makers with some of his own fervor for comprehensiveness. His intellectual reach, always insatiable, first led him into history to search for the roots of curriculum making and then out into contemporary education to search for its most remote flowering. Undoubtedly Rugg used this search for a framework which would reconcile all things in order to deal with his own profound ambivalence toward a culture which appeared to him to be both creative and technical. Since such a framework must deal somehow with the whole of knowledge, for which Rugg

---

niques of Curriculum-Construction," *Twenty-sixth Yearbook*, Part I (Bloomington, Ill.: Public School Publishing Co., 1926), p. vii.

had an enormous appetite, it was no accident that he strove to base the method of curriculum making on the foundational disciplines, adding sociology and eventually aesthetics to the traditional philosophy and psychology. Even the process itself by which the curriculum was made was not proof against his comprehensive approach. He wanted this process to be carried out by the most diverse and representative galaxy of artists, scholars, and technicians possible. The result of his efforts seems to have been to rescue curriculum making, for all time, from any hint of narrowness and superficiality and to launch it as a somewhat ambitious but undeniably universal undertaking.

Lastly, Rugg helped the profession see that attention to the method of curriculum making in itself lacked substance since method was neither dependent on nor derived from any particular set of values. For this reason, Dewey's vision of a school for a democratic social order had been somehow sidetracked as the educational technicians sought for a method of curriculum making which could be used to realize any and all visions. Anticipating the social upheavals of the thirties, Rugg urged the profession to turn to sociological analysis and aesthetic synthesis as sources of help on the question of what values the American school should work for. In particular, he challenged the analysis of adult activities as a method of identifying values, questioning whether an analysis of what is can ever show what ought to be.

6   Hollis L. Caswell

CASWELL'S BACKGROUND[1]

As a school administrator

Hollis Leland Caswell's first experience as a teaching-principal in Auburn, Nebraska, in 1922, was marked by a sense of excitement in seeing young people grow and in working with them that proved to be a powerful force in his future professional life. In this respect, he was in sharp contrast to Rugg, for whom teaching children was an afterthought. Caswell, who had taken a prelaw course at the University of Nebraska, became a teacher accidentally. Like a number who graduated during the depression of 1921, he had turned temporarily to schoolteaching, only to find in the potentialities of students who are challenged a lure pulling him on toward a career in professional education.

After four stimulating years as a teacher, Caswell was passed over reluctantly by a board which was choosing the superintendent of a larger high school, in favor of someone with a master's degree. Advised by Dean Sealock at Nebraska to choose Teachers College, Columbia University, for graduate work in education, Caswell at twenty-five selected tentatively a professional career in education from which, as he expressed it later, "once started there seemed no place to turn back."

Schooling

Influence of Strayer. The contact with both faculty and students at Teachers College[2] shook many of Caswell's preconceived ideas and

---

[1] The source for the background material on Caswell given in this section is a personal interview occurring on September 15, 1962.

[2] Among his fellow students were such men as: Walter Cocking, Assistant

revealed the depth and difficulty of educational problems. George Drayton Strayer was Caswell's major professor in school administration. Strayer, then at the peak of his professional career, was recognized as one of the principal architects of the new concept of school administration. As we have noted, before 1910, the administrator was an agent charged with carrying out the educational purposes of the community. By 1926, the notion had evolved that the administrator was the director of operations of a school system, employing procedures of scientific management. This was the view of school administration from which Bobbitt had derived his curriculum theory. Unlike Bobbitt, Strayer's ideas on the role of the school and the content of the curriculum had already jelled when he became interested in scientific management.[3] He had worked out a mixture of the ideas of the Herbartians and Dewey, with dashes of evolution and connectionism thrown in.[4] As a consequence, Strayer took a different tack from Bobbitt in 1910, throwing all his energies into making the operation of the school system the most efficient for the purpose.[5] He began to do field studies of schools in

---

Superintendent of Schools in St. Louis; Henry Hill, Superintendent in Little Rock, Arkansas; John Nuttall, Superintendent of Schools, New York; John Roe, Superintendent in Missouri; Oscar Buros, Professor of Education at Rutgers; Henry Linn, later Professor at Teachers College, Columbia University; and Paul Leonard, later President of San Francisco State College.

[3] In this respect Strayer was like Frank McMurry, with whom Strayer taught the same courses in curriculum and supervision jointly or in off-and-on years during his first five years at Teachers College. Strayer had identified the aim of education as social efficiency, a blend of social service and individual righteousness which would bring about group welfare by fostering individual welfare. He was essentially an environmentalist, holding that the school should so arrange the environment that the right responses would become habitual. Such habits, he contended, should be formed in relation to the educational objectives of health, mental development, morals, vocations, and leisure. He thought of the curriculum as the school subjects. George D. Strayer, *Brief Course in the Teaching Process* (New York: The Macmillan Co., 1911), pp. 5–7.

[4] Strayer himself traced his ideas to several sources: Dewey's course in educational philosophy, 1903, gave him his notion of the school as a miniature society, and his ideas of social service; the intellectual stimulus provided by his colleague, Frank McMurry, gave him his notions of the moral aim and of community betterment; and the work of another colleague, Edward Thorndike, reinforced earlier work Strayer had done with Cattell in psychology on the theory of stimulus-response and the importance of habits. George D. Strayer, *Brief Course in the Teaching Process* (New York: The Macmillan Co., 1911), pp. 7–13.

[5] Asked by Dean Russell in 1905 what he would really like to specialize in after finishing his degree, Strayer chose administration. At that time courses in administration were a dull sort of business, consisting of the personal reminiscing of men like Samuel Train Dutton and David Snedden on their solutions to administrative problems. Strayer and others who were at Teachers College,

order to develop a theory of good school operation as well as to improve the running of each school surveyed.[6]

Influenced by Thorndike to consider individual differences in pupils, Strayer was also led to develop the principle of equalization of educational opportunity, first stated in the Report of the Educational Finance Inquiry in 1921. Strayer insisted that such equality did not mean identity of opportunity but rather a school program to fit the needs of each child. By 1926, Paul Mort, who had studied under Strayer, was developing techniques for the intensive study of the problems and capacities of individual pupils. Profile charts made for each child, especially for nonpromotion cases, showed how the mechanical regulations imposed on them by school programs did them an injustice. Mort and Strayer supported regular promotions and tailor-made programs for individual children. The emphasis both men placed on what was really happening to children as they struggled with the school program gained Caswell's sympathy. Caswell assessed Strayer years later as a "broad-gauge person," whose crusading spirit, like Horace Mann's, rubbed off on those who knew him. Strayer's two great ideas—that education is profoundly important for the advancement of people and that the quality of education is measured by what the child really learns—were to become basic to Caswell's thinking about the curriculum.[7]

Survey experience. The survey or field-study movement had gathered a momentum, barely slackened by the war, that made it in 1926 a prime laboratory experience for graduate students in educational administration. Caswell, as Strayer's student, took part in extensive field work in school systems struggling with problems ranging from pupil accounting to the ventilation of school buildings. Caswell soon gravitated toward the work Mort was doing with Strayer on classification and progress of pupils, serving with Mort on a survey of schools in Lynn, Massachusetts,

---

Columbia University, during the first decade of the century (Lotus D. Coffman, Walter A. Jessup, Henry Suzzallo, Edward Elliott, and Ellwood P. Cubberley) changed all this. For a good source on the ideas they supplanted see Samuel Train Dutton and David Snedden, *The Administration of Public Education in the United States* (New York: The Macmillan Co., 1908).

[6] A good account of Strayer's influence may be found in Charles Robert Kelley, "Toward an Interpretation of the New Movement of 1915 in Educational Administration" (Doctoral dissertation, Teachers College, Columbia University, 1961).

[7] Caswell considers Strayer's philosophical position to have been more like that of William T. Harris than of the Herbartians, especially Strayer's view of education as a vital process, encompassing the importance of the individual as well as the social meaning of education.

in 1926–27. Mort, who was just starting his career as a teacher in 1928 and was working on a book called *The Individual Pupil*, impressed Caswell with his sensitivity to differences in children. This concern of Mort's was echoed by Thorndike in the courses Caswell took from him on the psychology of the elementary school subjects. Both men spoke directly to Caswell's desire to catch the individual student's interest, challenge his potential, and fit schoolwork to his abilities. This emphasis on the improvement of learning was to be shunted aside by the profession in the thirties in favor of a growing concern for the social role of the school. Recalling the shift, Rugg commented once, "As Thorndike astutely—and I thought wistfully—summed it up in an aside to me one day in the depression years—'So! Sociology's the thing now!' "[8] Yet Caswell, in spite of educational fashion, always considered that the child's interest and capacity were at the vital core of the work of the school.

Foundations courses. The efforts of some of the staff at Teachers College toward greater intellectual cohesion among themselves probably gave vitality to the courses offered in the foundational areas during the years Caswell was there. In 1927, a number of professors in education joined in an informal discussion group, with Kilpatrick as chairman.[9] Meeting bimonthly, they continued a search Rugg and Kilpatrick had begun several years before, for a better scholarly synthesis on which to reconstruct the American school. It was sorely needed, as Rugg never tired of pointing out. The early builders of American Education had lacked in 1900 a number of elements on which to establish schools to fit the twentieth century. The developments in the social sciences, particularly in psychology and sociology, were just beginning then. The challenge of industrial technology with its correlative social changes was imminent. And the resulting profound transformation which Dewey had hoped would occur in the basic disciplines and the arts had barely begun. Pooling their specialized insights, these educators tried to think through a better foundational base for American education. As Rugg himself commented, years later:

> Not only was the sky the limit—the uttermost reaches of men's changing culture of industrialism were too, and every new angle in the scholars' researches and interpretations in the sciences and the arts. We all revolu-

[8] Harold Rugg, *Foundations for American Education* (Yonkers-on-Hudson, New York: World Book Co., 1947), p. 723.

[9] Members were: William H. Kilpatrick, Harold Rugg, George S. Counts, John L. Childs, R. Bruce Raup, Goodwin Watson, Edmund de S. Brunner, Jesse Newlon, Harold F. Clark, F. Ernest Johnson, and others.

tionized our personal understandings and our theories of society and the culture and of the bio-psychology of the "Whole Person," and got glimpses of the meaning of the concepts of the new field-relativity physics.[10]

One of the members of this discussion group, R. Bruce Raup, was Caswell's professor of educational philosophy. After jolting many of Caswell's former ideas on democracy and social welfare, Raup introduced him to the wide scholarly basis on which such ideas should be formed. Caswell also learned important foundational ideas in William Russell's course on comparative education. Russell showed him how an educational system could be organized to advance the particular social goals and purposes of the culture that maintains it. Under Russell's guidance, Caswell began to think through his views on the function of education.[11]

Curriculum courses. Caswell was only well begun on graduate study when the *Twenty-sixth Yearbook* came out. The work of this committee made no particular impression on him then. He had taken the curriculum courses offered at Teachers College and had found them "pretty terrible." Rugg's course on the reconstruction of the elementary curriculum was a potpourri of the "scientific" approach to curriculum, observations on the project method, and recommendations on the formation of curriculum committees. Rugg and others[12] gave another course on curriculum foundations, which Caswell took when the course had been organized only a year. The staff who taught it were barely beginning to achieve a unity of discourse, and the course lacked structure. In assessing his graduate study in curriculum years later, Caswell felt that the extended course treatments in foundational areas by men like Raup, Russell, Mort, and Thorndike gave him his real insight into curriculum problems.

STATE CURRICULUM REVISION PROGRAMS

Curriculum course work

By an interesting coincidence, Caswell was not to be allowed a leisurely completion of his work for his degree. He had been hired as

[10] Harold Rugg, *The Teacher of Teachers* (New York: Harper, 1952), p. 225.

[11] This was Russell's first year as Dean of Teachers College. Caswell recalls that Russell would pose a problem, ask the students for their solution, and then show why what they thought was untenable. A paper on the function of education which Caswell wrote for Russell's course became the nucleus of the first chapter of Caswell's important work on the curriculum, *Curriculum Development.*

[12] Among them were Russell and Raup.

a professor of education at Peabody College for Teachers in Nashville, to begin to teach summer school courses in July, 1929. At the opening of the Spring Quarter, Charles McMurry, on the staff since 1915, died suddenly on the job. Bruce Payne, the President, urged Caswell to come immediately to teach McMurry's courses. With considerable trepidation, but encouraged by Strayer and Thomas Alexander, Caswell went. To his chagrin, one of his courses was on the curriculum. Remembering his former feelings of frustration with this course material, Caswell began to work with all his energy and imagination to do something better.[13]

In an attempt to infuse the process of curriculum making with vigor and scope, Caswell tried to give the members of his curriculum class a vision of education as a vital influence in the lives of children. He discovered that a number of his students were first-class educators, who knew teaching and children and who could contribute to his own background on public education.[14] He had a gnawing sense that much of the material written about the curriculum was not used by teachers, and he determined that the students in his courses were going to "get religion." He drew heavily on the work at Lincoln School and on his own insights gained from course work at Teachers College.[15] He sought to inspire teachers really to change the kinds of experiences children have and to try, through their teaching, to contribute positively to the improvement of society. He was to find Peabody an encouraging place to develop his ideas. Charles McMurry had managed in fifteen years to create an atmosphere there which was extraordinarily favorable to curriculum study. As we have noticed, McMurry's long-standing concern for the instructional act, the "smelting-point" in education, was somewhat out of line with the current interests in curriculum formulation. Unable to fit this emphasis into the method of curriculum making then in vogue, he had contented himself by reiterating it within the older curriculum assumptions. But his students had, as a result, become aware

[13] When Caswell expressed his feelings about the curriculum course to Payne, a student and colleague of Charles McMurry, Payne rejoined, "Your ignorance is better organized than your students'." Payne had long been interested in the curriculum. See Bruce R. Payne, *Public Elementary School Curricula* (New York: Silver, Burdett and Co., 1905).

[14] Caswell was referring to people like Clara L. Pitts and Daisy Parton, who were later active in the curriculum revision program in Virginia.

[15] He found Kilpatrick's book, *Education for a Changing Civilization,* very helpful, as well as ideas on the development of leaders gained from Russell's course, and the notion of the importance of the total culture, learned from Raup.

of its importance, and he had helped to develop in Peabody graduates a continuing climate of interest in instructional improvement.[16]

Establishment of Division of Surveys and Field Studies

Another fortuitous circumstance occurred at Peabody in 1929 which was to affect Caswell's interest in the curriculum. The General Education Board had been making surveys and field studies in the southern states for many years. They had decided that a field office in the South would be more effective and had made a grant to Peabody for this purpose. One of their old-time New York staff members, Frank Bachman, was sent to Peabody as the codirector of the newly established Division of Surveys and Field Studies. Caswell was asked to be his associate on the basis of his substantial field experience. Almost immediately Caswell received an invitation from the Department of Education of the State of Alabama to serve as a consultant in a curriculum revision program there.

Alabama

For one who had been relatively unimpressed with curriculum formulation during his graduate study, Caswell moved fast. By the next year, Alabama had its new *Course of Study for Elementary Schools*. In harmony with the current belief that involvement in the curriculum making process itself would provide the teacher with the necessary motive and understanding to carry the new curriculum into practice, the more than five thousand elementary teachers in Alabama had been invited to try out or contribute materials for the new course of study. Under the direction of a general committee, fifteen production committees in the different subject matter areas had set up general and specific objectives, including desirable content and methods to secure them. In the introduction to the course of study, the curriculum was referred to as the total instructional program, and the course of study was described as a handbook which would serve as a guide to teachers as they developed the curriculum. The recommendation was made that curriculum revision be continuous, especially in a changing society.[17]

[16] In 1933, Ullin Leavell of Peabody reported a memorial to Charles McMurry, in the shape of an organization called the McMurry Study Group, formed for the purpose of the exchange and evaluation of materials on curriculum construction. It was undertaken by some fifty of his former students and admirers because his "work in this field was an inspiration for many years." Society for Curriculum Study, "News Bulletin," IV (Sept. 25, 1933), p. 1 (Mimeographed).

[17] Department of Education, *Course of Study for the State of Alabama, 1930,* p. 7. Montgomery, Alabama.

The Alabama program was an example of statewide curriculum revision in the best current fashion, and everyone was pleased. But Caswell felt that something had been missing. His old desire to see that instruction was actually improved had somehow been frustrated. In spite of wide participation, the materials produced and their effect on practice had seemed too perfunctory and run-of-the-mill to warrant all the effort. He felt that there must be some better way of doing it than the one he had tried.

Florida

By the time he was again asked to be a consultant, in Florida in 1930, he had done some hard thinking. The idea had occurred to him of reviving an old plan of Jesse Newlon's which had been very successful in Denver in the early twenties. Before the Denver teachers had undertaken to plan a curriculum, they had spent time in preparatory study of the most up-to-date thinking on curriculum matters. They had read and discussed issues and problems, and had reviewed experimental studies. Heightened morale and enthusiasm on the part of the teachers had certainly been one result of this approach, yet the initial momentum had somehow bogged down.[18] True, the hoped-for outcome had been a course of study, complete with socially useful materials and motivating procedures. Had the need for teacher study and growth ceased once the materials had been produced? Perhaps the making of a course of study was too limiting a purpose. What if the center of gravity of curriculum making were shifted from the production of a course of study to the actual improvement of instruction? Then the need for continuous teacher study and growth would seem more logical. Caswell began to canvass all his intellectual resources to come up with study materials which would focus directly on the act of learning. The concept of "experience" recommended itself. During the decade in which Bobbitt's curriculum method was widely discussed, curriculum makers had talked about the activities and experiences children should have in order to realize curriculum objectives. Although such theorists had used the terms "activities" and "experiences" freely, they had not thought it important to make clear just what was meant by either one. It was clear, however, that activities and experiences were separate, self-

---

[18] An interesting account of the Denver approach is given in Lawrence A. Cremin, *The Transformation of the School* (New York: Alfred A. Knopf, 1961), pp. 299–303. Cremin attributes the lapse of the program into perfunctoriness to the ultimate sterility of an overemphasis on process.

contained units which could be strung along together in the hope that the child himself would give them continuity. This bits-and-pieces approach had been recently frowned on by the organismic psychologists and others.[19] What had Kilpatrick said? Not experiences but "experience is the unit element of curriculum-construction . . . the felt connection of actual experiencing teaches best."[20] There had been something also in Dewey's works about experience being both doing and undergoing.[21] If the teacher could be brought to regard the total, interacting experience of the child as the center of curriculum making, what would be the effect on instruction? Would his attention be compelled to the nature of the child? Would he search for ways by which to interest the child in the desirable experiences that the school offered? Could a continuity in the child's experience be achieved which had been difficult to establish through a series of activities? Even the popular "unit" approach had merely organized discrete elements of experience into larger segments.

Striving to incorporate into state curriculum revision some of his new insights, Caswell launched a study program for Florida teachers, based on the aim of instructional improvement. The results confirmed the value of the new emphasis. The course of study produced by the Florida teachers, unlike the one in Alabama, began boldly with the statement that "the purpose of this course of study is to help the teachers

[19] Dewey had earlier commented that, "there is no such thing as a fixed and final set of objectives, even for the time being or temporarily. Each day of teaching ought to enable a teacher to revise and better in some respect the objectives aimed at in previous work. . . . Education is by its nature an endless circle or spiral. It is an activity which includes science within itself. In its very process it sets more problems to be further studied, which then react into the educative process to change it still further, and thus demand more thought, more science, and so on, in everlasting sequence." *Sources of a Science of Education* (New York: Horace Liveright, 1929), pp. 75–77. One of the best criticisms of the mechanistic approach to the curriculum was that done by William Patty under the direction of William H. Kilpatrick. Although this study took eight years to be completed, it was begun at about the time that Caswell moved away from discrete curricular aims and activities toward the unified concept of experience. William Lovell Patty, *A Study of Mechanism in Education: An Examination of the Curriculum-making Devices of Franklin Bobbitt, W. W. Charters, and C. C. Peters, from the Point of View of Relativistic Pragmatism* (New York: Teachers College Contributions to Education, 1938).

[20] William Kilpatrick, "Statement of Position," *Twenty-sixth Yearbook of the National Society for the Study of Education*, Part II (Bloomington, Ill.: Public School Publishing Co., 1926), p. 126.

[21] Caswell found Dewey's *Art as Experience* very illuminating, especially Chapter III. Although Caswell may not have known it, some Herbartians had been groping toward his formulation. In the discussion following Charles McMurry's paper on correlation in 1896, Superintendent Dutton commented, "The

of Florida improve their instruction."[22] The organization of the program was by grades, not by subjects, the reason being:

> The child develops as a unit. His growth is a continuous process, advancing through successive stages and involving all his abilities. Each grade should represent a series of unified experiences for the child. All the English, mathematics, science and other subject matter presented in each grade should be so interrelated as to promote the unified development of all the abilities of the child.[23]

Each grade section of the course of study was prefaced with a statement of the developmental characteristics of the child at that age and a chart showing typical centers of interest from which units might be initiated. For example, it was suggested that third graders might be interested in community protection of health and life, especially the activities of the health department and the police, or that sixth graders might be interested in plagues and their control, such as smallpox and hookworm.

The general aim of education was "to promote and direct the adjustment and growth of the individual so that he may live worthily in an everchanging society."[24] Growth was to be made in the areas of the seven major social functions, as formulated by the Committee on the Reorganization of Secondary Education in 1918.[25] These functions were broken down into specific abilities, understandings, attitudes, and fixed associations which could be developed in the child as he studied each subject.

---

true course of study is the stream of activity that flows on in any school from day to day and from week to week. It is the quality of life that flourishes there." *Second Yearbook of the National Herbart Society for the Scientific Study of Teaching* (Bloomington, Ill.: Pantagraph Printing, 1896), p. 53. Dewey phrased the idea also when he said, "The reality of education is found in the personal and face-to-face contact of teacher and child. . . . It is in this contact that the real course of study, whatever be laid down on paper, is actually found." John Dewey, "The Situation as Regards the Course of Study," *Addresses and Journal of Proceedings of the National Education Association* (1901), p. 338.

[22] State Department of Public Instruction, Tallahassee, Fla. *Course of Study for Florida Elementary Schools* (1931), p. 5.

[23] State Department of Public Instruction, Tallahassee, Fla. *Course of Study for Florida Elementary Schools* (1931), p. 8.

[24] State Department of Public Instruction, Tallahassee, Fla. *Course of Study for Florida Elementary Schools* (1931), p. 6.

[25] They are: (1) health, (2) command of fundamental processes, (3) vocational efficiency, (4) citizenship, (5) worthy home membership, (6) worthy use of leisure, (7) ethical character. The committees felt that these classifications of human activities needed only a slight change of emphasis to be applied to the elementary school.

Caswell felt that the Florida work was a start in the right direction, although it still left hazy the connection between the child's interests and experiences and his social problems and needs. Attention to the social functions and centers of interest constituted a step ahead, but both seemed to vanish in the process of stating specific subject matter objectives. Sorely needed was some kind of overall curriculum design against which teachers could check the significance of the inevitable minutiae of daily practice.

Further, Caswell was still not completely satisfied with his emphasis on instructional improvement. The word "improvement" had an empty sound unless its user was moving in a clear direction. The frontier thinkers in foundations, whose works he had read at Teachers College, had urged that American national ideals be rescued from old and static formulations and be given vital content. Somehow true democratic conduct in the real world of practical action must be the outcome set by the school for youth.

Although the Florida experience had been a major breakthrough on procedure, broadening the base of participation, it had also taught him much about study groups mobilized on a large scale. He began to mature an organizational plan for curriculum making, which would effectively set a whole state to work without intimidating the least prepossessing and most traditional of its teachers. And he continued to develop a bibliography of first-rate materials on the curriculum. He felt a little like the teacher of an unfamiliar topic who must work hard to keep ahead of the students.

Virginia

Inception. The previous year, Sidney B. Hall, a professor at Peabody, had gone to Virginia to be the new State Superintendent of Public Instruction. As he left, he had asked Caswell to think about coming to Virginia to help him organize a program like Alabama's. One of Hall's most important acts in the ensuing year had been to carry out a reorganization of the Virginia State Department of Education, effective July, 1931. He had replaced the former Departments of Elementary and Secondary Education with a single Division of Instruction. It was an important step since it paved the way for a unified approach to statewide curriculum revision. As one of the first moves of its kind, however, it was a controversial one.[26]

[26] Caswell considered this move of Hall's to be prophetic. In the beginning, as school systems began to add curriculum specialists to their staffs and in-

147

Caswell went to Virginia determined to profit by his recent experiences in Florida and Alabama. He was to succeed and, in so doing, to forge a new kind of program of curriculum making as well as a new basic conception of the nature of the curriculum.

Study program. As a first step, in the fall, the sixteen thousand teachers and administrators in Virginia were invited, through their division organization,[27] to take part in a general study and discussion of issues in the curriculum. It was explained to them that the questions to be raised were matters of great importance in curriculum making but that there were no final answers to them. The hope was merely that a working consensus could be reached in the process which would foster the general staff cooperation necessary for a good curriculum program in Virginia.

Groups of convenient size, living near each other, met weekly some fourteen times between January and March. Each group selected a leader who assigned topics and helped secure materials. A secretary reported to the Division Superintendent. The study guide for this massive self-help extension course was a fifteen-page syllabus prepared by Caswell.[28] Carefully chosen readings were recommended under seven topics: (1) What is the curriculum? (2) Developments which have resulted in a need for curriculum revision; (3) What is the place of subject matter in education? (4) Determining educational objectives; (5) Organizing instruction; (6) Selecting subject matter; and (7) Measuring the outcomes of instruction. Sources cited were varied and important. They ranged from writings of Boyd Bode and John Dewey through

---

augurate curriculum revision programs, separate curriculum bureaus were established, set off from the rest of the administrative organization and directed by curriculum experts. Notable examples of this arrangement were St. Louis and Pittsburgh. Caswell recalls arguing publicly with Strayer in favor of the location of the curriculum bureau within the school organization, under the direction of the assistant superintendent of schools. According to Caswell, Pittsburgh was the first city in which an issue was really made of the place of the curriculum specialist in the administrative organization. Taking the curriculum bureau out of isolation from the on-going instructional program was a step toward establishing a division of instruction for the total system which would coordinate all curriculum improvement. This was the approach advocated from the first in Virginia. (Personal interview, Sept. 15, 1962).

[27] Divisions were the educational unit in Virginia. There were 109, each with a division superintendent who had charge of all the public schools in his division, whether city or county.

[28] Sidney B. Hall, D. W. Peters, and Hollis L. Caswell, "Study Course for Virginia State Curriculum Program," State Board of Education, *Bulletin XIV*, No. 2 (Richmond, Virginia, Jan. 1932).

William Ogburn and Ross Finney, Harold Rugg, William Kilpatrick and George Counts, to Franklin Bobbitt, the Denver Course of Study, Charles McMurry and the *Twenty-sixth Yearbook of the National Society for the Study of Education.* The emphasis given to the definition and interpretation of democratic ideals was equal to the stress laid on the growth and development of children.

Any sense of pressure was carefully avoided. Six thousand of the teachers did not take part at first, although the way was left open for them to do so later.[29] Division Superintendents were cautioned to work gradually. Since, according to the first bulletins of the program, "the major purpose of the State Curriculum Program is to improve classroom instruction in the State,"[30] a lockstep program would be self-defeating. One group might be far ahead of the average, another far behind. It soon appeared that the majority of the teachers were old-fashioned in their heavy reliance on a course of study. The new aim of instructional improvement implied that the course of study should be regarded as only one of several helpful aids to the teacher as he made the curriculum. The novelty of this viewpoint of curriculum making in the eyes of the teachers led Caswell to begin the state-wide program of curriculum development by making a state course of study for Virginia. True to his view that teachers must begin where they are on instructional improvement, he hoped that as they made a course of study together, they would learn the proper limits to its usefulness. If the course were well prepared, even when followed most slavishly by teachers, some improvements in child experience were bound to ensue. And those who freed themselves from overdependence on it would find it a helpful guide.

Committee work. The elaborate and smooth-running administrative machinery necessary to organize study groups and production committees for the course of study was in operation by the fall of 1932. Three state committees had been appointed in March by Superintendent Hall, one each on aims, principles, and definitions. A fourth committee on production was composed of the chairmen of the division production committees.[31] Working in the curriculum laboratory at Peabody during

[29] State extension courses in curriculum were offered. The State Teachers Colleges added courses in curriculum to their summer offerings. In 1931, only two offered curriculum work in the summer; in 1932, ten did.

[30] "Organization for Virginia State Curriculum Program," State Board of Education, *Bulletin XIV,* No. 5 (Richmond, Virginia, March, 1932), p. 5.

[31] Each division chairman was to appoint local chairmen to organize local production committees. These local chairmen formed the division production

the summer, under Caswell's direction, the State committees on aims, principles, definitions, and production had a handbook ready by July.[32] The work of these committees was critical since they would set the tone for the whole program. Caswell strove successfully to infuse their work with his new insights.

The determination of aims[33] seemed to Caswell a key operation, since on the work of this committee would depend whether or not "bold and creative efforts to put real content" into democracy, citizenship, and ethical character would be made.[34] The personnel of the Aims Committee were deliberately chosen to overlap to a considerable extent with that of the production committees. The plan was to give the same people, as far as possible, the responsibility for both determining ends and devising means. The committee produced over sixty general aims for elementary education during their summer at Peabody.[35] Their bibliography alone filled five and a half very closely printed pages. It ranged widely in the field of education and out, including such different items as Frank Lloyd Wright's *Autobiography* and Thorstein Veblen's *The Theory of the Leisure Class*.[36]

They had taken the standard beginning step of the already classical approach of the curriculum maker. Working according to the method, the committee stated the aims "in terms of the ways that people think,

---

committee. It was a system in which everyone, right down to the last teacher, was thoroughly articulated.

[32] "Procedures for Virginia State Curriculum Program," State Board of Education, *Bulletin XV,* No. 3 (Nov. 1932). The source for the date of its issuance and other information on the history of the program is Sidney B. Hall, "Brief Description of Virginia Program for Improving Instruction," State Board of Education, *Bulletin XXI,* No. 4 (Jan. 1939), pp. 10–17.

[33] The Principles Committee and Definitions Committee served largely to clarify the initial work of the Aims Committee.

[34] The phrase is one of Count's from the *American Road to Culture.* This challenge was apparently the lodestar for the work of the committee on aims. "Procedures for Virginia State Curriculum Program," State Board of Education, *Bulletin XV,* No. 3 (Nov. 1932), p. 14.

[35] Twenty-four understandings analyzed into 150 generalizations; 18 attitudes, analyzed into 100 characteristics; 8 appreciations, analyzed into 30 characteristics; and 12 automatic responses analyzed into 115 habits and skills. "Procedures for Virginia State Curriculum Program," State Board of Education, *Bulletin XV,* No. 3 (Nov. 1932), pp. 17–41.

[36] It included, among other items, Bobbitt's *Curriculum-Making in Los Angeles* which contains the fruit of years of activity analysis by himself and his students. Caswell deliberately made the list as varied as he could, covering the whole range of writings from conservative to progressive. "Procedures for Virginia State Curriculum Program," State Board of Education, *Bulletin XV,* No. 3 (Nov. 1932), pp. 42–47.

live, and act. . . . When the individual reaches the stage of growth in which the understandings, attitudes, appreciations, and automatic responses listed here constitute his personality he will be the integrated personality, the socially adaptable person, the cultured man capable of living the good life."[37]

Yet the spirit of this group, like the times themselves, had changed. Shocked by the depression, the committee strove to reassert man's ability to direct his social life toward a better realization of his ideals. The committee chose to be guided by the principle that the school had a major responsibility to "discover and define the ideals of a democratic society and provide for the continuous redefinition and re-interpretation of the social ideals in light of economic, political, and social changes."[38] The aims chosen were permeated by the spirit of traditional social reform with a modern dash of sociological and economic analysis. Sample generalizations were, "Opportunities for exploitation increase as interdependence grows. . . . The methods of science are now applied to social problems. . . . Religion is an agency of group control. . . . The present social order is not fixed and permanent." Sample attitudes were, "The tendency to question authority constructively. . . . The disposition to be free from prejudice."[39]

Caswell had the sensitivity of the good administrator toward the power of the lay public over schools in a democracy as well as toward its duties in regard to them. He and Superintendent Hall distributed copies of the aims widely to men's and women's clubs, chambers of commerce, and the press—requesting discussion and comments. Hall also called a public meeting in the Chamber of the House of Delegates, inviting representatives of many organizations to attend. He and Caswell explained the aims, urged their further study, and welcomed written suggestions.[40]

Using the statement of aims as their compass, several hundred teachers, working in production committees, began to develop appropriate experience units. Supervisors and college staffs cooperated by

[37] "Procedures for Virginia State Curriculum Program," State Board of Education, *Bulletin XV*, No. 3 (Nov. 1932), pp. 15–17.
[38] "Procedures for Virginia State Curriculum Program," State Board of Education, *Bulletin XV*, No. 3 (Nov. 1932), p. 12.
[39] "Procedures for Virginia State Curriculum Program," State Board of Education, *Bulletin XV*, No. 3 (Nov. 1932), pp. 20, 22, 24, 29. This might mean advocating racial tolerance in a Southern community.
[40] "Brief Description of Virginia Program for Improving Instruction," State Board of Education, *Bulletin*, XXI, No. 4 (Jan. 1939), p. 12.

making extension courses and summer school workshops available for the committee work. By the following summer, enough material had accumulated to make a mimeographed tryout edition of the course of study feasible. Working that summer at a curriculum laboratory at Peabody, the newly-formed Elementary Reviewing and Unifying Committee undertook to arrange this material by grades and by subjects.

The curriculum design.[41] Ever since he had been the consultant on the Florida program, Caswell had been seeking an overall design that would be better than the traditional grade and subject arrangement. He wanted a pattern by which teachers could judge whether a given unit was relating the child to the culture in a meaningful way. After much study, he felt he had come up with some ideas, and he sent a careful memorandum of them to the Reviewing Committee. He asked the members to consider the possibility of a better way of organizing the new curriculum materials that were being prepared.

The content of the memorandum was largely exploratory. At first, Caswell had begun to work on the problem of design from the point of view of the child. He sensed that most children had a tremendous mass of interests based largely on previous experience and that it was relatively rare for a child to have a dominant interest. Children usually seemed quite as concerned about the Congo and long division as they did about making boats. He contended that only by knowing youngsters thoroughly could a teacher get at these experiences to which the child had devoted his energies and attention in the past. He theorized that it was possible to select from this broad range of interests those which had cultural importance without doing violence to the child.

Caswell had then turned to current theory in organismic psychology and cultural anthropology, particularly as derived from contemporary studies of American culture, for help in the selection from children's interests of those that had social significance. Both disciplines stressed wholeness, the psychological wholeness of experience and the wholeness of a given culture pattern. The anthropologist had theorized that man discharges his social functions in an integrated pattern. Caswell suggested that if these functions could be used as the categories of learning, suitably adapted to the child's age and development, the child's learning would also be integrated. Although in the beginning, he said, the child might employ the modes of social behavior in crude form, he would gradually reconstruct and refine them in practice, giving sequence to

[41] The material in this section is based on a personal interview with Caswell, Sept. 15, 1962.

his learning. Caswell further suggested that the content of the functions and the values they served should be those of the culture in which they were found.

Further, Caswell was influenced by Boyd Bode's work, *Progressive Education at the Crossroads*, to recognize the "necessity of using the traditional subjects in a curriculum based on social functions as a means of helping pupils organize their knowledge for future use, discover generalizations of wide applicability, and fill in gaps in their knowledge."[42] He suggested to the Reviewing Committee that an adequate curriculum design should give attention to content as well as social functions and children's interests. He hoped that the objectives which had been worked out by the Committee on Aims would give the teacher a content framework against which to check the child's progressive organization of his concepts in the direction of mastery of the fields of organized knowledge.

Caswell had asked Paul Hanna, who was then active in the affairs of Lincoln School, to meet with him and the Reviewing Committee on the memorandum. Discussion showed that the real problem was helping teachers apply the vague criteria of subject matter, child interest, and social meaning to the daily task of instruction. Some sort of guidance chart was requested which would show a cross-hatching of the three major factors. Hanna was asked to shape up on the basis of his experiences in Lincoln School what he thought would be good centers of interest. Caswell offered to work on the social functions and the relevance of subject matter.

The final design adopted by the Committee for the Course of Study had scope and sequence, or both a space and a time dimension. It was a grid, the vertical items being the scope, and the horizontal ones the sequence by grades.[43] With a few exceptions, the social functions selected as the scope (the space dimension) were worked on in some form in every grade. For example, first graders who learned how to cross a street properly were having experiences that fell within the category of the protection and conservation of life.[44] The sequence of experiences (the

[42] Caswell thought of the concept of experience as providing a balanced picture of these three important elements: the interests of the child, the social functions, and organized knowledge in terms of logical relationships. Whatever the changing fashion in curriculum theorizing, Caswell says he always held to the prime importance of these three basic factors.

[43] Sidney B. Hall, D. W. Peters, Helen Ruth Henderson, and Hollis L. Caswell, *Tentative Course of Study for Virginia Elementary Schools* (Richmond, Va.: State Board of Education, 1933), pp. 40–43.

[44] First and second graders, however, did not work on religion or education.

time dimension) was arranged according to the centers of interest, ranging from home and school life in the first grade to the effects of the machine upon our living in the sixth. Specific activities or units of work were the result of the conjunction on the grid of a social function with a center of interest.[45]

For example, in the fourth grade, the function of "the expression of aesthetic impulses" in conjunction with the center of interest—"the effects of discovery upon our living"—resulted in the question, "How is recreation influenced by frontier living?", which might suggest a detailed activity like "designing a sampler." The aims of education infused the activities with content which was zealously recorded for the teacher through an intricate bookkeeping system. All of the 457 items in the statement of aims were coded, and each suggested activity bristled with letters, reminding the teacher of the aims it involved.[46]

The tryout edition was sent to fifty-two divisions in September, 1933. In harmony with the policy of the program, the use of this material was left voluntary.[47] On the basis of a very favorable reaction to the tryout edition, a Tentative Course of Study was produced in 1934 for general use in the schools.

An assessment. Even after thirty years, the reader of the published materials captures the spirit of excitement that pervaded the work in

[45] The functional phases of social life which constituted the scope were: (1) Protection and conservation of life, property, and national resources, (2) Production and consumption of goods and services, (3) Recreation, (4) Expression of aesthetic impulses, (5) Transportation and communication, (6) Exchange of goods and services, (7) Expression of religious impulses, (8) Education, (9) Extension of freedom, and (10) Distribution of rewards of production. The centers of interest which constituted the sequence were: Grade I, Home and school life; Grade II, Community life; Grade III, Adaptation of life to environmental forces of nature; Grade IV, Adaptation of life to advancing physical frontiers; Grade V, Effects of discovery upon our living; Grade VI, Effects of the machine upon our living; Grade VII, Extension of provision for cooperative living. Sidney B. Hall, D. W. Peters, Helen Ruth Henderson, and Hollis L. Caswell, *Tentative Course of Study for Virginia Elementary Schools* (Richmond, Va.: State Board of Education, 1933), pp. 40–43.

[46] It was a formidable-looking document, and required several pages of explanation on how to use it. Once understood, however, its workings were really quite simple. A fellow consultant, F. W. Stemple, discussing his plans for curriculum revision in West Virginia praised the Virginia program but said, half in jest: "We just can't use it. Our teachers are overwhelmed, for it is so far removed from what they have been accustomed." *Curriculum Journal*, VII (April, 1936), p. 24.

[47] Some of these "volunteers," had been spurred on by local pride. In the spring of 1934, a ground swell of reluctance to install the new course of study was traced to an initial failure to involve principals and superintendents properly

Virginia. Although the program there became a prototype for Caswell's later work in other states, and his ideas found their smoothest and most complete expression in the Mississippi report in 1939, none of the other programs seems to give off the sheer vitality and enthusiasm of the one in Virginia. Years later, Caswell himself assessed the effect of the program on the schools in Virginia as threefold: (1) it enlarged the vision of teachers and increased their competence; (2) it greatly increased the quantity of modern instructional materials used in the schools; (3) it increased the amount of supervision and improved its quality. He further described it as the first program which sought to achieve a social orientation of the curriculum, that would be meaningful to children and youth. These are fair judgments, and he might have added that the program touched off a series of state curriculum revision programs, modelled on the one in Virginia.

Whatever the future effect of these programs, which is outside the scope of this study, the immediate result was to dramatize on a statewide scale the new focus upon the improvement of instruction. As Caswell himself was to phrase it years later, "We drew a bead on the experience of the learner." Attention swung to the teacher as the person who exerts the most crucial influence on child experience. Aims ceased to be static formulas and became whatever actually guided the child's experience. Bobbitt's concept of the curriculum as composed of experiences had come to life and become the pivot on which theorizing about the curriculum would soon move.

This shift in focus was probably too thoroughgoing to be clearly perceived in the beginning by either the teachers in Virginia or the profession at large. A lack of clarity was not to be counted a failure, however, since the concept itself was a "process" concept and growth in understanding is intrinsic to any "process." In this sense, the teachers were learners like the children, and their "curriculum" was as much an experience as was the children's. To some observers, the program in Virginia suggested that the new concept of the curriculum as the experiences the child actually undergoes would prove to be a fruitful one. The following description by Charles W. Knudsen, one of Caswell's colleagues, helps to clarify this statement:

---

in the program. A memo was issued to the effect that: (1) application must be made for permission to try out the tentative course of study; and (2) that only those systems would be accepted that could demonstrate a high level of teacher competence and adequate libraries and supervision. All but a few applied, and about a dozen were denied.

155

Observation of Virginia teachers' work and conferences with teachers lead the writer to believe that many of them, sensing their ineptitude in directing learning units, are likely to consider the planning of the first unit they direct as a task that stands alone. They feel, and perhaps rightly so, that the difficulties involved in selecting, planning, gathering materials for, evaluating, and determining the scope of one unit is enough for one task. As soon as they have convinced themselves that they can successfully conduct one unit, they are ready to tackle the problem of sequence. They accept the principle that curriculums should provide for consecutive and progressive growth, but they are not confident in the early steps of unit development that they can solve successfully the problem of sequence. As one of the principals expressed the case for his teachers, "At first their units were short, dealing with small problems, but as their skill increased the units became longer and more comprehensive. Based on pupil interests, these units began to grow naturally one out of the other.[48]

THE CURRICULUM SOCIETY

These emerging ideas about curriculum were too good to keep imbedded in state programs, making them largely unavailable to the very teachers who might profit the most from them. They also deserved the analysis and refinement that critical scholarship in education was now able to give. Caswell had a ready pen,[49] and he set about to report in the professional magazines the new curriculum design and other innovations.

Articles on the curriculum had so far jostled elbows in journals with articles on every kind of educational subject. Charters had been one of the first to feel a real need for a separate publication on the curriculum. In 1923, he admitted that his collection of studies in curriculum at the end of his book was not definitive. "But with no central magazine

[48] Society for Curriculum Study, *The Changing Curriculum*, ed. Henry Harap (New York: Appleton-Century, 1937), p. 199. As we have seen, teacher involvement in curriculum improvement had been in the air for at least fifteen years, beginning with Newlon's work in Denver. Caswell's conception of the curriculum process was to render the teacher indispensable to curriculum making, but the nature of this teacher involvement had still not been made clear. Interesting developments in psychology and sociology which had been maturing since the early twenties were to enable curriculum theorists like Alice Miel, a student of Caswell, to illuminate the nature of teacher involvement and to revolutionize the procedures used to secure it. See Alice Miel, *Changing The Curriculum: A Social Process* (New York: D. Appleton-Century Co., 1946). Miel recalls that Stuart Courtis, with whom she studied at the University of Michigan, organized his college classroom democratically, as early as 1927, and tried to apply the new ideas on group process to the preparation of teachers.

[49] During his six years at Peabody, he wrote some twenty-five magazine articles alone.

existing devoted to curriculum construction, or other central agency, it is impossible to be certain that all significant studies have been secured. Some of the studies have been found quite by accident," he commented.[50] The Curriculum Bureau established at Teachers College in 1926 was an attempt at a clearing house in curriculum, but its field was narrow. The Bureau's reports helped the profession keep abreast of developments in courses of study, but there were other gaps to be filled. The new ideas in curriculum were in danger of becoming fragmentary and vague without the stimulus of wide critical review.

By 1928, Henry Harap had become quite disturbed at the lack of an organized methodology in the expanding field of curriculum making. Professor of Education at the Cleveland School of Education, he took a first step toward meeting this need by publishing a book on the subject.[51] More important, he and other like-minded university professors and field leaders persuaded themselves that there was a real need for a systematic exchange of ideas on curriculum making. They began to meet to share views and news. The word got around, and the interest was so wide and enthusiastic that by 1932 they had begun to call themselves the Society for Curriculum Study.[52] Membership was limited to curriculum directors, administrative officers in charge of curriculum making, supervisory officers in charge of curriculum making, special or general consultants in curriculum revision, authors or investigators in curriculum making, and instructors in curriculum making.[53] The purpose of the Society was to "enable those interested in curriculum making to be of mutual help to each other, and to advance the movement of thorough and progressive curriculum revision."[54] Harap, now at Western Reserve, had offered to get out a little, mimeographed news sheet or bulletin for the Society so that the members could keep in touch with each other's projects and know when meetings would be held. It soon became apparent that the Society filled a real need. Everybody who was anybody in curriculum study joined

[50] Wallace Werrett Charters, *Curriculum Construction* (New York: The Macmillan Co., 1923), p. 169.

[51] Henry Harap, *The Technique of Curriculum Making* (New York: The Macmillan Co., 1928).

[52] Walter Cocking, Edgar Dale, and Rudolph Lindquist were also active in organizing this group. At first the name was the Society of Curriculum Specialists, but this title did not quite express their scholarly intent.

[53] Since these specializations had been in existence for less than a decade, this list is quite impressive.

[54] Society for Curriculum Study, "News Bulletin," III (March 25, 1932), p. 10 (mimeographed).

it. By 1934, they had 250 members and had organized their first, full-dress annual meeting, complete with theme and speakers.[55]

The Bulletin

This group provided opportunities par excellence for a young man like Caswell to have his new ideas appraised critically as well as talked about and tried in other places.[56] One of the early customs of the Society was to canvass the membership for squibs on their current curriculum projects, of whatever nature, and the Bulletin always carried long lists of items of professional interest such as a progress report by Hollis L. Caswell to the effect that during 1932 he was a general consultant in Virginia and Florida and Director of the Curriculum Laboratory at Peabody.[57] All sorts of issues were aired in the Bulletin, from the relationship of the curriculum to the present economic crisis, to whether the child-centered school really had a technique of curriculum making. The Society announced that a total of forty-four doctoral theses on curriculum was reported in 1932–33.[58] In 1934, Bobbitt gave a summary of his theory of the curriculum and offered to arrange a composite theory on the basis of similar summaries from one hundred course thinkers, if the summaries were expressed in approximately fifty concise and unambiguous statements.[59] The Bulletin covered a wide scope. A sample issue might contain both an attack by Jesse Newlon on the Hegelianism of Harris and a proposal by Paul Hanna that the Society sponsor a series of teaching materials on contemporary society, the *Building America Series.*[60]

[55] Society for Curriculum Study, "News Bulletin," V (April 9, 1934), pp. 1–4; (Sept. 25, 1934), pp. 20–25. (mimeographed).

[56] Paul Hanna, consultant in social science in the Virginia Program from the staff of Teachers College, Columbia University, influenced Caswell's thinking and helped spread his ideas. As early as 1932, Hanna, Newlon, Kilpatrick, and Hopkins had organized a student/faculty discussion group at Teachers College on issues in the curriculum, among them the program in Virginia. Later Hanna was consultant to the Santa Barbara Public Schools in California, developing a curriculum based on social functions. Society for Curriculum Study, "News Bulletin," III (Dec. 7, 1932), pp. 2–3. (mimeographed).

[57] Society for Curriculum Study, "News Bulletin," IV (Jan. 30, 1933), p. 10. (mimeographed).

[58] Society for Curriculum Study, "News Bulletin," IV (May 29, 1933), pp. 6–7. (mimeographed).

[59] Whatever happened to this magnificent plan, it assuredly would not be considered today as a useful way of arriving at a general theory! Bobbitt's "method" in 1918 was a "theory" by 1934. Society for Curriculum Study, "News Bulletin," V (Jan. 12, 1934), pp. 2–4, 9. (mimeographed).

[60] The same Society also sponsored: *A Challenge to Secondary Education* (1935), *Integration* (1937), *The Changing Curriculum* (1937), and *The Com-*

Supervisors' reaction

The supervisors for a long time stood aloof from this Society even though their interests were quite similar.[61] As we have noted, a special interest in the curriculum was at first a sideline for administrators, supervisors, and professors of education. This led to some unexpected consequences. One of them was that each one's approach to the new movement reflected his wider conflicts with the others over the division of labor in educational leadership. When the existence of the new specialist in curriculum began to make sense in response to the expanded enterprise of curriculum making, more confusion ensued. His appearance threatened to complicate the problem by injecting another kind of person into a relationship that was already hazy.

While the intricacies of this problem deserve fuller treatment, at this point our concern is limited largely to the effect of the conflicts on the new Society. Although all groups sensed the challenge of the new specialist, the supervisors felt it most, since they had traditionally been charged with the improvement of instruction. The real power of their role, however, had always been unclear. Theoretically the supervisor was a line officer above the principal,[62] but, by working agree-

---

munity School (1938). While these were not exactly yearbooks, much of the planning and work on them went on as part of the work of the Society. *Curriculum Journal* VI (May 22, 1935), p. 1; VII (April 1936), pp. 17–21; (Dec. 1936), pp. 8–10.

[61] They had their own organization, the National Conference on Educational Method, and magazine, *The Journal of Educational Method*, both started in 1921.

[62] In practice, all disapproved of the line function of the supervisor. The National Society for the Study of Education in their yearbook on *The Relation of Principals and Superintendents to the Training and Improvement of their Teachers*, published in 1908 were very categorical in their statements on this problem. The Annual Report of the School Committee of Boston, issued in 1896 had said, "A clear and distinct line of separation should be drawn between the duties of supervisor and the duties of principal. Were this done, conflict, repetition, and overlapping of duties would, in the interests of unity, vigor and economy, be avoided." The authors of the yearbook agreed with this and went on to say, "A visiting supervisor should work through the principal, advising with him rather than with the teachers direct. In no case should the supervisor issue orders to the teacher. It should be her business to point out to the principal the needs of the various teachers; to give assistance to these teachers in ways which the principal may decide. This process, while indirect, and hence slow, tends to place responsibility and hence, ultimately, to produce a high degree of efficiency." (Page 21). By 1935, Paul Revere Pierce, reviewing the history of this conflict, observed, "The general supervisor has been, from the beginning, the superior line officer of the principal; actually he has rarely exercised his prerogatives except in routine matters. Superintendents have seldom clothed the general supervisors with defined supervisory powers, and the supervisors, except in

ment, he had become a staff person with advisory power only. He had found it difficult to sustain this staff role, since, like the old-time factory foreman, he was held accountable by the superintendent for quality teaching. His real job had become one of inspection, and he had depended for power largely on the rewards and punishments he could command. At times he had even been asked to "rate" teachers.[63] His role had become neither line nor staff but an uneasy compromise between them.

The new focus on process and product, initiated around 1910, should have made the old line function obsolete. Administrators, supervisors, and teachers (according to this view) were all co-partners in a common task—that of improving the final product, the educated adult. As this focus slowly gained acceptance, the curriculum specialist, unencumbered by an older pattern, had much less trouble with the new role than did the supervisor. It seemed possible that unless the supervisor could accommodate himself to a new function, the curriculum specialist might replace him.

At about the same time as the curriculum specialists began to meet, the supervisors' organization made efforts of their own to deal with the problems posed by the new concept of the curriculum. In 1929, the National Conference on Educational Method was accepted as a department in the National Education Association. Its new name was the Department of Supervisors and Directors of Instruction,[64] and its first yearbooks dealt with the problem of the role of the supervisor.[65] After tracing the history of supervision and surveying actual supervisory practices, the yearbooks showed a gradual move toward evaluating the

---

sporadic cases, have not sought them." *The Origin and Development of the Public School Principalship* (Chicago: The University of Chicago Libraries, 1935), pp. 104–05.

[63] William H. Burton, clarifying the role of the supervisor in 1922 in his book *Supervision and the Improvement of Teaching* (New York: D. Appleton and Co., 1922), listed teacher rating as one of five areas in which superintendents frequently delegated authority to supervisors, p. 9ff.

[64] The name of their magazine was changed to *Educational Method*.

[65] A nucleus of such men as Ernest Melby, Archie Threlkeld, Stuart Courtis, Orville Brim, and Franklin Bobbitt, kept prodding the organization toward the emphasis on curriculum development. See especially "Educational Supervision," *First Yearbook of the National Conference on Educational Method* (1928), pp. 216–18, 244, 250; "Scientific Method in Supervision," *Second Yearbook of the National Conference of Supervisors and Directors of Instruction* (1929); "Current Problems of Supervisors," *Third Yearbook of the National Conference of Supervisors and Directors of Instruction* (1930), pp. 207–08.

supervisor and strengthening the teacher.[66] This willingness to explore the newer concept of supervision gave the organization fresh vigor, but it was clear that the Society for Curriculum Study was the real going concern. They were not defending an old territory but were discovering a new one, and their organization had all the vitality and freshness of any pioneering enterprise.[67] The concepts they were developing had a pertinence and challenge that made it likely that they would replace older concepts in supervision.

LANDMARK WORKS

Curriculum Development

In the meantime, Caswell had become involved in six more curriculum revision programs operating out of Peabody, three in cities and three in states. They provided the perfect seedbed for his ideas, which became so well-matured by 1935 that he felt ready to put them into book form. The volume, *Curriculum Development,* embodying a comprehensive statement of the frontier thinking of the period, shortly became a "must" for all those interested in the curriculum.[68]

Most of its contents are already familiar to us. The opening chapter described the challenge of contemporary life to the school. After an analysis of present-day social problems worthy of Rugg, Caswell called on the school to cooperate with other social institutions in rediscovering and redefining democratic ideals. Chapters on principles, definitions,

[66] Unfamiliar with the emerging focus on instructional improvement, the teachers did not understand well the survey question on the evaluation of the supervisor in the study done by Ernest Melby, as reported in the *Second Yearbook.* Since they obviously thought that the supervisor was not supposed to help them but to judge them, they were startled and confused by the idea that they should judge him on the help he had given them. Some of the original leadership in the Department of Supervisors phrased it well, fifteen years later, when they said that everyone had had to get used to the idea that "the improvement of teachers is not so much a supervisory function in which teachers participate as it is a teacher function in which supervisors cooperate." A. S. Barr, W. H. Burton, and L. J. Brueckner, *Supervision,* (2nd ed., New York: Appleton-Century Crofts, Inc., 1947), p. 10.

[67] Some within the Department of Supervisors and Directors of Instruction resisted broadening the scope of the Department to include those curriculum theorists who were not directly supervising instruction.

[68] That year Caswell was nominated to the Executive Committee of the Society for Curriculum Study. Doak Campbell lent the weight of his professional reputation to the volume by appearing as coauthor, but Caswell made it clear that the work was largely his, and it will be so treated in this study. Something similar occurred in the preparation of *Readings in Curriculum Development.*

and aims, gave a reasoned and scholarly exposition of the nature and sources of each. The curriculum design of scope and sequence was described, followed by a close analytical discussion of pupil purposes, activities, subject matter, teaching procedures, and evaluation, all considered as elements in the curriculum. The book closed with a thorough, well-organized presentation of the nature of a program of curriculum development as undertaken by a school wishing to improve its own curriculum.

It was a new kind of book in curriculum. More than a handbook, it was an attempt to structure a complete field of study, erecting a conceptual framework and fitting into it in a coherent way almost everything in curriculum making which had gone before.[69] As we have already noticed in examining the statewide curriculum programs, the key to the structure lay in the concept of experience. After reminding the reader that by 1935 the curriculum had come generally to mean "the experiences in which pupils are expected to engage in school, and the general order of sequence in which these experiences are to come,"[70] Caswell went on to warn that the curriculum was more than the experiences which were made available to the child. The curriculum consisted rather of the experiences the child actually underwent:

Experience is a process; it is the living through of actual situations. The process of living through situations involves the reaction of a variety of elements. The presence of these elements in different proportions and relationships determines the type and strength of the reaction or experience. It is possible through analysis to determine what these elements are and to examine evidences of each, but when they come into relationship and reaction takes place it becomes impossible to distinguish clearly one from the other, or to discover in the outcome the characteristics of the elements involved. The observable characteristics of the situation are a process and an outcome, different in character from any of the elements in the process. Thus, the process of experiencing results in changes in

[69] Since it did not espouse an extreme position of any kind, as some felt that curriculum books should do in those confused times, it was considered by a few to be too encyclopedic. A reviewer commented that it would be useful in classes as a source book, but that it lacked an integrated point of view "which he knew the authors had." He had missed the point, or perhaps he got it without realizing it. The book was not a polemic but a text. W. Featherstone, "Review of *Curriculum Development*," *Curriculum Journal*, VI (Nov., 1935), pp. 29–30.

[70] Quoted from Frederick G. Bonser, *The Elementary School Curriculum* (New York: The Macmillan Co., 1920), p. 1. Caswell's own definition reads, "The curriculum is held to be composed of all the experiences children have under the guidance of teachers." Hollis L. Caswell and Doak S. Campbell, *Curriculum Development* (New York: American Book Co., 1935), p. 69.

an individual which are unities different from any of the elements which went to make up the experience.[71]

Thus a curriculum which is, in essence, the learner's experience as it is actually going on in school is a living process of interaction of the elements of that experience. The development of this curriculum occurs when the teacher guides the process by bringing all these varied elements in the learner's experience into desired relationships. This means that the child always had a "curriculum," but his school curriculum should be normative. The teacher is the chief curriculum maker, but in a certain sense anyone is a curriculum maker who contributes to the child's curriculum, i.e. to his interacting "experience." The janitor who scolds the child for accidentally breaking a milk bottle, the superintendent who decides that the budget does not permit modelling clay for the first grade, the parent who attacks the schools for teaching communism, are all contributing to the curriculum.

Curriculum development then is continuous since it is built right into the instructional process. However, intensive curriculum programs (like the one in Virginia) may be instituted at any time to serve as starting points for curriculum improvement. Such programs must be organized so that the wide variety of people who affect the curriculum realize their responsibilities and opportunities. Desirably, curriculum programs should pass from an intensive phase to a continuous one.

Aware that he was writing a fundamental book in a new field, Caswell tried also to conceptualize the field itself. After stressing that curriculum development can best take place when the teacher is assisted by an orderly program, he went on to say:

> This is the task of curriculum development. It can be accomplished only through assistance from many workers and many fields of study. Philosophy, sociology, psychology, and the subject matter fields must all be called upon for help. The materials from these fields, however, cannot be employed by an additive method. Each field contributes its share of materials—raw materials for curriculum making—but mere compilation by no means represents the process of curriculum development. Materials must be so selected and arranged as to become a unity in the experience of the learner. The process is one of synthesis rather than compilation. In providing for this synthesis lies the peculiar task of curriculum development. This task is in clear contrast to the work in most fields of study where the major emphasis is given to organization or development of materials within particular cultural limitations. Thus, curriculum consid-

---

[71] Hollis L. Caswell and Doak S. Campbell, *Curriculum Development* (New York: American Book Co., 1935), p. 81.

ered as a field of study represents no strictly limited body of content, but rather a process or procedure.[72]

This comment suggests that Caswell expected the curriculum maker to know more content from a wider variety of fields than most. He also expected from him "knowledge" of the process of curriculum development in the sense of "experience" with it. The body of content of the new field of study, as Caswell defined it, would consist of: (1) a recognition of the relevance of content from many fields to the curriculum process; (2) knowledge about the process, such as its definition, description, analysis, and elaboration; and (3) actual experience with the process in action.

The nature of this process of curriculum development, representing as it does a new field of study, deserves some extended attention. The legitimate descendent of Bobbitt's method, it appears to be a moving thing which comes alive and proceeds only as a variety of people participate in it and make it move. It assumes a slightly different face for each participant, but the unitary nature of the whole process demands the cohesive and interrelated participation of each member. All must do their part, or the whole enterprise will fail. Participation is the key word with which to describe the process. The emphasis on participation alone might imply, however, that the task is a standardized one, bits of which may be parcelled out to various participants. Each one would then master his particular part of the general technique or process. This is not at all what Caswell means. He makes it clear that he conceives of the curriculum process as essentially a matter of judgment rather than of technique. The elements of the curriculum process are experiential, and a major characteristic of human experience is human purpose and human control. Continuous judgment is required to keep this experience going in the direction toward which the curriculum process is fixed, i.e. the democratic ideal. Thus, no specific techniques can be formulated nor any fixed plan of action proposed, although standards of quality can be freely applied. Such terms as "evolving," "reconstruction," "development," and others are Caswell's explicit recognition of the experiential quality of the process of curriculum development.

His conception is more analogous to the attempt a person makes to keep in balance a scale which is continually being added to or taken

---

[72] Hollis L. Caswell and Doak S. Campbell, *Curriculum Development* (New York: American Book Co., 1935), pp. 69–70.

from. This process requires continuous judgment, action following judgment, and rejudgment as the result of action—all intended to keep matters in harmony with the original end in view. The weigher, as the result of experiences in the process of weighing, would become gradually more expert at making judgments and more identified with the success of the attempt. He might slowly develop some guides to action peculiarly appropriate to his scales and the kinds of objects he is weighing. His rules, however, would be helpful to other weighers only in a very general fashion since scales, objects, and weighers vary. This analogy is admittedly quite limited, but it has some usefulness.

We might say then that the curriculum process, as described by Caswell, requires the continuous judgment of the participant in relation to the end in view and that this judgment is continually improved through the participation in the process itself.

Five aspects of this process may be distinguished. They are not discrete, but we may examine them as though they were: They are: (1) the curriculum—a learner's process; (2) curriculum development—a curriculum worker's process; (3) curriculum improvement—a curriculum worker's process; (4) participation in curriculum programs—the widest possible participation in this process; and (5) control of conduct—a learner's process.

The curriculum—a learner's process. Experience, which is a process in itself, is the curriculum process in its most basic and meaningful form. It is a selective process in terms of a goal or value. That is, the curriculum process consists of the learner's experience, but not all the learner's experience is the curriculum process. Only that part of his experience which is guided by teachers comprises the curriculum process.

Curriculum development—a curriculum worker's process. The curriculum process described above is brought about by a process of organization and coordination of the elements of that experience. This organizing process is called curriculum development. When an "orderly program is provided to assist the teachers in bringing [all] these varied elements [in the experience of the learner] into suitable relationships,"[73] then curriculum development occurs. Such an orderly program will not just happen but must be planned for and carried out by curriculum workers. Although teachers are curriculum workers, yet there are

---

[73] Hollis L. Caswell and Doak S. Campbell, *Curriculum Development* (New York: American Book Co., 1935), p. 69.

curriculum workers who do not teach. All together bring about the process of curriculum development.

Curriculum improvement—a curriculum worker's process. Curriculum improvement, another process, is useful in the process of curriculum development and is, in fact, gained by participation in it. Curriculum improvement is the process of acquiring an evolving "know-how" or technique of curriculum development. The immediate sources of this "know-how" are the "general experience of teachers and . . . technical studies by specialists in various fields."[74] When teachers and other curriculum workers try out new materials as they work in curriculum programs, their experiences are an especially valuable source of techniques of curriculum development. The repository of this technique is the person involved, that is the curriculum worker, as he becomes increasingly proficient at curriculum development.

Participation in curriculum programs—the widest possible participation in this process. As we have seen, a curriculum program means the evolving plan or design which organizes all the elements of the learner's experience. Part of this program includes the administrative organization which coordinates the relationships of all the individuals who in some way affect the curriculum process. This organization, or curriculum program, structures the interrelationships of the people and their activities within a school system which is working, as a unit, to develop and improve the curriculum. The list of participants includes: (1) the initiator—usually the superintendent; (2) curriculum specialists who know the content of curriculum as a field of study; (3) the curriculum director who "directs the orderly program which assists the teacher" and which results in curriculum development; he also directs the administrative organization, or curriculum program, by providing for the development of relationships between supervisor, administrator, teacher, child, and public; (4) teachers; (5) children; and (6) lay public. Participation in this curriculum program, which is the planned coordination of many efforts, is a process which (it is assumed) works a change in the character and personalities of the participants. These programs may have an intensive phase when they are first initiated, followed by a continuing phase later.

Control of conduct—a learner's process. As we have seen, the curriculum process consists of all the learner's experience which is guided

---

[74] Hollis L. Caswell and Doak S. Campbell, *Curriculum Development* (New York: American Book Co., 1935), p. 76.

by the teacher. Experience implies not only what is happening to the learner but also what he purposes. His conduct, under the teacher's guidance, is seen to be increasingly subject to his own control as he is helped to choose and act appropriately in real situations in social life. As he continues on into adult life to control his conduct in the direction of the democratic ideal, he is helping to mold the social order. This control of conduct is that aspect of the curriculum process by which the whole process itself is finally evaluated. As Caswell himself commented:

> Integrations of habits and knowledge which represents desired types of conduct can be developed only by guiding the child in situations which require such conduct . . . there is only one way to learn to be honest, and that is to be honest . . . having secured one [act that exemplifies the desired type of conduct] the chances are slightly better than before that situations requiring the same type of conduct will be met as desired . . . more and more habits and knowledge become a part of the control of conduct and the chances increase that in all new situations he will exhibit the desired trait."[75]

Caswell fits the traditional concepts of curriculum and method into this framework by regarding them as elements of the process. In and of themselves, they do not constitute the curriculum since the essence of the curriculum is an ongoing interrelationship of parts. Every bit of the educational endeavor becomes grist to the mill. The curriculum worker must become an expert at relationships. He must "know" the process of curriculum development in an operational sense, having learned it in the same way as he believes the learning process should function for children. He must have undergone personality modification as he made increasingly better and more informed choices in day-by-day situations.

The Changing Curriculum

By 1936, Caswell was Chairman of the Executive Committee of the Society for Curriculum Study, and Rudolph D. Lindquist, another active Society member, was President of the Department of Supervisors and Directors of Instruction. The time seemed propitious for a rapprochement between the organizations, and, at the instigation of their leaders, the proposal was made that each group appoint members to a joint committee to make a report on the real changes in the curriculum field

---

[75] Hollis L. Caswell and Doak S. Campbell, *Curriculum Development* (New York: American Book Co., 1935), pp. 378–79.

167

that had occurred in the thirties. The committee met[76] and made a rather "safe" outline, obviously anticipating some communication problems. But the expected difficulties did not materialize. At the second meeting, rapport was such that the Committee discarded its first plans and proceeded to construct an outline for a real progress report. When it came out in 1937, called *The Changing Curriculum*, it constituted another landmark book like the *Twenty-sixth Yearbook*.[77] As they worked with the curriculum specialists, the supervisors began to recognize in the new curriculum concept of instructional improvement a clarification of the role of the supervisor.[78]

Like the committee that worked on the *Twenty-sixth Yearbook*, this group also began with a survey, a sound procedure in a matter as mutable as the curriculum. They found evidence of a. fresh wave of curriculum development programs, seven-tenths of which had been initiated since 1932. A quarter of the school systems said they had curriculum directors, most of whose offices had been created since 1931. Statewide curriculum programs were reported underway in thirty-two states.[79]

This group was not satisfied with measures of quantity but sought evidences of quality of content in the programs as well. One of the committee members offered a list of recent trends in curriculum practices which she had gleaned from an analysis of educational magazines, curriculum yearbooks, and recent professional books.[80] These were rephrased as descriptive statements of points of view, and schoolmen were asked to tell to what extent each item represented the beliefs of their school. Analysis of the answers showed strong leanings toward

[76] Committee members were: Edith Bader, Orville Brim, Prudence Cutright, Will French, Harold Hand, Charles Knudsen, Ernest Melby, Paul Rankin, Laura Zirbes, and Henry Harap, Chairman.

[77] A sense of historic continuity led one of the authors to nominate the *First Yearbook of the National Herbart Society* in 1895 as the first, the *Twenty-sixth Yearbook of the National Society* as the second, and their own report as the third of the landmark books on the curriculum during the previous forty years. Society for Curriculum Study, *The Changing Curriculum*, ed. Henry Harap (New York: Appleton-Century, 1937), pp. 55–56.

[78] The success of this joint effort was one of the factors which contributed to the eventual merger in 1942 of the Society for Curriculum Study with the Department of Supervisors and Directors of Instruction to form the Department of Supervision and Curriculum Development (known today as the Association for Supervision and Curriculum Development).

[79] Society for Curriculum Study, *The Changing Curriculum*, ed. Henry Harap (New York: Appleton-Century, 1937), pp. 1–3.

[80] Laura Zirbes, *Curriculum Trends: A Preliminary Report and a Challenge* (Washington, D. C.: Association for Childhood Education, 1935).

several characteristics of the new field. Many thought that the curriculum should educate for the reconstruction of American life through the democratic process; that learning is active, self-directive, and creative; that the teacher is the key person in curriculum development; and that a wider scope of needs, interests, and purposes should be included in the curriculum.[81]

A chapter tracing the historical development of curriculum organization devoted particular attention to the work of Caswell on scope and sequence and characterized it as a "sharp break with curriculum development" as it had been traditionally conceived.[82] Its author found enough other scope and sequence patterns that had been developed since the one in Virginia to enable him to compare them critically.

In addition, the report contained descriptions and critical analyses of state, county, and city curriculum development programs, including a discussion of teacher education. There were chapters on administrative organization, planning, learning units, and evaluation of programs.

In conclusion, the editor, Henry Harap, touched on Rugg's concern of a decade before by saying:

> In the past the school has kept itself aloof from social realities. When the rate of social change could be measured in generations, the failure of the school to adjust itself was not noticeable. Today, the rapidity of change demands that the school shall keep in close touch with contemporary social processes. Democracy requires that the school shall help to discover how to re-establish that equality of opportunity which is the dream of a free nation.[83]

To this observation he added a challenge, not as much to the curriculum specialist as to that newly important person in curriculum making—the teacher:

> The emerging school challenges the teacher to become a scholar in a broader and deeper sense than heretofore. It is not enough to be at home in one branch of knowledge or on one level of education. The learning enterprises in the curriculum lead into many byways of experience, knowledge, and skill unknown to the conventional school. They call for a teacher who has the resourcefulness and power and courage to pursue the unpredictable lines of inquiry of a new learning enterprise.

[81] *The Changing Curriculum,* ed. Henry Harap (New York: Appleton-Century, 1937), pp. 5–17.

[82] *The Changing Curriculum,* ed. Henry Harap (New York: Appleton-Century, 1937), p. 92.

[83] *The Changing Curriculum,* ed. Henry Harap (New York: Appleton-Century, 1937), p. 339.

The teacher of tomorrow will be essentially an experimenter with an inquiring mind and a growing attitude. He will conceive of life as a continually developing process to which he and his pupils may make an easy adjustment. He will follow the facts wherever they may lead and transmit something of his enthusiasm for truth to all those who work with him.[84]

If the above sounds like a heavy program for average teachers, Caswell tried to make it lighter for them. Caswell was so convinced of the value of the initial study phase of the curriculum programs that he began to turn the really impressive bibliography he had collected into a book of readings. He hoped that, by placing side by side the strongest arguments he could find for various positions underlying curriculum decisions, he might stimulate and even force teachers to examine their views and think through their judgments. *Readings in Curriculum Development,* when it came out in 1937, became a standard reference work for students of the curriculum, and it served to strengthen the growing emphasis on the foundations of the curriculum.

APPOINTMENT TO TEACHERS COLLEGE

In 1938, Dean Russell of Teachers College, Columbia University, announced a comprehensive reorganization plan which had been some time in preparation. We are interested in it because it furnished a final proof of the coming-of-age in education of the field of curriculum. The departments had formerly been organized to represent the different school levels, from primary to college. There had also been departments of supervision and curriculum, whose course offerings were scattered out among many of the other departments. As we have seen, the comprehensive nature of the new curriculum field had begun to cut across area and level lines such as these, causing them to appear obsolete. Supervisors were now considered to have a curriculum role to play, and teachers had become the chief curriculum makers on any level. Even special methods in subject matter areas were being judged on the basis of their effect on the total curriculum.

The reorganization abolished these area and level departments and divided professors, courses, and students on the one hand into the Department of Educational Administration for those preparing for administrative posts, and on the other into the Department of Cur-

[84] *The Changing Curriculum,* ed. Henry Harap (New York: Appleton-Century, 1937), pp. 338–39.

riculum and Teaching for those preparing for supervisory posts.[85] It was more than coincidence that Jesse Newlon, Chairman of the Division of Instruction within which the major reshuffling took place, had been active for years in curriculum development. In his annual report as Chairman of Instruction, Newlon in discussing the coming changes explained:

> In all this Teachers College has a twofold responsibility—the responsibility of leadership in bringing about desired changes in the curriculum, and the responsibility of reconstructing its own curriculum for the professional education of teachers for the new school.[86]

Caswell, who had been brought from Peabody the year before specifically to organize the new Department of Curriculum and Teaching, became its official head at the time of the reorganization in 1938.[87]

AN ASSESSMENT

Meeting Dewey's challenges

Of Dewey's four challenges, Caswell seems to have met best the second one, in which Dewey suggested the need for a reordering of the curriculum organization so that knowledge would be acquired by the child as he satisfied his individual and social purpose. As we have seen, Caswell's curriculum pattern of scope and sequence was a creative attempt to locate within a framework three basic elements of the curriculum—children's interests, social functions, and organized knowledge.

The great importance given to the social functions in this design suggests that they might prove to be the principal basis for the organization of knowledge in the curriculum. Caswell hoped that a checklist of the major concepts drawn from the bodies of organized knowledge

[85] William F. Russell, *Report of the Dean for the Academic Year Ending June 30, 1938*, Teachers College, Columbia University, p. 7. This move was a confirmation of the position Sidney Hall and Caswell had taken years before in Virginia on the need to coordinate administratively all efforts at instructional improvement. The departments in the teaching of the different subjects did maintain a segmentation of the curriculum. However, some measure of coordination was sought. These departments involved too many faculty, about seventy-five, to have had them all in one department.

[86] *Report of the Dean, for the Academic Year Ending June 30, 1936*, Teachers College, Columbia University, p. 43.

[87] Caswell became Head of the Division of Instruction also, relieving Newlon who had been Chairman of both Instruction and Foundations.

would provide the direction in which the child's maturing grasp of functional knowledge would move. Although events were to prove whether this hope was justified, Caswell must be credited with having given serious attention to Dewey's second challenge, to make the organization of knowledge adequate to the carrying out of human purposes.

Although Caswell did not make any special contribution toward Dewey's third challenge, to shape a kind of school organization which would permit the child's growth to be continuous, his curriculum concept did make the search for such an organization seem logical. At least, Caswell called attention to the importance of the child's actual experience and encouraged educators to think of ways of improving this experience.

By the late thirties, the teacher had become indispensable to curriculum making. This development was a reversal of the position of the teacher in the institutional hierarchy of Dewey's day. Although Caswell alone had not brought this change about, his work dramatized the change on a statewide scale and left the way open for a better implementation of the teacher's role in the next decade.

Caswell's contribution

To begin, Caswell helped lead the trend to give curriculum making departmental status in colleges preparing teachers, supervisors, and curriculum directors. This move gave a needed continuity to the new professional activity, curriculum making, by assuring that a systematic preparation of the specialist would replace the current rather haphazard pattern of studies. Departmental status also served to enhance the visibility of curriculum as a field of study, although the presence of technicians working in the schools and the large body of literature on the curriculum had already helped to call professional attention to curriculum making. In addition, administrative recognition gave more assurance that knowledge about curriculum making would be systematically gathered, increased, and disseminated. Strategically, the administrative change was a good one.

In the second place, Caswell developed further the idea of method in curriculum making. He took two notions, one already advanced by Bobbitt, and the other by Rugg, worked them together and subtly transformed them.

The first notion Caswell used, with a significant change, was like Bobbitt's metaphor of the ideal man as the finished product of a process of refinement called education. The activities of Caswell's ideal man were "democratic," a term not yet in Bobbitt's vocabulary. For Caswell, the democratic man was by definition primarily less an individual than a social and political entity. The events of the thirties, domestic and foreign, foreseen by Rugg in his concept of social lag, had served to make social reconstruction stand out sharply for Caswell as the need of the times. Democratic man's chief contribution, he felt, was to bring about such social reconstruction. Thus, Caswell found most interesting those activities in Bobbitt's list by which the ideal man helped correct society's evident ills.

The second notion Caswell used resembled Rugg's idea that the key concepts most helpful in the solution of social problems should be identified. However, Caswell, unlike Rugg, was not content merely to foment sharp and critical thought about social ills. Aware that thought was no guarantee of action, Caswell tried to prepare the child for the social action needed to redress these ills. He surmised that social evils were probably the result of disorders of the social functions. If the key ideas were woven right into the child's performance of the social functions from the very beginning, he felt that the future citizen would be better able to use knowledge to control conduct.

Caswell's attempt to forge a method of curriculum making which would be responsive to current social needs may have been naïve. Knowledge organized around the normal exercise of social functions, and around the correction of these functions when they go wrong, is by nature static. It does not provide for either the creation of new knowledge or the appearance of new problems, both of which result, as a rule, only when the knower is enabled somehow to step in an intellectual and attitudinal way outside of the given problems and solutions. Dewey's notion of the progressive reorganization of subject matter[88] did contain this dynamic element. In Dewey's approach to content by way of purpose, whether child or adult, the solution of problems was not an end in itself but rather a challenge to identify emerging purposes and problems. The content distilled from this entire process was to be progressively organized so as to serve the newly emerging purposes and problems. Such knowledge is both critical and creative and is quite different from that knowledge which serves correctional and restorative ends, as implied in Caswell's approach. But whatever the success of Caswell's attempt to make knowledge func-

[88] Arno Bellack should be credited with calling the profession's attention recently to the crucial importance of this much neglected concept of John Dewey's.

tional, he did give fresh attention to the need to develop and improve the method of curriculum formulation.

In the third place, Caswell focused attention on the process by which the wide variety of individuals interact in order to make the curriculum. Using the statewide curriculum programs as laboratories in which to study the method of curriculum making in operation, Caswell became realistic about the gap between theory and practice. Guessing that the social and intellectual interaction of the human beings involved in making the curriculum was a key factor, he devised a technical approach to curriculum making that would focus attention on this interaction. He dramatized this approach by ruling out all views of the curriculum except that of the actual experiences undergone by the learner, as directed by the school. This definition gave importance to all the human beings who directly or indirectly affect this guided experience. To insure that they would not be in ignorance of their influence and unwittingly affect the curriculum unwisely, he devised a decision-making technique in curriculum involving all these people. He theorized that all would become more conscious of the complexity of the process, and more involved in its success, as they made a greater number of decisions that were increasingly important in their effect.

Although Caswell probably did not originate the idea but rather gave it currency, it was a brilliant and timely contribution. As a programmatic definition,[89] it took attention away from the course of study and put it on the children in a compelling way. It served to bring the curriculum maker up against the sharp reality of the child's actual interaction with knowledge, a favorite focus of the McMurrys and Dewey. It made the curriculum maker aware of the influence on this interaction of many factors hitherto disregarded, not the least of which was the role of the teacher. The definition proved, however, to be more useful in pointing out where to look than in explaining what to see. Such a focus was valuable to many, but to some the notion that the curriculum was the experience undergone by the learner proved to be a mystical one. Its components were still stubbornly resistant to isolation, observation, and study. The curriculum maker was forced inevitably back on the earlier inquiries, still unsettled, concerning the role of the apperceptive mass, or problem solving, or some other entity. He also had to decide whether what he found in the child's experience

---

[89] See for this concept Israel Scheffler, *The Language of Education* (Springfield, Ill.: C. C. Thomas, 1960), pp. 19–30.

was socially desirable, a problem which was yet to be dealt with satisfactorily.

Attention to process also raised questions about the teacher's new role. Caswell's notion of teacher involvement in an interactive process was not quite the same as the older idea, advanced by Bobbitt, that the teacher should carry out instructions laid down by a controlling science. Teacher involvement often leads to truly creative teacher behavior and is a standing challenge to the notion of a controlling science. Otherwise teacher involvement easily becomes a token operation, and the teacher is urged to become "involved" only in order to increase his loyalty, not in order to conduct an exhilarating search for fresh insights. Yet the new definition did serve to restore all these problems to an important place and to reinterpret them in terms of the process of human interaction.

Finally, Caswell provided the profession with a valuable and wide-scale tryout of a curriculum design which would guide the teacher who was trying to take concepts from the fields of organized knowledge and make them available as resources in the solution of social problems. Caswell's realism about the teacher struggling with the realities of teaching is reminiscent of the concern of the Herbartians. However inadequate the design, it was a specific proposal, and its trial would reveal strengths and weaknesses on which to build.

7   Summary

THE PROBLEM

The purpose of this study is to explore some aspects of those changes in thought about the curriculum from 1895 to 1937 which contributed to the establishment of the curriculum as a specialized field of study. At particular times during these years, the thinking of certain educators was judged to be particularly influential on the rest. From this group of leaders, seven figures were selected, each of whom could be said to have affected the thinking of his contemporaries about the curriculum. Each one's writings during his influential period were examined to discover: (1) how he perceived the educational situation, and why he became interested and involved in the study of the curriculum; (2) what proposals he made about the curriculum; and (3) how relevant to the educational situation his proposals proved to be. It was hoped that a study of the changing emphases of these selected thinkers would cast some light on the outlines of emerging thought about curriculum making. A brief summary of the major proposals of each figure follows.

In the opinion of Charles and Frank McMurry, who helped found the Herbart Society, the content of the elementary school program, as taught in 1895, showed itself to have been collected haphazardly. In response to a variety of pressures, subjects had been added, and new methods had been tried, until the curriculum had become overcrowded and disjointed. A more methodical approach was sought by the Mc-Murrys, who had studied the pedagogy of Johann Herbart as developed and adapted to the elementary school by German educators. Herbartian theory outlined a systematic way to select and organize content and promised to give needed order and system to the curriculum. Although pure Herbartianism was never a success in the United States, the

McMurrys and others succeeded in focusing the profession's attention on the method by which instructional content is selected and organized.

The study of Herbartian ideas by the profession coincided with the initial development and spread of the educational theories of John Dewey. His pedagogy was based on an experimental theory of knowing and an instrumental theory of knowledge, both basically contradictory to the metaphysics and psychology underlying Herbartian pedagogy. The vigorous clash of doctrine which ensued resulted in two legacies to the profession: (1) an awareness of the need to use method in selecting and organizing content; and (2) a vision of the nature and purpose of a democratic school which would give direction to the concern for method. Dewey's challenge to the profession to make this vision a reality may be thought of as setting educators four major tasks: (1) to rework the organization of knowledge to accommodate cultural change; (2) to reform the basic curriculum organization to fit new views of knowledge and value; (3) to develop school programs and schedules harmonious with American educational purposes; and (4) to shape a staff organization appropriate to a democratic school.

During the first decade of this century, elements of a more systematic approach to the curriculum and an enlarged vision of the potentialities of the school may be seen in the growing demand that schooling be more effective in bringing about a gradual improvement in the general cultural level. The new experts at educational measurement undertook to meet this demand by streamlining the curriculum, eliminating content which was socially useless. This piecemeal approach was replaced shortly by a more methodical one suggested by Franklin Bobbitt in 1913. Working from an analogy with industrial processes, Bobbitt proposed a way to formulate the curriculum so that the student would develop both the ability to live and the ability to produce in the modern world. Bobbitt and W. W. Charters, another theorist, contended that an analysis of the desirable activities of the mature adult would disclose the nature of the experiences the child should have in order to become that adult. Although their method of curriculum making was challenged by other methods, they succeeded in establishing the basic importance of a method of curriculum making.

During the twenties, the method of curriculum making was tested on a wide enough front so that important relevant elements were considered, ranging from the nature of the child to the needs of society. Harold Rugg explored the usefulness of the method in reconciling apparent contradictions between basic elements. Recalling the need for a psychological and philosophical framework for the curriculum as urged earlier by Dewey and the Herbartians, Rugg proposed that sociology and aesthetics be added to the list. Rugg actively promoted efforts leading to a synthesis of thought about curriculum making.

Using statewide curriculum programs as laboratories for the study of curriculum making, Hollis Caswell sought during the thirties for a theoretical framework for the curriculum which would harmonize children's interests, social functions, and organized knowledge. He found it in the concept of curriculum making as a process, in which all the relevant elements are contained. He suggested that the process of curriculum making wore a different aspect for each participant, ranging from the child whose curriculum is composed of the experiences he undergoes under the guidance of the school, to the curriculum director whose major responsibility is the coordination of the forces which affect the child's curriculum. Caswell theorized that the mastery of such a process would depend on experience with it as well as specialized knowledge relevant to it. His formulation of the curriculum process as a dynamic one whose elements should be in a state of creative balance was useful to the increasing variety of people involved in curriculum making. Caswell helped lead the trend to give curriculum making administrative recognition as a field of study on the college level.

CONCLUSION

Throughout any chronicle such as this one, of a series of changing emphases, run certain connections between the episodes, which give a sense of continuity to the whole. One of the most tempting of these connections is that of cause and effect. It is possible, for example, to find considerable evidence to support the view that each one of our educators successively took up the task of curriculum making where the previous one left off. If the McMurrys can be credited with having alerted the profession to the need for method in selecting and organizing content, then Dewey's vision of a democratic school can be seen as supplying precisely the direction that the Herbartians lacked. Bobbitt and Charters can then be viewed as having contributed to the earlier search for method when they formulated theirs. Rugg, then, appears as the prophet, pointing out the value limitations of mere method, and Caswell can be credited with trying to make the method more operational. Doubtless, elements of truth inhere in such a cause-and-effect

179

interpretation. Doubtless also, such an explanation is, at base, too simple. Certainly there is much evidence that suggests that each man, if asked, might have judged his own contributions in quite a different manner than the hindsight with which the writer of this paper has viewed them. For these leaders did not know that they were helping to shape a field; they were busy on a number of different concerns, and often they intended their contribution to be used for quite another purpose than the one to which subsequent events have assigned it. Although a good plot can be found for the events of the period, such a story probably leaves out much more of interest than it includes.

Quite another kind of connection between events is given by several persistent interests which run like threads throughout the whole period. These interests appear often as agreements or unsolved problems, rarely as issues. Although there are a number of them, four should be mentioned which seem to have been especially persistent and significant.

The first interest, the nature of knowledge, is a philosophical one, rarely recognized in so many words, but permeating the consideration of even the most trivial curriculum problem. As we have seen, the American Herbartians assumed knowledge to be essentially immutable and eternal, structured as it was by universal ideals. They thought of knowledge as stable, waiting to be perceived by human beings. Bobbitt and Charters shared the Herbartian's view of knowledge as stable, although they sought for this knowledge in the good life as lived in their own time, rather than within a universal framework of ideals. They gave universality to knowledge by relying on human consensus. The greatest good for the greatest number was their touchstone of truth.

Dewey, on the other hand, viewed knowledge as essentially dynamic, since it was basically instrumental to man's purpose. Dewey agreed on the large degree of commonality in individual and social goals. He did not stop there, however, but instead took into deliberate account the role of the novel and unpredictable in human experience, both as found in the environment and within the human psyche. As a result, he viewed knowledge as continually evolving.[1]

Rugg seems to have been ambivalent on this issue. He shared with Dewey the courage to "start thinking," but he showed a curious re-

[1] "Let us admit the case of the conservative," he commented years later in *Characters and Events: Popular Essays in Social and Political Philosophy*, I (New York: Henry Holt and Co., 1929), p. 1. "If we once start thinking no one can guarantee what will be the outcome, except that many objects, ends, and institutions will be surely doomed. Every thinker puts some portion of an apparently stable world in peril, and no one can wholly predict what will emerge in its place."

luctance to abandon his own creative thoughts once clarified, and seems to have been convinced that his own thoughts would be the best thoughts for other men. He appears to have had confidence only in the dynamic nature of his own knowledge. Caswell alone, in his preoccupation with the curriculum process and the concept of curriculum as experience, was able to take a position on the nature of knowledge that was almost completely laissez faire.

The second interest, the nature of knowing, was also philosophical. In a variety of ways, all shared the notion developed by the Herbartians that knowing was essentially an active process. The Herbartians had first challenged an earlier assumption that knowing was passive, by viewing the mind as an active entity creating its own knowledge. They also assumed that knowledge would direct conduct. Given their mixture of a dynamic view of knowing and a static view of knowledge, we are not surprised to find their pedagogy psychologically dynamic and sociologically static. They capitalized on the active nature of the child's mind in order to get him to learn certain given knowledge and thus to behave in a certain way. In the same vein, Bobbitt and Charters exploited the child's perception of social utility as a means of acquiring knowledge. Rugg relied more on the aesthetic and emotional aspects of the psyche to furnish the motive power. Because of the nature of Caswell's central concerns, the problem of the nature of knowing was no more pertinent to them than the question of the nature of knowledge had been. Dewey alone, although he shared the others' view of knowing as active, believed in the dynamic nature of knowledge. This conviction led him to trust experimentation as a way of arriving at truth. As a result, his pedagogy was in the true sense both psychologically and sociologically dynamic.

A third interest, that of the limits of each newly emerging specialization, was a political one. During the period in which the Herbartians and Dewey were most active, pedagogy was still a unified area of competence. By the time Bobbitt and Charters had begun to be influential, several new specializations were beginning to compete with each other for influence on instructional improvement. Educational administrators exploited school surveys; educational psychologists turned to account the new measurement techniques; supervisors in the various subject fields improved the textbooks; and free-lance teachers developed creative schools which were a standing challenge to existing practice. It is interesting to speculate why, by the late thirties, this initiative for instructional improvement had passed clearly and irrevocably to quite a different group from any of the above—namely, the curriculum specialists. It is possible that they were more thoroughgoing in their approach to the problem, unencumbered as they were with other concerns such as administration or measurement. It is also possible that the momentum of the American trend, begun a century before, to make schooling really matter in the cultural growth of the nation bore the question of what to teach to the forefront of everyone's attention and compelled educators to put extensive and serious attention on the problem of the widest possible dissemination of new knowledge and value.[2] Perhaps it was felt that a new group would have a fresher and less stereotyped approach to what was essentially a new problem—the creative blend of new kinds of content with the traditional, in the education of all kinds of learners.

A fourth interest, that of "giving common efficacy to the experiences of genius," (a phrase of Dewey's) was primarily a technological one. It was invincibly American both to value novelty and spontaneity and immediately try to give it technical form so that it could be mass produced and distributed. One of the real enigmas of this period is the failure of Colonel Parker's undeniable pedagogical genius to exert a greater influence on practice than it did. Possibly an aesthetic approach to his inspired teaching would have been better than a technological one. Perhaps literary accounts would have been preferable to the attempt to routinize his experience according to Herbartianism and make it available for teacher training. Maybe all those whom Rugg later called artist-teachers suffered this same fate. Certainly the prevailing tendency of the whole period was to analyze and routinize fresh insights about the curriculum. Possibly neither the creative approach nor the technological one needed to dominate, but both could have coexisted harmoniously and fruitfully.

This study has discussed some of the steps by which the concept

---

[2] The revolutionary effect of changes in content was noted by Thomas H. Briggs when he said, "Although the importance of the curriculum has always been recognized, it is only at long intervals that material changes are made in it. One would not go far wrong in asserting that the history of education is written in terms of these changes in subject matter." *Curriculum Problems* (New York: Macmillan Co., 1926), p. 1. Caswell's surprise, apropos of chicken-culling in Bavaria in 1957, at the small extent to which education seemed to have affected the everyday living of the people there, reflects the American belief, perhaps naïve but typical, that education should make a difference in the quality of the smallest detail of daily life. See "Achievement and Challenge: a Century of American Education," *National Education Association Journal*, 46 (March, 1957), p. 142.

of the curriculum has changed in the last forty years from that of a static body of knowledge to that of a fluid interacting process, also steps by which the qualifications of the curriculum maker have changed from those of a generalist to those of a specialist. It is hoped that the insight which has been gained into the nature of these changes will be helpful to those who explore this development further.

The story of the establishment of the field of specialization of curriculum making ends in 1938, at a point which serves perhaps only to whet the reader's appetite all the more for what happened after that. In general, in the ensuing quarter of a century, there has been remarkably little basic change in the field. The forms with which it was established were securely constructed and continue to endure. The work of these shapers of the field seems in most respects still fresh and timely. Their special interests still persist, giving continuity to current thought on curriculum.

In fact, present thinkers, unhampered by the experiences of the shapers as they groped blindly toward a formulation that was still ahead of them, seem freed to undertake more sophisticated sorts of speculation about curriculum making. A case in point is the current interest in curriculum theory. The solid work done by the shapers of the curriculum making field has made it possible for current theorists to avoid some of the older dilemmas. For example, the Herbartians inherited a tradition in which the educational philosopher was the principal theorist. Clearly and persuasively he identified education with the search for the good life, yet a theory of instruction that might implement this search was not available. The teacher relied mainly on narrow, practical guides to action, or on his own inspiration of the moment. The fact that the techniques of instruction he used might be crucial to the very nature of the values he wished to develop was not yet made clear. The Herbartians initiated the search for a theory of instruction to replace the rule of thumb. But it was Bobbitt and those who followed him who first saw the need for a theoretical reconciliation between both values and instructional theory. Bobbitt and others realized that only when values are related to instruction does the theorist have a way of making a curriculum, and, unless he relates them, he may have a curriculum but no grasp of how to make another or even to improve the one he has. Bobbitt, relying on metaphor to help him grasp this theoretical relationship, drew an analogy between curriculum making and the industrial process. It is interesting to speculate to what extent Rugg's thought reflected a metaphorical view of the world as a great stage, or how much Caswell's imagination was fired by images of the processes of chemical interaction.

These early theorists sensed the need to visualize or theorize, if you will, about the relationship between values and the actual instructional process. Interestingly enough, the emphasis of such theorizing has seemed to oscillate, over-concentrated at one point in values, at another in instruction. A good clear statement of educational values would be met with the cry for attention to the means to carry them out. Technical attention would be given to instruction, and another theorist would show how sterile such attention really was. If the period is looked at as a whole, this shifting pattern of interest in either values or instruction, philosophies or techniques, becomes apparent. The positive note here is that the field of curriculum making, historically considered, offers precisely that formulation which, if developed, should steady these shifts and make it possible for the curriculum maker to realize the full potential of his field.

Bibliography

For the convenience of the reader, individual items within the categories of yearbooks and reports of national committees have been arranged according to the date of publication.

Alabama, State of, Department of Education. *Course of Study for Elementary Schools,* 1930.

Baker, Melvin C. *Foundations of John Dewey's Educational Theory.* New York: King's Crown Press, Columbia University, 1955.

Barr, Arvil S., Burton, W. H., and Brueckner, L. J. (eds.). *Supervision,* 2nd ed. New York: Appleton-Century-Crofts, Inc., 1947.

Bobbitt, Franklin. "A City School as a Community Art and Musical Center," *Elementary School Teacher,* XII (November, 1911), 119–26.

Bobbitt, Franklin. *The Curriculum.* Boston: Houghton Mifflin Co., 1918.

Bobbitt, Franklin. *Curriculum-Making in Los Angeles.* Chicago: The University of Chicago, 1922.

Bobbitt, Franklin. "Elimination of Waste in Education," *Elementary School Teacher,* XII (February, 1912), 259–71.

Bobbitt, Franklin. *How to Make a Curriculum.* Boston: Houghton Mifflin Co., 1924.

Bobbitt, Franklin. "The Supervision of City Schools," *Twelfth Yearbook of the National Society for the Study of Education,* Part I. Chicago: University of Chicago Press, 1913.

Bode, Boyd H. *Progressive Education at the Crossroads.* New York: Newson and Co., 1938.

Bonser, Frederick G. *The Elementary School Curriculum.* New York: The Macmillan Co., 1920.

Boston Public Schools. *Course of Study,* 1916.

Brett, George S. "History of Psychology," *Encyclopedia Britannica* (14th ed.), XVIII, 706–20.

Briggs, Thomas S. *Curriculum Problems.* New York: The Macmillan Co., 1926.

Brown, Elmer E. *The Making of Our Middle Schools.* New York: Longmans, Green and Co., 1902.

Bryson, Lyman. *The Next America: Prophecy and Faith.* New York: Harper, 1952.

Burris, William P. *The Public School System of Gary, Indiana.* United States Bureau of Education, Bulletin 1914, No. 18. Washington, D.C.: Government Printing Office, 1914.

Burton, William H. *Supervision and the Improvement of Teaching.* New York: D. Appleton and Co., 1922.

Butler, Nicholas M. *The Meaning of Education and Other Essays and Addresses.* New York: The Macmillan Co., 1898.

Callahan, Raymond E. *Education and the Cult of Efficiency.* Chicago: University of Chicago Press, 1962.

Caswell, Hollis L. "Achievement and Challenge: a Century of American Education," *National Education Association Journal,* XLVI (March, 1957), 139–43.

Caswell, Hollis. *City School Surveys: An Interpretation and Appraisal.* New York: Teachers College, Columbia University, Bureau of Publications, 1929.

Caswell, Hollis. *Curriculum Development.* New York: American Book Co., 1935.

Caswell, Hollis. *Readings in Curriculum Development.* New York: American Book Co., 1937.

Charters, Wallace W. *Curriculum Construction.* New York: The Macmillan Co., 1923.

Charters, Wallace W. *Methods of Teaching: Developed from a Functional Standpoint.* Chicago: Row, Peterson and Co., 1909.

Charters, Wallace W. *Teaching the Common Branches: A Textbook for Teachers of Rural and Graded Schools.* Boston: Houghton Mifflin Co., 1913.

Chicago Public Schools. *Course of Study,* 1904.

Counts, George S. *American Road to Culture: A Social Interpretation of Education in the United States.* New York: John Day Co., 1930.

Cremin, Lawrence A. *The Transformation of the School: Progressivism in American Education 1876–1957.* New York: Alfred A. Knopf, 1961.

DeGarmo, Charles. *Herbart and the Herbartians.* New York: Charles Scribner's Sons, 1895.

DeGarmo, Charles. "Most Pressing Problems Concerning the Elementary Course of Study," *First Yearbook of the National Herbart Society for the Scientific Study of Teaching.* Bloomington, Ill.: Pantagraph Printing and Stationery Co., 1895, 5.

DeGarmo, Charles. "The Principles upon Which the Co-ordination of Studies Should Proceed." *Journal of Proceedings and Addresses of the National Educational Association,* 1895, 88–89.

Dewey, Jane M. (ed.). "Biography of John Dewey," *The Philosophy of John Dewey.* Edited by Paul Arthur Schilpp. Evanston: Northwestern University, 1939.

Dewey, John. *Art as Experience.* New York: Minton, Balch and Co., 1934.

Dewey, John. *Characters and Events: Popular Essays in Social and Political Philosophy,* I. New York: Henry Holt and Co., 1929.

Dewey, John. *The Child and the Curriculum*. Chicago: The University of Chicago Press, 1902.

Dewey, John. "Democracy in Education," *Elementary School Teacher*, IV (Dec., 1903), 193–204.

Dewey, John. *Democracy and Education: An Introduction to the Philosophy of Education*. New York: The Macmillan Co., 1916.

Dewey, John. *The Educational Situation*. Chicago: The University of Chicago Press, 1902.

Dewey, John. "Ethical Principles Underlying Education," *Third Yearbook of the National Herbart Society for the Scientific Study of Teaching*. Chicago: The University of Chicago Press, 1897, 7–34.

Dewey, John. (ed.). *Elementary School Record*, I–IX. Chicago: The University of Chicago Press, 1900.

Dewey, John. "From Absolutism to Experimentalism," *Contemporary American Philosophy*. Edited by George P. Adams and William P. Montague. New York: The Macmillan Co., 1930, 13–30.

Dewey, John. "How Much Freedom in New Schools?" *New Republic*, LXIII (July 9, 1930), 204–06.

Dewey, John. *How We Think*. Boston: Houghton Mifflin Co., 1910.

Dewey, John. *Interest and Effort in Education*. Boston: Houghton Mifflin Co., 1913.

Dewey, John. "Interest as Related to Will," *First Yearbook, Second Supplement of the National Herbart Society for the Scientific Study of Teaching*. Bloomington, Ill.: Pantagraph Printing and Stationery Co., 1895.

Dewey, John. "Interest as Related to Will," *First Yearbook, Second Supplement of the National Herbart Society for the Scientific Study of Teaching*. Second edition. Chicago: The University of Chicago Press, 1895.

Dewey, John. *The Method of the Recitation: A Partial Report of a Course of Lectures Given at the University of Chicago*. Oshkosh, Wisconsin: Oshkosh Normal School, 1899.

Dewey, John. *Moral Principles in Education*. Boston: Houghton Mifflin, 1909.

Dewey, John. "Pedagogy as a University Discipline," *University Record*, I (Sept. 25, 1896), 361–63.

Dewey, John. *Pedagogy: Philosophy of Education Syllabus*. Chicago: The University of Chicago Press, 1898–99.

Dewey, John. *Psychology*. New York: Harper, 1886.

Dewey, John. *Psychology and Social Practice*. Chicago: The University of Chicago Press, 1901.

Dewey, John. "The Relation of Theory to Practice in the Education of Teachers," *Third Yearbook of the National Society for the Scientific Study of Education*, Part I. Chicago: The University of Chicago Press, 1904.

Dewey, John. *The School and Society*. Chicago: The University of Chicago Press, 1900.

Dewey, John. "Shortening the Years of Elementary Schooling," by Louis Soldan. "Discussion," *School Review*, XI (January, 1903), 4–20.

Dewey, John. "The Situation as Regards the Course of Study," *National Education Association, Journal of Proceedings and Addresses*, 1901, 332–48.

Dewey, John. *Sources of a Science of Education*. New York: Horace Liveright, 1929.

Dewey, John, and Dewey, Evelyn. *Schools of Tomorrow*. New York: E. P. Dutton and Co., 1915.

Dorfman, Joseph. *Thorstein Veblen and His America*. New York: The Viking Press, 1934.

Dutton, Samuel T., and Snedden, David. *The Administration of Public Education in the United States*. New York: The Macmillan Co., 1908.

Edmunds, Henry H. "History of the Herbartian Movement in the United States and Its Relation to Present Trends in Education." Typewritten. Milner Library, Illinois State Normal University, 1929.

Edwards, Newton, and Richey, Herman. *The School in the American Social Order*. Boston: Houghton Mifflin Co., 1947.

Eliot, Charles. "Shortening and Enriching the Grammar School Course," *Journal of Addresses and Proceedings of the National Educational Association*, 1892, 617–25.

Elliott, Edward. "The Education and Training of Secondary Teachers," *Fourth Yearbook of the National Society for the Scientific Study of Education*, Part I. Chicago: The University of Chicago Press, 1905.

Featherstone, William. "Review of *Curriculum Development*," *Curriculum Journal*, VI (November, 1935), 29–30.

Felmley, David. *Semi-Centennial History of the Illinois State Normal University, 1857–1907*. Normal, Ill.: David Felmley, 1907.

Fenner, Mildred S. *National Education Association: History*. Washington, D. C.: National Education Association, 1945.

Florida, State of, Department of Public Instruction. *The Course of Study for Florida Elementary Schools, Grades I–VI*, 1931.

Frank, Waldo D. (ed.). *America and Alfred Stieglitz: A Collective Portrait*. New York: Doubleday, Doran and Co., 1934.

Gagné, Robert M. "Military Training and Principles of Learning," *American Psychologist*, XVII (February, 1962), 83–91.

Hailman, W. N. "The New Education," *Education*, V (November, 1884), 174–81.

Hall, Sidney B. *Brief Description of Virginia Program for Improving Instruction, 1931–1939*. Bulletin of the State Board of Education, XXI, No. 4, (January, 1939).

Hall, Sidney B. *Organization for Virginia State Curriculum Program*. Bulletin of the State Board of Education, XIV, No. 5, (March, 1932).

Hall, Sidney B. *Study Course for Virginia State Curriculum Program*. Bulletin of the State Board of Education, XIV, No. 4, (January, 1932).

Hall, Sidney B., Peters, D. W., and Caswell, H. L. *Procedures for Virginia State Curriculum Program*. Bulletin of the State Board of Education, XV, No. 3, (July, 1932).

Hall, Sidney B., Peters, D. W., Henderson, H. R., and Caswell, H. L. *Tentative Course of Study for Virginia Elementary Schools.* Richmond, Virginia: State Board of Education, September, 1933.

Handlin, Oscar. *John Dewey's Challenge to Education: Historical Perspectives on the Cultural Context.* New York: Harper, 1959.

Harap, Henry. *Curriculum Trends at Mid-Century.* Cincinnati: South-Western Publishing Co., 1953.

Harap, Henry. *The Technique of Curriculum-Making.* New York: The Macmillan Co., 1928.

Harper, Charles A. *Development of the Teachers College in the United States with Special Reference to Illinois State Normal University.* Bloomington, Ill.: McKnight and McKnight, 1935.

Herbart, Johann F. *The Science of Education.* Translated by Henry and Emmie Felkin. Boston: D. C. Heath and Co., 1892.

Herbart, Johann F. *Psychology.* Translated by Margaret K. Smith (from the second revised German edition, 1834). New York: D. Appleton and Co., 1891.

Joint Committee on Curriculum of the Department of Supervisors and Directors of Instruction and the Society for Curriculum Study. *The Changing Curriculum.* D. Appleton Century Co., 1937.

Joncich, Geraldine M. (ed.). *Psychology and the Science of Education: Selected Writings of Edward L. Thorndike.* New York: Teachers College Press, Teachers College, Columbia University, 1962.

Kelley, Charles R. "Toward an Interpretation of the New Movement of 1915 in Educational Administration." Unpublished doctoral dissertation, Teachers College, Columbia University, 1961.

Kilpatrick, William H. "Dewey's Influence on Education," *The Philosophy of John Dewey,* ed. Paul Arthur Schilpp. Evanston: Northwestern University, 1939. 445–74.

Kilpatrick, William H. *Education for a Changing Civilization.* New York: The Macmillan Co., 1926.

Kilpatrick, William H. "Tendencies in Educational Philosophy," *Twenty-Five Years of American Education.* Edited by Isaac L. Kandel. New York: The Macmillan Co., 1924, 55–90.

Krusé, Samuel A. "Late Charles A. McMurry Met the Acid Test of the Master Teacher," *School and Society,* LVIII (September 4, 1943), 171–72.

Lange, Karl. *Apperception.* Edited by Charles DeGarmo. Boston: D. C. Heath, 1893.

Leavell, Ullin. "Peabody's Modern Founder": Charles Alexander McMurry," *Peabody Journal of Education,* XXII (March, 1945), 262–3.

Levermore, C. H. "The 'New Education' Run Mad," *Education,* VI (January, 1886), 290–98.

Lindner, Gustav. *Empirical Psychology.* Translated by Charles DeGarmo. Boston: D. C. Heath, 1889.

Lowry, Charles D. "The Relation of Principals and Superintendents to the Training and Improvement of Their Teachers," *Seventh Yearbook of the National Society for the Study of Education*, Part I. Chicago: The University of Chicago Press, 1908, 11–66.

McClellan, James. "The Contributions of Herbart," *Progressive Education*, XXIX (March, 1952), 168–70.

McCluskey, Neil. *Public Schools and Moral Education: the Influence of Horace Mann, William Torrey Harris and John Dewey*. New York: Columbia University Press, 1958.

McKenny, Charles. "The McMurrys in American Education." *Peabody Journal of Education*, V (March 1928), 261–68.

McMurry, Charles A. *Conflicting Principles in Teaching and How to Adjust Them*. Boston: Houghton Mifflin Co., 1914.

McMurry, Charles A. *A Course of Study for the Eight Grades of the Common Schools, Including a Handbook of Practical Suggestions to Teachers*. Bloomington, Ill.: Public School Publishing Co., 1895.

McMurry, Charles A. *Course of Study in the Eight Grades*. Vol. I. New York: The Macmillan Co., 1906.

McMurry, Charles A. *Course of Study in the Eight Grades*. Vol. II. New York: The Macmillan Co., 1906.

McMurry, Charles A. *The Elements of General Method*. Rev. ed. New York: The Macmillan Co., 1903.

McMurry, Charles A. *A Geography Plan for the Grades of the Common School*. Winona, Minnesota: Jones and Kroeger, 1891.

McMurry, Charles A. *How to Conduct the Recitation and the Principles Underlying Methods of Teaching in Classes*. Chicago: A. Flanagan Co., 1890.

McMurry, Charles A. *How to Organize the Curriculum*. New York: The Macmillan Co., 1923.

McMurry, Charles A. *Pioneer History Stories: For Third and Fourth Grades*. First series. Winona, Minnesota: Jones and Kroeger, 1891.

McMurry, Charles A. *Practical Teaching: Large Projects in Geography*, Book I. Richmond, Virginia: Johnson Publishing Co., 1925.

McMurry, Charles A. "A Reply to Dr. White's Paper," *Second Yearbook of the National Herbart Society for the Scientific Study of Teaching*. Bloomington, Ill.: Pantagraph Printing, 1896.

McMurry, Charles A. *Special Method in Arithmetic*. New York: The Macmillan Co., 1905.

McMurry, Charles A. *Special Method in Geography for Third and Fourth Grades*. Bloomington, Ill.: Public School Publishing Co., 1895.

McMurry, Charles A. *Special Method in History: a Complete Outline of a Course of Study in History for the Grades Below the High School*. New York: The Macmillan Co., 1903.

McMurry, Charles A. *Special Method in Language in the Eight Grades*. New York: The Macmillan Co., 1905.

McMurry, Charles A. *Special Method for Literature and History of the Common Schools*. Bloomington, Ill.: Public School Publishing Co., 1896.

McMurry, Charles A. *Special Method in Natural Science for the First Four Grades of the Common School*, 3rd. ed. Bloomington, Ill.: Public School Publishing Co., 1896.

McMurry, Charles A. *Special Method in Primary Reading*. New York: The Macmillan Co., 1903.

McMurry, Charles A. *Special Method in the Reading of the Complete English Classics in the Grades*. Bloomington, Ill.: Public School Publishing Co., 1894.

McMurry, Charles A. *Teaching by Projects: A Basis for Purposeful Study*. New York: The Macmillan Co., 1920.

McMurry, Charles A., and McMurry, Frank M. *The Method of the Recitation*. Bloomington, Ill.: Public School Publishing Co., 1897.

McMurry, Dorothy. *Herbartian Contributions to History Instruction in American Elementary Schools*. New York: Teachers College, Columbia University, Bureau of Publications, 1946.

McMurry, Frank. "Concentration," *First Yearbook of the National Herbart Society for the Scientific Study of Teaching*. Bloomington, Ill.: Pantagraph Printing and Stationery Co., 1895, 28–69.

McMurry, Frank. "Some Recollections of the Past Forty Years of Education," *Peabody Journal of Education*, IV (May, 1927), 325–32.

Marshall, Helen. *Grandest of Enterprises, 1857–1957*. Normal, Ill.: Illinois State Normal School, 1956.

Mayhew, Katherine Camp, and Edwards, Anna Camp. *The Dewey School: The Laboratory School of the University of Chicago 1896–1903*. New York: D. Appleton Century Co., 1936.

Mayo, Arthur B. "The Concept of Vocational Education in the Thinking of the General Educator, 1845–1945," University of Illinois Bulletin 1946, No. 62. Urbana: University of Illinois, July, 1946.

Melvin, A. Gordon. *Education: A History*. New York: John Day Co., 1946.

Meriam, Junius L. *Child Life and the Curriculum*. Yonkers-on-Hudson, New York: World Book Co., 1920.

Meriam, Junius L. *Normal School Education and Efficiency in Teaching*. New York: Teachers College Contributions to Education, 1905.

Miel, Alice Marie. *Changing the Curriculum: A Social Process*. New York: D. Appleton Century Co., 1946.

Mississippi, State of, Department of Education. *Program for the Improvement of Instruction: Curriculum Reorganization*. Bulletin No. 6 (October, 1939).

Monroe, Paul. *A Text-Book in the History of Education*. New York: The Macmillan Co., 1905.

Morehouse, Frances. *Practice Teaching in the School of Education, University of Illinois, 1893–1911*. University of Illinois School of Education Bulletin 1912, No. 7. Urbana: University of Illinois, 1912.

National Conference on Educational Method. "Educational Supervision." *First Yearbook*. New York: Teachers College, Columbia University, 1928.

National Conference of Supervisors and Directors of Instruction. "Scientific Method in Supervision." *Second Yearbook*. New York: Teachers College, Columbia University, 1929.

National Conference of Supervisors and Directors of Instruction. "Current Problems of Supervisors." *Third Yearbook*. New York: Teachers College, Columbia University, 1930.

National Education Association, Department of Supervisors and Directors of Instruction. "The Evaluation of Supervision." *Fourth Yearbook*. New York: Teachers College, Columbia University, 1931.

National Education Association, Commission on the Reorganization of Secondary Education. *Preliminary Statements*. United States Bureau of Education Bulletin 1913, No. 41. Washington, D.C.: Government Printing Office, 1913.

National Education Association, Commission on the Reorganization of Secondary Education. *The Social Studies in Secondary Education*. United States Bureau of Education Bulletin 1916, No. 28. Washington, D.C.: Government Printing Office, 1916.

National Education Association, Commission on the Reorganization of Secondary Education. *Cardinal Principles of Secondary Education*. United States Bureau of Education Bulletin 1918, No. 35. Washington, D.C.: Government Printing Office, 1918.

National Education Association, Department of Superintendence. "The Status of the Superintendent." *First Yearbook*. Washington, D.C.: National Education Association, 1923.

National Education Association, Department of Superintendence. "The Elementary School Curriculum." *Second Yearbook*. Washington, D.C.: National Education Association, 1924.

National Education Association, Department of Superintendence. "Research in Constructing the Elementary School Curriculum. *Third Yearbook*. Washington, D.C.: National Education Association, 1925.

National Education Association, Department of Superintendence. "The Nation at Work on the Public School Curriculum." *Fourth Yearbook*. Washington, D.C.: National Education Association, 1926.

National Educational Association. "Report of a Committee on a Course of Study from Primary School to University." *Addresses and Journal of Proceedings*, 1876, 58–68.

National Educational Association. "Report of the Committee of Educational Value of Common School Studies." *Journal of Proceedings and Addresses*, 1886, 403–20.

National Educational Association. *Report of the Committee of Ten on Secondary School Studies: with the Reports of the Conferences Arranged by the Committee*. United States Bureau of Education. Washington, D.C.: Government Printing Office, 1893.

National Educational Association. "Report of the Committee of Fifteen." *Journal of Proceedings and Addresses*, 1895, 232–37.

National Educational Association. "Report of the Sub-Committee on the Correlation of Studies in Elementary Education." *Journal of Proceedings and Addresses*, 1895, 287–350.

192

National Educational Association. *Report of the Committee on Economy of Time in Education.* United States Bureau of Education, Bulletin 1913, No. 38. Washington, D.C.: Government Printing Office, 1913.

National Herbart Society for the Scientific Study of Teaching. *First Yearbook.* Bloomington, Ill.: Pantagraph Printing and Stationery Co., 1895.

National Herbart Society for the Scientific Study of Teaching. *Second Yearbook.* Bloomington, Ill.: Pantagraph Printing and Stationery Co., 1896.

National Herbart Society for the Scientific Study of Teaching. *Third Yearbook.* Chicago: University of Chicago Press, 1897.

National Society for the Study of Education. "The Education and Training of Secondary Teachers," *Fourth Yearbook*, Part I. Chicago: University of Chicago Press, 1905.

National Society for the Study of Education. "The Relation of Principals and Superintendents to the Training and Improvement of their Teachers." *Seventh Yearbook.* Chicago: The University of Chicago Press, 1908.

National Society for the Study of Education. "The Supervision of City Schools." *Twelfth Yearbook*, Part I. Chicago: University of Chicago Press, 1913.

National Society for the Study of Education. "Minimum Essentials in Elementary-School Subjects—Standards and Current Practices." *Fourteenth Yearbook*, Part I. Chicago: The University of Chicago Press, 1915.

National Society for the Study of Education. "Second Report of the Committee on Minimal Essentials in Elementary-School Subjects." *Sixteenth Yearbook*, Part I. Chicago: University of Chicago Press, 1917.

National Society for the Study of Education. "Third Report of the Committee on Economy of Time in Education." *Seventeenth Yearbook*, Part I. Bloomington, Ill.: Public School Publishing Co., 1918.

National Society for the Study of Education. "The Measurement of Educational Products." *Seventeenth Yearbook*, Part II. Bloomington, Ill.: Public School Publishing Co., 1918.

National Society for the Study of Education. "Fourth Report of the Committee on Economy of Time in Education." *Eighteenth Yearbook*, Part II. Bloomington, Ill.: Public School Publishing Co., 1919.

National Society for the Study of Education. "The Social Studies in the Elementary and Secondary School." *Twenty-second Yearbook*, Part II. Bloomington, Ill.: Public School Publishing Co., 1923.

National Society for the Study of Education. "The Foundations and Technique of Curriculum Construction." *Twenty-sixth Yearbook*, Part I. "Curriculum-Making: Past and Present." Bloomington, Ill.: Public School Publishing Co., 1926.

National Society for the Study of Education. "The Foundations and Technique of Curriculum Construction." *Twenty-sixth Yearbook*, Part II. "The Foundations of Curriculum-Making." Bloomington, Ill.: Public School Publishing Co., 1926.

Ogburn, William. *Social Change with Respect to Culture and Original Nature.* New York: B. W. Huebsch, 1922.

Page, David P. *Theory and Practice: of Teaching or the Motives and Methods of Good School Keeping.* New York: A. S. Barnes and Co., 1858.

Parker, Francis W. *Talks on Pedagogics: An Outline of the Theory of Concentration.* New York: E. L. Kellogg and Co., 1894.

Parker, Francis W. *Talks on Teaching.* New York: A. S. Barnes, 1893.

Parker, Samuel C. *A Textbook in the History of Modern Elementary Education: With Emphasis on School Practice in Relation to Social Conditions.* Boston: Ginn and Co., 1912.

Patty, William Lowell. *A Study of Mechanism in Education: An Examination of the Curriculum-Making Devices of Franklin Bobbitt, W. W. Charters and C. C. Peters, from the Point of View of Relativistic Pragmatism.* New York: Teachers College, Columbia University, 1938.

Paulsen, F. *German Education.* New York: Charles Scribner's Sons, 1908.

Payne, Bruce R. *Public Elementary School Curricula: A Comparative Study of Representative Cities of the United States, England, Germany and France.* New York: Silver, Burdett and Co., 1905.

Pierce, Paul. *Origins and Development of the Public School Principalship.* Chicago: University of Chicago Libraries, 1935.

President's Research Committee on Social Trends. *Recent Social Trends in the United States.* New York and London: McGraw-Hill Book Co., Inc., 1933.

Rein, Wilhelm. *Outlines of Pedagogics.* Translated by C. C. and Ida J. Van Liew.

Rice, Joseph. "The Futility of the Spelling Grind." *Forum,* XXIII (April, 1897), 163–72.

Rosenkranz, Karl. *Pedagogics as a System.* Translated by Anna C. Brackett. St. Louis: R. P. Studley Co., 1872.

Rugg, Harold and Ann Shumaker. *The Child-Centered School: An Appraisal of the New Education.* Yonkers-on-Hudson, New York: World Book Co., 1928.

Rugg, Harold. *Foundations for American Education.* Yonkers-on-Hudson, New York: World Book Co., 1947.

Rugg, Harold. "Francis Wayland Parker and His Schools," *Yearbook of Education: Education and Philosophy.* Yonkers-on-Hudson, New York: World Book Co., 1957, 405–12.

Rugg, Harold. "Is the Rating of Human Character Practicable?" *Journal of Educational Psychology,* XII, XIII (Nov., Dec., 1921, Jan., Feb., 1922), 425–38.

Rugg, Harold. *Statistical Methods Applied to Education.* Boston: Houghton Mifflin Co., 1917.

Rugg, Harold. *The Teacher of Teachers: Frontiers of Theory and Practice in Teacher Education.* New York: Harper, 1952.

Rugg, Harold. *That Men May Understand: An American in the Long Armistice.* New York: Doubleday, Doran and Co., 1941.

St. Louis Public Schools. *Course of Study,* 1902.

Scheffler, Israel. *The Language of Education.* Springfield, Ill.: C. C. Thomas, 1960.

Slade, James P. "Country Schools," *Education*, III (January, 1883), 234–47.

Society for Curriculum Study. *A Challenge to Secondary Education: Plans for the Reconstruction of the American High School*, Edited by Samuel Everett. New York: D. Appleton Century Co., 1935.

Society for Curriculum Study. *The Community School*, Edited by Samuel Everett. New York: D. Appleton Century Co., 1938.

Society for Curriculum Study. *Integration: Its Meaning and Application*. New York: D. Appleton Century Co., 1937.

Soldan, F. L. "What is a Fad?" *American Education*, V (December, 1901), 201–07.

Spencer, Herbert. *Education: Intellectual, Moral and Physical*. New York: D. Appleton and Co., 1861.

Stevenson, John A. *The Project Method of Teaching*. New York: The Macmillan Co., 1921.

Stratemeyer, Florence. *The Effective Use of Curriculum Materials*. New York: Bureau of Publications, Teachers College, Columbia University, 1931.

Strayer, George D. *Brief Course in the Teaching Process*. New York: The Macmillan Co., 1911.

Strayer, George D. "The Financing of Education in the State of New York," *The Educational Finance Inquiry Commission*. New York: The Macmillan Co., 1923.

Strayer, George D. "Tribute to Frank McMurry, *School Executive*, LVI (Sept., 1936), 4.

Taylor, Frederick W. *The Principles of Scientific Management*. New York: Harper, 1911.

Teachers College, Columbia University. *Announcement*, 1926.

Teachers College, Columbia University. *Report of the Dean for the Academic Year Ending June 30, 1936*.

Teachers College, Columbia University. *Report of the Dean for the Academic Year Ending June 30, 1938*.

Thayer, Vivian T. *Passing of the Recitation*. Boston: D. C. Heath, 1928.

Thorndike, Edward L. *An Introduction to the Theory of Mental and Social Measurements*. New York: Teachers College, Columbia University, 1904.

Trainer, John. *How to Grade and Teach a Country School*. Decatur, Ill.: Burgess, Trainer and Co., 1885.

Trillingham, Clinton C. *The Organization and Administration of Curriculum Programs*. Los Angeles, Cal.: University of Southern California Press, 1934.

Ufer, Christian. *Introduction to the Pedagogy of Herbart*. Translated by J. C. Zinser. Boston: D. C. Heath, 1894.

United States Bureau of Education. "Report of the Committee of the National Council of Education on Economy of Time in Education," *Bulletin*, No. 38, 1913.

University of Illinois, School of Education. *Bulletin No. 7*, 1912.

White, Emerson E., "Isolation and Unification as Bases of Courses of Study," *Second Yearbook of the National Herbart Society for the Scientific Study of Teaching.* Bloomington, Ill.: Pantagraph Printing, 1896.

White, Morton. *The Origin of Dewey's Instrumentalism.* New York: Columbia University Press, 1943.

Wundt, Wilhelm M. *Outlines of Psychology.* Translated by Charles Judd. New York: G. E. Stechart and Co., 1897.

Ziller, Tuiskon. *Basis of the Doctrine of Instruction as a Moral Force.* 1865.

Zirbes, Laura. *Curriculum Trends: A Preliminary Report and a Challenge.* Washington, D. C.: Association for Childhood Education, 1935.

Index

academies, rise of, 9
activity analysis, 5; Bobbitt's concept of, 84; Charters's concept of, 92, 97; curriculum making and, 102
Adams, George P., 49 n., 99 n.
administration, in curriculum making, 100
adult, "ideal," 81
Alabama, curriculum revision in, 143–144
Alexander, Thomas, 142
American Historical Association, 109
American Institute of Instruction, 42
analogy, industrial, use of by Bobbitt, 80, 103, 183
Angell, Norman, 14
apperception, child study and, 32, 69; in Herbartian theory, 24
Apperception (Lange), 17, 25 n.
application, in Herbartian theory, 18–20
association, in Herbartian theory, 18–19
Ayres, Leonard, 73 n.

Bachman, Frank, 143
Bader, Edith, 168 n.
Bagley, William C., 75, 114, 127, 129
Baker, James, 68 n., 74
Baker, Melvin C., 49 n., 69 n.
Ballou, Frank, 90
Barr, A. S., 161 n.
Beard, Charles A., 116, 125
behavior response, 72
Bellack, Arno, 173 n.
Bellamy, Edward, 113

Bismarck, Otto von, 21
Boas, Franz, 125
Bobbitt, Franklin, 4–5, 67–90, 93, 120–121, 129, 138, 149, 150 n., 160 n., 164, 172, 178, 180–183; assessment of, 99–104; background of, 76–80; curriculum definition of, 85–86; curriculum-making method of, 80–90; Gary experiment by, 78–79
Bode, Boyd, 94 n., 148, 153
Bonser, Frederick Gordon, 102 n., 111 n., 127, 162 n.
books, *see* textbooks
Boston, public schools, 90
Brief Course in the Teaching Process (Strayer), 138 n.
Briggs, Thomas H., 182 n.
Brim, Orville, 160 n., 168 n.
Brooks, Sarah, 39 n.
Brown, Elmer E., 7, 9 n., 25 n., 30 n.
Brueckner, L. J., 161 n.
Bruner, Herbert, 102 n., 111 n.
Brunner, Edmund de S., 140 n.
Bryson, Lyman, 73 n.
Bureau of Curriculum Research, Columbia University, 111
Buros, Oscar, 138 n.
Burris, William P., 41 n., 79 n.
Burton, W. H., 160 n., 161 n.
Butler, Nicholas Murray, 29, 30 n., 114 n., 116 n.

Caldwell, Otis, 108 n., 111 n., 117
Calkins, N. A., 13
Callahan, Raymond E., 79 n.

197

Campbell, Doak S., 161 n., 162 n., 163 n.
Carnegie Institute of Technology, 93
Caswell, Hollis L., 5, 70 n., 179; assessment of, 171–175; background of, 137–141; work in Virginia, 147–156; writings of, 156, 161–170
Cattell, James McKeen, 71, 116
Changing Curriculum, The (Harap), 168–170
character, knowledge and, 43; *see also* morality
Charters, Werrett Wallace, 5, 76, 90–99, 120, 178, 180–181; activity analysis of, 92; assessment of, 99–104; background of, 90–93; on curriculum content, 94–95
Chicago, University of, 53, 59–60, 73 n., 75, 78, 90, 115
Chicago Principals Association, 89
child, interaction and activities of, 84–85, 119; moral development of, 69; occupation of in school, 57; personal experience of, 55, 86, 119
Child-Centered School, The (Rugg & Shumaker), 122–123
child growth, apperception and, 32; "creative," 119; sequence of, 57–58; stages in, 57–58
child-study movement, 7, 69
childhood experiences, in Bobbitt's curriculum concept, 86
Childs, John L., 140 n.
citizenship, education for, 54
Civil War, 9, 42
civilization, understanding of, 118–119
Clark, Harold F., 140 n.
Clark University, 7, 78
classroom phenomena, 39; *see also* school
clearness, in Herbartian system, 18–19
Cocking, Walter, 106, 137 n., 157 n.
Coffman, Lotus D., 114, 139 n.
college courses, curriculum study in, 110–111
college teachers, curriculum making and, 3; *see also* teacher
Committee for the Course of Study, 153
Committee of Fifteen, 27, 30, 68
Committee of Ten, 26–27, 68 n., 107

Committee on Articulation of High School and College, 107
Committee on Economy of Time, 74 n.
Committee on the Culture Element in Education, 69, 73
Committee on the Reorganization of Secondary Education, 107, 146
Comte, Auguste, 49
conduct, control of, 166–167
Cooke, Morris L., 80 n.
Cooperative Plan of Curriculum Revision, 110
core subject, 21
correlation, apperception and, 24; discussion of by Herbartian Society, 31–36; knowledge and, 33–34, 109
Counts, George S., 140 n., 149
Courtis, Stuart A., 76, 128, 160 n.
Cremin, Lawrence A., 53, 144 n.
Cubberley, Ellwood P., 139 n.
cultural anthropology, 152
culture epochs, theory of, 32–33
curriculum, Bobbitt's definition of, 85–86; Caswell's treatise on, 162–163; childhood experiences and, 86; content in, 9–10, 94, 101; division of labor and, 85–86; growth of, 12; haphazard adoption of, 12–13; job analysis and, 93–99; as learner's process, 165; psychology and, 71–73; scientific management and, 79–80, 138; social implications of, 88; teacher's role in, 3, 98, 107; technique, refinements in, 70; unease about, 8–16; unity and clarity as problems in, 36; *see also* curriculum making
Curriculum, The (Bobbitt), 82–83, 88, 99 n.
Curriculum Bureau, Teachers College, 157–158
Curriculum Committee on Correlation, 109
Curriculum Construction (Charters), 94
curriculum courses, in various states, 140–143
curriculum development, as curriculum worker's process, 165–166; German experience in, 16–23

Curriculum Development (Caswell), 161

curriculum lag, 127, 132

curriculum making, Bobbitt's method in, 80–90; Charters's procedure in, 97–99; "conscious experience of man" in, 55; development of, 1–6; industrial processes and, 4, 80, 103, 183; as new specialization, 101; Rugg's criticism of, 120–121; society and, 102–103; subjects in, 106–109; teacher's participation in, 3, 98, 107, 166

curriculum pattern, Charters's concept of, 96

Curriculum Problems (Briggs), 182 n.

curriculum revision, by states, 106, 140–143

curriculum society, 156–161

"curriculum technique," course in, 106

Cutright, Prudence, 168 n.

Dale, Edgar, 157 n.

Dana, Henry, 116 n.

DeGarmo, Charles, 7, 17 n., 21 n., 22 n., 25 n., 29, 30 n., 31–35, 39, 42, 68 n.

Democracy and Education (Dewey), 65, 112

Denver, curriculum making in, 106, 144

Denver Course of Study, 149

Department of Curriculum Construction, National Society for the Study of Education, 126

Department of Curriculum and Teaching, Teachers College, 171

Department of Superintendence, 109

Department of Supervisors and Directors of Instruction, 160, 167

Detroit, curriculum making in, 106

Dewey, Jane M., 48 n., 53 n.

Dewey, John, 4, 40 n., 38 n., 41, 69, 78, 84, 90–91, 94, 108, 112, 127–128, 136, 140, 145, 148, 172–173, 179–182; contribution of, 63–65; criticism of Herbartians, 51–52; four basic challenges of, 99, 135, 171; interest in Herbartian ideas, 47; philosophy of, 49–50; teaching career of, 59–60; writings of, 59–60

division of labor, in curriculum, 85–86

Division of Surveys and Field Studies, Peabody College, 143

Dutton, Samuel Train, 138 n., 139 n., 145 n.

Edmunds, Henry Hugh, 7 n., 17 n.

education, citizenship and, 54; Dewey's introduction to, 47–50; efficiency movement in, 67; ethical principles underlying, 53; foundation courses in, 140; measurable standards of, 80, 99 (*see also* measurement, psychological); morality and, 42, 53, 84; psychology and, 71–73; as science, 73 n., 82; "smelting point" of, 36, 142; social need and, 82, 92; as social policy, 56; and technological change, 64, 83; truth and, 100

"educational situation," 105–112

"educative process," concept of, 129

Edwards, Newton, 13 n., 14 n., 57 n., 71 n.

efficiency movement, 67

Elementary School Record, 56–57

Elements of General Method (Charles McMurry), 43

Eliot, Charles W., 26 n., 68, 71

Elliott, Edward, 9 n.

equal difference theorem, 73 n.

Ethical Principles Underlying Education (Dewey), 53

fads, 35, 37

fairy tales, 32

Featherstone, W., 162 n.

Felkin, Emmie, 25 n.

Felkin, Henry, 25 n.

Felmley, David, 7 n.

Fenner, Mildred S., 90 n.

field-study movement, 139

Finney, Ross, 149

Fisher, George, 71

Florida, curriculum revision in, 144–147

Foundations and Techniques of Curriculum-Construction (NSSE Yearbook), 131

French, Will, 168 n.

Gagné, Robert M., 97 n.

Galton, Francis, 71
Gary (Ind.) experiment, 71
Gates, Arthur I., 111 n.
General Education Board, Peabody College, 143
General Method, course in, 38
geography, ideas of, 34
George Peabody College for Teachers, *see* Peabody College for Teachers
Germany, curriculum development in, 16–23, 177
grammar, time studies in, 93
growth, *see* child growth

Hailmann, Eudora, 25 n.
Hall, Florence, 25 n.
Hall, G. Stanley, 48 n., 78
Hall, Sidney B., 147, 148 n., 149, 150 n., 151, 153 n., 154 n., 171 n.
Hand, Harold, 168 n.
Handlin, Oscar, 69 n.
handwriting, 13, 71
Handwriting Scale (Ayres), 75 n.
Handwriting Scale (Thorndike), 72
Hanna, Paul, 153, 158
Harap, Henry, 121 n., 157, 167 n., 168 n., 169, 170 n.
Harper, Charles A., 7 n., 15 n.
Harper, William Rainey, 130
Harris, William Torrey, 7, 17, 26 n., 28–29, 33, 44, 48, 139 n., 158
Hegel, Georg Wilhelm Friedrich, 48 n., 49, 51 n.
Henderson, Helen Ruth, 153 n., 154 n.
Herbart, Johann, 4, 17–18, 25 n., 30, 41, 51, 177
Herbart Society, 7, 68, 123, 177; Dewey and, 50–51, 53; formation of, 8, 30–31; reorganization of, 58; *see also* National Herbart Society for the Scientific Study of Teaching
Herbartianism or Herbartian theory, 4, 16–21, 108, 177–178, 180; assessment of, 38–46; Bobbitt and, 76; critique of, 50–56; the McMurrys' contribution to, 23–24, 40–46; psychological aspect of, 50–52; as "schoolmaster's psychology," 54; teacher training in, 21–23; terminology of, 39
Herrick, Cheesman, 108 n.

Hill, Henry, 138 n.
Hillegas, Milo Burdette, 102 n.
history, ideas of, 34–35
Hopkins, L. Thomas, 102 n.
Horn, Ernest, 76, 91 n., 102 n., 112 n.
Hosic, James, 108 n.
Humanistic revival, 20

Illinois, University of, 14, 114
Illinois State Normal University, 15, 36
Individual Pupil, The (Mort), 140
industrial processes, curriculum making and, 4; job analysis and, 93–99
Introduction to the Theory of Mental and Social Measurements (Thorndike), 72

Jackman, Wilbur, 30 n.
James, Edmund, 7, 17 n.
James, George, 25 n.
James, William, 48 n., 49, 71
Jena, University of, 21–22, 24
Jessup, Walter A., 139 n.
job analysis, curriculum and, 93–99
Johns Hopkins University, 47 n.
Johnson, F. Ernest, 140 n.
Johnson, Marietta, 111 n.
Joncich, Geraldine M., 71 n.
Jones, Thomas, 108 n.
Judd, Charles H., 72, 75, 120–121, 127–128

Kandel, Isaac L., 40 n., 63 n.
Kant, Immanuel, 51
Kelley, Charles Robert, 80 n., 139 n.
Kiehle, D. L., 9 n.
Kilpatrick, William H., 18, 38 n., 40, 49, 50 n., 52 n., 62, 108 n., 127, 129, 131, 140 n., 145, 149
Kingsley, Clarence, 108 n.
Klemm, L. R., 25 n.
knowledge, character and, 43; as "connective tissue," 95; correlation and, 109; divisions of, 33; social purpose and, 61; will and, 20; *see also* education
Knudsen, Charles W., 155, 168 n.
Krusé, Samuel A., 8 n.

laboratory school, curriculum of, 56–58
Lang, Ossian, 25

Lange, Karl, 16, 21, 25 n.
learned societies, formation of, 9 n.
Leavell, Ullin, 8 n., 143 n.
Leonard, Paul, 138 n.
Levermore, C. H., 9 n.
Lincoln School, New York, 112 n., 116, 118–119, 142, 153
Lindner, Gustav, 25 n.
Lindquist, Rudolph D., 157 n., 167
Linn, Henry, 138 n.
Lippman, Walter, 114
Looking Backward (Bellamy), 112
Lukens, Herman, 7, 25 n.
Lynn, Mass., survey, 139–140

McCluskey, Neil, 48 n.
McKenny, Charles, 44 n., 45 n.
McMurry, Charles, 4, 7–8, 16, 18, 22–28, 30 n., 33 n., 47, 56 n., 90, 92, 133 n., 142, 143 n., 145 n., 149, 174, 177, 179; contributions of, 40–46, 62–65
McMurry, Dorothy, 25 n., 39 n., 46 n.
McMurry, Frank, 4, 7–8, 11, 13–16, 18, 19 n., 21 n., 24–28, 30 n., 32, 36–38, 47, 56 n., 90, 112 n., 138 n., 174, 177, 179; contributions of, 40–46, 62–65
McMurry Study Group, 143 n.
Mann, Horace, 8, 13, 139
Marshall, Helen E., 7 n.
Mays, Arthur B., 69 n.
Meaning of Education, The (Butler), 114 n.
Mearns, Hughes, 122
measurement, psychological, 71–75, 80, 99
measurement movement, 114–115
Melby, Ernest, 160 n., 168 n.
memorizing, emphasis on, 10–11
Meriam, Junius L., 39 n., 76, 90–91, 102 n., 112 n.
Methods of Teaching (Charters), 91
Michigan, University of, 14, 47 n.
Miel, Alice, 156 n.
Mississippi Valley, history of, 34
Missouri, University of, 76, 90
Monroe, Paul, 9 n.
Montague, William P., 49, 99 n.
morality, education and, 42, 53–54, 69, 84
Mort, Paul, 139
Mossman, Lois C., 102 n.

National Conference on Educational Method, 159 n., 160
National Council for the Social Studies, 109
National Council of Teachers of English, 109
National Education Association, 25, 26 n., 27 n., 28 n., 29 n., 30 n., 69, 70 n., 74 n., 90, 108 n., 130, 135, 160
National Herbart Society for the Scientific Study of Teaching, 4, 30
National Society for the Scientific Study of Education, 58
National Society for the Study of Education, 5, 67–68, 106 n., 107 n.; *Twenty-sixth Yearbook* of, 123–134
Nebraska, University of, 137
Neo-humanism, 20
Newlon, Jesse, 140 n., 144, 158, 171
New School for Social Research, 116
New York University, 13
nineteenth century, curriculum changes in, 8–16
Normal School Education and Efficiency in Teaching (Meriam), 39 n.
normal schools, teaching methods in, 14
Northern Illinois State Normal School, 36
Noss, Theo., 25 n.
Nuttall, John, 138 n.

Ogburn, William F., 132, 149
Ohio State University, 93 n.
organism, total response of, 71
Organization and Administration of Curriculum Programs (Trillingham), 105 n.
Oswego Normal School, 12

Page, David, 15
Parker, Francis Wayland, 7, 11, 27, 29, 35–36, 49, 54 n., 112 n., 113, 182
Parker, Samuel Chester, 12 n., 13 n., 19 n., 22 n., 25 n., 67 n.
Patty, William Lovell, 145 n.
Paulsen, F., 20 n.
Payne, Bruce, 142

Peabody College for Teachers, 36, 44, 142–143, 147, 149–150, 152, 158, 171
pedagogy, university chairs in, 13
penmanship, 13, 71
Pestalozzi, Johann H., 12, 96
Peters, D. W., 148 n., 153 n., 154 n.
Philippine Normal School, Manila, 77
Pierce, Paul Revere, 159 n.
platoon system, 79
Pope, Arthur Upham, 115
Practikum, 22
Primary Object Lessons (Calkins), 13
Principles of Scientific Management, The (Taylor), 79 n.
profile charts, 139
Progressive Education at the Cross-roads (Bode), 153
"progressive" schools, 65 n., 111–112
psychology, contributions of, 71–73; organismic, 152
Psychology (Dewey), 48

Rankin, Paul, 168 n.
Raup, R. Bruce, 111 n., 140 n.
Rein, Wilhelm, 22 n., 23, 25 n., 30
research, objective, 118
Rice, Joseph, 71
Rickey, Herman, 13 n., 14 n., 71 n.
Robinson, James Harvey, 108, 116, 125
Roe, John, 138 n.
Rosenkranz, Karl, 15–16
Rugg, Harold, 5, 8 n., 10 n., 46 n., 48 n., 73 n., 90 n., 91 n., 105–136, 140, 149, 172–173, 178–179, 183; background of, 112–117; childhood conflicts, 112–113; contribution of, 135–136; curriculum-making, criticism by, 120–121; shift of interest, 116–117; social studies series, 117–120; and *Twenty-sixth Yearbook,* 123–134
Russell, James Earl, 7, 111 n., 138 n., 141
Russell, William F., 171 n.

St. Louis, curriculum making in, 106
St. Louis Public Schools, 15, 48, 89
St. Louis Teachers Association, 13
Scheffler, Israel, 174 n.

Schilpp, Paul Arthur, 17 n., 38 n., 40 n., 48 n., 52 n., 53 n.
school, child-centered, 120–122, 127; as embryonic community life, 78–79; society-centered, 127
school organization, attention to, 8
school system, "controlling science" in, 89
Schools of Tomorrow (Dewey), 112
science, in school system, 73, 82, 89
scientific management, 79–80, 138; prevision in, 89
Seeley, Levi, 25 n., 30 n.
Sheldon, Edward, 26 n.
Shumaker, Ann, 122
"smelting point," in education, 36, 142
Smith, Margaret K., 25 n.
Smith, Perry, 112 n.
Smith-Hughes Act, 93 n.
Snedden, David, 111 n., 138 n., 139 n.
social behavior, tabulation of, 5
Social Change (Ogburn), 132 n.
social issues, research in, 118
social life, knowledge and, 61; transformation of, 63
social need, education and, 82, 92
social studies, in curriculum making, 108–109; Rugg's series in, 117–120
social usefulness, 75
society, curriculum content and, 102–103
Society for Curriculum Study, 157, 159–161, 167
Soldan, F. Louis, 13, 35, 89
Spanish American War, 77
spelling, 71
Spencer, Herbert, 68
standards, measurable, 82; *see also* measurement
state curriculum revision programs, 141–156, 179
Statistical Methods Applied to Education (Rugg), 115
Stevenson, John Alford, 87 n.
Stoy, Karl, 21 n., 30
Stratemeyer, Florence, 111 n.
Strayer, George D., 8 n., 76, 111 n., 137–138, 142, 148 n.
study courses, curriculum making and, 105–107
superintendent, role of, 109–110

supervisor, reaction to Society for Curriculum Study, 159–161
survey movement, 75, 139
Suzzallo, Henry, 74 n., 139 n.
Swarthmore College, 7
system, in Herbartian theory, 18–20

Taylor, Frederick Winslow, 79, 93
Taylor, Katharine, 112 n.
teacher, versus administrator, 100; in curriculum making, 3, 98, 107; reliance on textbooks by, 10
Teacher of Teachers, The (Rugg), 114 n., 141 n.
Teachers College, Columbia University, 5, 7, 38, 59, 71–72, 75, 90, 110–111, 116, 131, 137; Curriculum Bureau, 157; Department of Curriculum and Teaching, 171
teacher training, Charters's experiments in, 90; in Herbartian theory, 21–23; McMurry role in, 36–38
technological change, knowledge and, 64, 83
tests and scales, 71–75; *see also* measurement
textbooks, changes in production of, 1830–1900, 9–10; in curriculum study, 3
That Men May Understand (Rugg), 113 n., 118 n., 119 n.
Thayer, Vivian T., 8 n., 39 n.
Theoretikum, 22
Theory and Practice of Teaching (Page), 15
Theory of the Leisure Class, The (Veblen), 150
thinking, versus knowledge, 44
Thorndike, Edward Lee, 67, 71–73, 75, 111 n., 139–140
Threlkeld, Archie, 160 n.

time, economy of, 92–93
Toronto, University of, 90
Trainer, John, 11 n.
Transformation of the School, The (Cremin), 144 n.
Trillingham, Clinton C., 105 n.
truth, education and, 100
Turner, Frederick Jackson, 125
Twenty-sixth Yearbook, 124–136, 149
type studies, 35, 37, 39 n.

Ufer, Christian, 16, 21, 25 n.

value conflicts, social implications of, 87–88
Van Liew, C. C., 7, 25 n., 30 n.
Van Liew, Ida J., 25 n.
Veblen, Thorstein, 125, 150
Virginia, curriculum revision in, 147–156
Virginia State Department of Education, 147

Watson, Goodwin, 140 n.
Webb, Sidney and Beatrice, 117
Western Reserve University, 157
Whipple, Guy, 114
White, Emerson E., 33 n., 35 n.
White, Morton, 49 n.
will, knowledge and, 20
Wirt, William, 78
Wright, Frank Lloyd, 150
Wundt, Wilhelm, 71, 72 n.

Yearbook Committee, 124–131

Ziller, Tuiskon, 17–18, 20–22, 30
Zinser, J. C., 25 n.
Zirbes, Laura, 168 n.

203

Augsburg College
George Sverdrup Library
Minneapolis, Minnesota 55404